Global Sustainability
and the Responsibilities
of Universities

Published by Economica Ltd,
49, rue Héricart
75015 Paris
France

© Economica Ltd, 2012

First published 2012

Printed in France

Luc E. Weber and James J. Duderstadt (eds)
Global Sustainability and the Responsibilities of Universities
ISBN 978-2-7178-6113-6

Global Sustainability and the Responsibilities of Universities

Edited by

Luc E. Weber

James J. Duderstadt

ECONOMICA

Glion Colloquium Series N°7

London • Paris • Genève

Titles in the Series

Governance in Higher Education: The University in a State of Flux
Werner Z. Hirsch and Luc E. Weber, eds, (2001)

As the Walls of Academia are Tumbling Down
Werner Z. Hirsch and Luc E. Weber, eds, (2002)

Reinventing the Research University
Luc E. Weber and James J. Duderstadt, eds, (2004)

Universities and Business: Partnering for the Knowledge Economy
Luc E. Weber and James J. Duderstadt, eds, (2006)

The Globalization of Higher Education
Luc E. Weber and James J. Duderstadt, eds, (2008)

University Research for Innovation
Luc E. Weber and James J. Duderstadt, eds, (2010)

Global Sustainability and the Responsibilities of Universities
Luc E. Weber and James J. Duderstadt, eds, (2012)

Other publications of the Glion Colloquium

The Glion Declaration I: The University at the Millennium
The Glion Colloquium, (1998)

The Glion Declaration II: Universities and the Innovative Spirit
The Glion Colloquium, (2009)

Challenges Facing Higher Education at the Millennium
Werner Z. Hirsch and Luc E. Weber, eds, American Council on Education/
Oryx Press, Phoenix and IAU Press/Pergamon, Paris and Oxford, (1999)

CONTENTS

PREFACE

Over the past decade, the Glion Colloquium has established itself as an influential resource in addressing both the challenges and roles of the world's research universities. Launched in 1998 by Professors Luc Weber (University of Geneva) and Werner Hirsch (University of California), the Colloquium brings university leaders and influential participants from business and government from around the world to Glion-above-Montreux, Switzerland, every two years to consider the future of higher education. Topics have included the rapidly changing nature of research universities, university governance, the interaction between universities and society, collaboration between universities and business, and the globalization of higher education. The papers presented and associated discussions at each colloquium have subsequently been published in a series of books available through publishers or downloadable in full-text format on the Glion Colloquium website at http://www.glion.org.

Although the early colloquia primarily involved participants from Europe and North America, in recent years the event has been extended to achieve a true global participation involving university leaders from around the world. The VIII Glion Colloquium was held in June 2011 to consider the roles that could be played by the world's research universities in addressing the various challenges of global sustainability in the broadest sense, e.g., climate, environmental, economic, health, poverty and geopolitical. Of particular interest was the degree to which the imperatives of global sustainability were driving change in higher education around the world. This included considerations not only of how research universities were adapting to the imperatives of global sustainability (e.g., social diversity, resource management, academic programs, research and scholarship), but also how they could develop new curricula, student experiences, research paradigms, social engagement and international alliances to better address the challenges of global sustainability, while producing globally identified citizens. The Colloquium also considered longer-term possibilities that might pose even greater threats to global sustainability and how universities could prepare their graduates for such eventualities.

While history has always been characterized by periods of both change and stability — war and peace, intellectual progress and decadence, economic prosperity and contraction — today the pace and magnitude of such changes have intensified, driven by the powerful forces of globalization, changing demographics, rapidly evolving technologies and the expanded flows of information, technology, capital, goods, services and people worldwide. Economies are pushing the human exploitation of the Earth's environment to the limits; the military capacity of the great powers could destroy the world population many times over, business corporations have become so large that they can influence national policies, the financial sector has become so complex and unstable that it has the capacity to trigger global economic catastrophes in an instant, and corrupted regimes leading to failed states still appear in all parts of the world. Many believe that the impact of human activities, ever more intense, globally distributed and interconnected, threatens the very sustainability of humankind on Earth, at least in terms that we currently understand and enjoy.

While the fruits of development and modernity are indisputable, the negative consequences of these recent developments appear to be increasingly serious. For example, there is compelling evidence that the growing population and invasive activities of humankind are now altering the fragile balance of our planet. The concerns are multiplying in number and intensifying in severity: the destruction of forests, wetlands and other natural habitats by human activities, the extinction of millions of species and the loss of biodiversity; the buildup of greenhouse gases and their impact on global climates; the pollution of our air, water and land. We must find new ways to provide for a human society that presently has outstripped the limits of global sustainability.

So, too, the magnitude, complexity and interdependence (not to mention accountability) of business practices, financial institutions, markets and government policies now threaten the stability of the global economy, as evidenced by the impact of complex financial instruments and questionable market incentives in triggering the collapse of the global financial markets that led to the "Great Recession" of the past two years. Again, the sustainability of current business practices, government policies and public priorities must be questioned.

Of comparable concern are the widening gaps in prosperity, health and quality of life characterizing developed, developing and underdeveloped regions. To be sure, there are some signs of optimism: a slowing population growth that may stabilize during the 21st century, the degree to which extreme poverty appears to be receding both as a percentage of the population and in absolute numbers, and the rapid growth of developing economies in Asia and Latin America. Technological advances such as the "green revolution" have lifted a substantial portion of the world's population from extreme poverty. Yet it is estimated that one-sixth of the world's population still live in extreme poverty, suffering from diseases such as malaria, tuberculosis, AIDS, diarrhea and others that prey on bodies weakened by chronic hunger, claiming more than 20,000 lives daily. These global needs can only be addressed by the commitment of developed nations and the implementation of technology to alleviate poverty and disease.

The world's research universities have for many years been actively addressing many of the important issues associated with global sustainability. The "green revolution" resulting from university programs in agricultural science has lifted a substantial portion of the world's population from the ravages of extreme poverty. University scientists were the first to alert the world to the impact of human activities on the environment and climate, e.g., the impact of CFCs on atmospheric ozone depletion; the destruction of forests, wetlands and other natural habitats by human activities leading to the extinction of millions of biological species and the loss of biodiversity; and the buildup of greenhouse gases, such as carbon dioxide and their impact on the global climate. University biomedical research has been key to dealing with global health challenges, ranging from malaria to Nile virus to AIDS, and the international character of research universities, characterized by interactional programs, collaboration and exchanges of students and faculty, provide them with a unique global perspective. Universities are also crucial to developing academic programs and culture to produce a new generation of thoughtful, interdependent and globally identified citizens. These institutions are evolving rapidly to accept their global responsibilities, increasingly becoming universities not only "in" the world, in the sense of operating in a global marketplace of people and ideas, but "of" the world, accepting the challenge of extending their public purpose to addressing global concerns. To quote from the 2009 Glion Declaration:

"The daunting complexity of the challenges that confront us would be overwhelming if we were to depend only on existing knowledge, traditional resources, and conventional approaches. But universities have the capacity to remove that dependence by the innovations they create. Universities exist to liberate the unlimited creativity of the human species and to celebrate the unbounded resilience of the human spirit. In

a world of foreboding problems and looming threats, it is the high privilege of univer-
sities to nurture that creativity, to rekindle that resilience, and so provide hope for all
of Earth's peoples."

The opening session of the colloquium considered the unusually broad
range of global sustainability issues. While most attention is focused on the
changes humankind is forcing upon the natural world, one must also question
the sustainability of human societies themselves (Weber). This requires
broader considerations than the natural sciences. The arts and humanities
help us to define sustainability. The social sciences are essential to the study
of social organizations and communities. Key to this broader understanding is
the ability to accurately estimate values of different practices and options
(Cohon). For example, how do we value the welfare of future generations and
hence our intergenerational responsibilities? Here our traditional social and
economic organizations, such as governments and corporations, tend to come
up short in weighing the full range of externalities that should influence policy
development and economic decisions (Biersteker). Even our schools and universities fall short because of the degree to which considerations of values and
ethics have largely disappeared from our academic programs, particularly in
professional schools such as business administration (Morand). At its core,
the theme of global sustainability implies a sense of equity and hence depends
upon the mediating power of the law (Leroy). Here research universities can
work with international development agencies such as the World Bank to
provide innovative approaches to the legal challenges of sustainable development.

The particular complexities of global sustainability issues were the topic of
the second session. Despite the increasing confidence on the part of the scientific community that the activities are changing the climate of the planet,
there remains substantial public opinion that denies the reality of both climate change and human impact. Part of the challenge in shaping both public
understanding and policy concerning global climate change issues is the difficulty of conducting rational discussion of concepts such as severity of consequences and probability of occurrence (Vest). In those rare instances in which
both public understanding and scientific agreement have converged, effective
policies have been developed, such as the Montreal Protocol addressing depletion of the ozone layer by limiting the emissions of CFCs. Yet today, we have
a difficult time in engaging in open discussions on issues such as global sustainability when a substantial part of our population denies the reality of the consequences of human activities on global climate. In part, this may be due to
the difficulty we have in comprehending the timescales, magnitudes and paradigm shifts characterizing such processes (Duderstadt). We tend to think of
climate change on geological timescales and policy on political election

cycles. Furthermore, the magnitude of investment required to transform our carbon-dependent energy economy is staggering, amounting to tens of trillions of dollars. Finally, we lack the international policy forums and governance structures necessary for decisive action (Harayama and Carraz). Clearly, universities have important roles in conducting the research necessary to address uncertainties, serving as an honest broker providing impartial scientific information, and as role models in fostering sustainable campus environments (Eichler and Aebischer).

The implications of these characteristics for university teaching and learning formed the topic of the third session. Today, sustainability is more than a state of mind. It has evolved into a core value and strategy (Katehi). It was noted that the current generation of college students — the Millennials — was much more inclined toward social engagement (Munroe-Blum and Rueda). Social entrepreneurship would become an increasingly important theme at both the local and international level. We must prepare our students for both the unpredictable and the unknown. This requires a sustainable university, a multidisciplinary curriculum, and a research-based education (Beretz). Yet, it was also noted that since, even in developed nations, only a small fraction of the population benefited from college education, the real focus to achieve greater public awareness and global citizenship must begin at the primary and secondary school level (Johnson). The most essential element of a solution to global sustainability is our youth.

The fourth session focused on the research contributions of universities. Although we are rapidly developing the research tools to address global sustainability challenges, there is a mismatch in the cadence between their evolution and our evolving state of readiness to respond (Killeen). Universities around the world are evolving to address many of these issues. European universities are facing many changes: more autonomy and less bureaucracy; the harmonization of degrees through the Bologna Process; stimulated competition (e.g., the German Excellence Initiative); region-wide competition for research grants; and the challenges of "massification" — increasing the fraction of college-educated citizens from 5% to 45% of the population or greater (Huber). Furthermore, European universities continued to face the challenges of limited mobility of faculty, students and ideas that would drive a contemporary renaissance. It was suggested that grand challenges were needed to inspire scholars (Winckler and Fieder). Yet, the university cannot confine its activities to traditional education and research, since these must be translated into policy recommendations and action before we are overtaken by the consequences of indecision.

The fifth session concerned the capacity of research universities to adapt to the challenges and needs of their broader societies. The evolution of Mexico's Technologico de Monterrey System into a truly "citizen-oriented" university, deeply imbedded in the society it serves, provided a profound example of how a university could (and must) focus on the needs of its society to thrive (Rangel), embracing a new paradigm of University 2.0, based on growth and intimate engagement with society. So too, IIT Madras provided a provocative example of how a university can achieve a dynamic equilibrium with its social, ecological, and economic environment while evolving to serve a rapidly growing nation (Ananth). The challenge of meeting the extraordinary demographic change in which Europe's population is declining (with a loss of 42 million over the next 20 years), with very significant implications for immigration (Nazaré). This would require many research universities to develop a broader portfolio of academic programs, including more applied disciplines similar to those of the "Fachhochschulen" and polytechnic universities.

The theme of the sustainability of universities themselves and their changing relationship with government, students, the public and other stakeholders was also explored in this session. The globalization of higher education is a major force driving change, since it is no longer good enough to achieve leadership in one's own country. Furthermore, there has been an important paradigm shift in which the traditional role of government to provide for the purposes of universities has been inverted to become the role of universities to provide for the purposes of government (Newby and Flett). Governments increasingly regard universities as delivery agencies for public policy goals. It was stressed that universities had to remember the very serious nature of the current global financial crisis (Niland). In the same way that globalization would continue to reshape the landscape for the sustainability of the research university as we know it today, such a severe and enduring financial crisis could well attack the "DNA" of research universities and threaten to hollow out its academic core.

In addition to the colloquium sessions focused on global sustainability, a special panel discussion was organized involving the leadership of university organizations throughout Europe (Huber, Newby, Rapp, Schiesser and Winckler). The evolution of the European University Association was reviewed, illustrating its growing influence on the Bologna Process of integration and enhancement of higher education in Europe. The roles of smaller organizations of research universities, such as the League of European Research Universities and the Russell Group (U.K.) in addressing particular challenges such as massification, demographics and mission profiling were also discussed.

The VIII Glion Colloquium was arranged under the auspices of the University of Geneva and the Graduate Institute of International Studies and Development in Geneva and made possible by the generous support of the National Science Foundation of the United States, Rio Tinto Alcan of Canada, Credit

Suisse and the Swiss Federal Institute of Technology (ETH-Board, ETHZ and EPFL), as well as the University of Geneva. We are also particularly grateful for the efforts of those who contributed to the colloquium and to the production of this book, in particular Natacha Durand and Manuela Wullschleger of the University of Geneva for their kind and efficient help, as well as Edmund Doogue in Geneva, who provided rigorous editorial assistance.

Luc Weber   James Duderstadt
University of Geneva   *University of Michigan*

CONTRIBUTORS
AND
PARTICIPANTS

CONTRIBUTORS

AEBISCHER, Patrick

Professor Patrick Aebischer was trained as an MD (1980) and a Neuroscientist (1983) at the Universities of Geneva and Fribourg in Switzerland. From 1984 to 1992, he worked at Brown University (U.S.) as an Assistant and then Associate Professor. In 1992, he returned to Switzerland as a Full Professor at the Centre Hospitalier Universitaire Vaudois (CHUV) in Lausanne. Patrick Aebischer has been President of the Ecole Polytechnique Fédérale de Lausanne (EPFL) since 2000 and pursues his research in the field of neurodegenerative diseases.

ANANTH, M. S.

Prof. M. S. ANANTH served as Director, Indian Institute of Technology Madras, from 2001 to July 2011. He obtained his Ph.D. in Chemical Engineering from the University of Florida in 1972. He has been a Visiting Professor at Princeton University, at the University of Colorado and at the National Institute of Standards and Technology in Boulder, as well as at RWTH, Aachen, Germany. He is currently a member of the Scientific Advisory Committee to the Cabinet and the National Manufacturing Competitiveness Council and visiting Professor of Chemical Engineering, Indian Institute of Science, Bangalore.

BERETZ, Alain

Professor of pharmacology, Alain Beretz was vice-president of Université Louis Pasteur in Strasbourg, in charge of industrial relations, before being elected in December 2008 as President. In this office, he was one of the actors of the innovative merger of the three universities in Strasbourg, and was elected president of the single Université de Strasbourg in January 2009. He is a member of the board of directors of the League of European Research Universities (LERU).

BIERSTEKER, Thomas

Thomas Biersteker is the Gasteyger Chair in International Security at the Graduate Institute, Geneva, where he directs the Programme for the Study of International Governance. Author/editor of nine books, including *Countering the Financing of Terrorism* (2007) and *The Emergence of Private Authority in Global Governance* (2002), his current research focuses on international relations theory and on the design of U.N. targeted sanctions. He directed the Watson Institute for International Studies at Brown University between 1994 and 2006. He received his M.S. and Ph.D. from the Massachusetts Institute of Technology (MIT).

CARRAZ, René

René Carraz is a research fellow at BETA, Strasbourg University. He holds a Ph.D. in Economics. He teaches and does research on science, technology and innovation. Recent work includes studies of university-industry linkages in Japan and Asia, the effects of patents on university researchers and the role of patents and publications in university strategy.

COHON, Jared

Jared Cohon has been president of Carnegie Mellon University since 1997. He came to Carnegie Mellon from Yale, where he was dean of the School of Forestry and Environmental Studies from 1992 to 1997. He started his teaching and research career in 1973 at Johns Hopkins, where he was a faculty member in the Department of Geography and Environmental Engineering for 19 years. Dr Cohon earned a B.S. degree in civil engineering from the University of Pennsylvania in 1969 and a Ph.D. in civil engineering from MIT in 1973.

DUDERSTADT, James J.

James J. Duderstadt is President Emeritus and University Professor of Science and Engineering at the University of Michigan. A graduate of Yale and Caltech, Dr Duderstadt's teaching and research areas include nuclear science and engineering, applied physics, computer simulation and science policy. He has served as chair of numerous National Academy and federal commissions, including the National Science Board, the Nuclear Energy Advisory Committee of the U.S Department of Energy and the Policy and Global Affairs Division of the National Research Council.

EICHLER, Ralph

Professor Ralph Eichler is President of the ETH Zurich. He obtained his doctorate in Physics from ETH Zurich. After being active as a researcher in the U.S. (Stanford University and LAMPF/Los Alamos Meson Physics Facility) and Germany (DESY/German Electron Synchrotron, Hamburg), as well as at the ETH Zurich and the Paul Scherrer Institute (PSI), he became a Professor of Physics at ETH Zurich in 1989. He was spokesman for the international collaboration H1 and took on leading roles at PSI, firstly as Deputy Director from 1998 to 2002 and as Director from 2002.

FLETT, Alastair

Alastair Flett is the Senior Executive Coordinator at the University of Liverpool. Educated at the University of York and University College London, he has worked in strategic and operational planning in Higher Education for the last nine years.

FIEDER, Martin

Dr Martin Fieder is an Anthropologist and Behavioral Biologist. His research interests are in the fields of human sociobiology, evolutionary demography, organization and higher education management. Martin Fieder has been working for more than 10 years at the Rectorate of the University of Vienna, with a special focus on organization, strategic planning and international benchmarking.

HARAYAMA, Yuko

Yuko Harayama, holder of a Ph.D. in Education Sciences and a Ph.D. in Economics, is the Deputy Director of the OECD's Directorate for Science, Technology and Industry, and a professor of Science and Technology Policy at the Graduate School of Engineering of Tohoku University. In Japan, she served as a Member of the Council for Science and Technology Policy at the Cabinet Office and a member of different commissions related to Science and Technology at the Ministry of Education, Culture, Sport, Science and Technology and the Ministry of Economy, Trade and Industry.

HUBER, Bernd

Professor Dr Bernd Huber, born in Wuppertal/Germany, is Professor for Public Finance, and, since 2002, President of Ludwig-Maximilians-Universität

(LMU) München. His research focuses on Public Finance, Government Debt, European Fiscal and Monetary Integration, International Taxation and Labour Markets. Among his numerous functions, he is a member of the Scientific Council to the German Ministry of Finance and of the "Zukunftsrat" (Council on Future Challenges) to the Bavarian State Government. Prof Huber has been the chairman of LERU, the League of European Research Universities, since 2008.

JOHNSON, Roberta

Roberta Johnson is executive Director, National Earth Science Teachers Association Boulder, Colorado. She directs the National Earth Science Teachers Association and leads the award-winning *Windows to the Universe* project. She served for a decade as the founding Director of Education and Outreach at the University Corporation for Atmospheric Research. Prior to that, she was a research scientist at the University of Michigan and a research physicist at SRI International. She regularly serves as an advisor to federal agencies, international organizations and professional societies.

KATEHI, Linda P. B.

Chancellor of the University of California, Davis, Linda P.B. Katehi is a member of the National Academy of Engineering, American Academy of Arts and Science, and many other national and international boards; she holds 19 U.S. patents and has co-authored more than 650 publications. Prior to joining UC Davis, she was a top administrator at the Universities of Illinois Urbana-Champaign, Purdue and Michigan.

KILLEEN, Timothy L.

Timothy L. Killeen has been the Assistant Director for the Geosciences at the National Science Foundation since July 2008. He oversees the Geosciences directorate which supports research in the atmospheric, geospace, earth and ocean sciences. From 2000 to 2008, Dr Killeen was director of the National Center for Atmospheric Research. He received a Ph.D. in Atomic and Molecular Physics from University College London in 1975.

LEROY, Anne-Marie

Anne-Marie Leroy is currently the Senior Vice President and General Counsel, World Bank Group. Other positions she has held are: Partner at the Denton Wilde Sapte LLP Paris office (2005-09); Judge of the Conseil d'Etat (1986-1991, 2002); judge of the Inter-American Development Bank Administrative Tribunal (2003); Director of Legal and International Affairs, French Ministry of National Education (1991); Department Head in charge of Governance and Civil Society, OECD (1998); Senior Advisor to Prime Minister Lionel Jospin (1998). She graduated from the Paris Institute for Political Science and the National School for Public Administration.

MORAND, Pascal

Pascal Morand is a graduate of HEC and holds a doctorate in Economics. Since 2006, he has been Dean of ESCP Europe. From 1987 to 2006, he was Director General of the Institut Français de la Mode (IFM). He is a trustee of the Board of the Ecole Nationale Supérieure de Création Industrielle (ENSCI-Les Ateliers), and a member of the Scientific Board of COE-Rexecode. His research and publications deal with international economics and their relationship with culture.

MUNROE-Blum, Heather

Heather Munroe-Blum is Principal and Vice-Chancellor (President), McGill University. She holds a B.A., B.S.W. (McMaster University); M.S.W. (Wilfrid Laurier University); Ph.D. in epidemiology (University of North Carolina-Chapel Hill). She is a member of the boards of the Association of American Universities; Association of Universities and Colleges of Canada (AUCC); AUCC Committee on University Research (Chair); Canada Pension Plan Investment Board; Yellow Media Inc. She is also a member of Canada's Science, Technology and Innovation Council; U.S. National Research Council's Committee on Research Universities; Canada Foundation for Innovation; Trilateral Commission. She is an Officer of the Order of Canada and of the National Order of Quebec, as well as a Specially Elected Fellow of the Royal Society of Canada.

NAZARÉ, Maria Héléna

Rector of the University of Aveiro during the period of 2002-2010 and chair of the Portuguese Rectors Conference Committee for research and knowledge — transference, Maria Héléna Nazaré currently chairs the Higher Education Committee of the Portuguese National Education Council, is the Treasurer and Vice-President of EUA since 2009, a member of the Administration Board of Portugal Telecom, President of the Advisory Board of Fundação Galp Energia, President of the Portuguese Physics Society and President-elect of European University Association.

NEWBY, Howard

Sir Howard Newby is the Vice-Chancellor of the University of Liverpool. He is the former Vice-Chancellor of the University of the West of England, Chief Executive of HEFCE, Vice-Chancellor of the University of Southampton,

Chairman and Chief Executive of ESRC, President of Universities U.K., and President of the British Association for Advancement of Science. He was made a CBE in 1995 for services to social science and received a knighthood in 2000 for services to higher education.

NILAND, John

John Niland is Professor Emeritus (in Economics) at the University of New South Wales, where he was Vice-Chancellor and President from 1992-2002. He has been President of the Australian Vice-Chancellors' Committee and a Member of the University Grants Council of Hong Kong. Currently he is Deputy Chairman of Singapore Management University, Chairman of Campus Living Villages Limited and an Independent Director of Macquarie Group Limited.

RANGEL, Rafael

Rafael Rangel took Master and Ph.D. degrees from the University of Wisconsin. He is the Chancellor of Monterrey Tech a private educational system with 130,000 students, 64 Campus and 13,000 faculty members. He is the recipient of Honorary Doctorates from the universities of North Carolina, British Columbia, Thunderbird, Georgetown, Carnegie Mellon, Arizona State and Florida International; and winner of the Gold Medallion from Instituto de Empresa, and Orden Isabel la Catolica from the Kingdom of Spain.

RUEDA, Carlos

Carlos Rueda is a Ph.D. candidate at the Desautels Faculty of Management at McGill University. He is currently working on management and leadership development under the advisory of Henry Mintzberg and Paola Perez-Aleman. He graduated with a B.A. in Economics from Universidad del Pacifico (Lima, Peru), and completed the Global Competitiveness Leadership Program at Georgetown University. In 2010, he was elected as a Sauvé Scholar at McGill University.

VEST, Charles M.

Charles M. Vest is president of the U.S. National Academy of Engineering and president emeritus of the Massachusetts Institute of Technology. He is the author of a book on holographic interferometry and two books on higher education. He holds 17 honorary doctorates, received the 2006 National Medal of Technology from President George W. Bush, and the 2011 Vannevar Bush award from the U.S. National Science Board.

WEBER, Luc E.

Luc Weber was professor of Public Economics at the University of Geneva and an adviser to the Swiss Government from 1975 onwards. Elected Vice-Rector of the University of Geneva in 1982, Prof. Weber became Rector a few years later, as well as Chairman of the Swiss Rectors' Conference. He also served many international organizations: member of the Board the European University Association, Vice-president of the International Association of Universities and Vice-president and President of the Steering Committee for Higher Education and Research of the Council of Europe. He is co-founder of the Glion Colloquium.

WINCKLER, Georg

Prof. Georg Winckler studied economics at Princeton University and at the University of Vienna, taking his Ph.D. in 1968. In 1978 he became Professor of Economics and in 1999 Rector of the University of Vienna (re-elected in 2003 and 2007). He was President of the Austrian Rectors' Conference and Vice President and President of the EUA. Since April 2008 he has been a member of ERAB and, since February 2009, a member of the PEOPLE Advisory Group, European Commission, Brussels.

PARTICIPANTS

The following personalities participated in the eighth Glion Colloquium and contributed comments and statements to the discussion:

Michel BENARD, University Relations Manager for Google

Yves FLUECKIGER, Vice-Rector University of Geneva

Jovan PAVLEVSKI, President of Economica, Paris

Jean-Marc RAPP, Rector Emeritus of the University of Lausanne and President of the European University Association (EUA)

Fritz SCHIESSER, President of the ETH Board, Switzerland.

PART I

•••••••••••••

Elements of Global
Sustainability

CHAPTER 1

Universities, hard and soft Sciences: all key Pillars of global Sustainability

Luc Weber

PREAMBLE

Imagine you are an economic historian writing at the end of the 21st century about the second half of the 20th and first decade of the 21st. You will probably write that this period was characterized by an unprecedented increase in prosperity in the Western World, the rapid emergence of new, giant economic powers, an increasing interdependence due to globalization and, globally, relative peace. In brief, the well-being of the world's population increased rapidly thanks to prosperity and to global peace.

However, we cannot also exclude today the possibility that the period will — on the contrary — be described in very gloomy terms; this would certainly be the case if, for example, one or more of the following events take place in the years to come:

- the well-documented phenomenon of climate deterioration provokes famines and mass migration, as well as a great increase in natural disasters,
- fears about nuclear power generated by the dramatic consequences of the earthquake and tsunami in Japan lead to a deep energy crisis,
- the growing aspirations of populations for more freedom, equality and democracy in many developing countries lead to more instability due to ineffective political regimes,

3

- a global economic and financial meltdown generated by the incapacity to reverse the unprecedented measures taken by central banks and governments to prevent the 2008 financial and banking crisis turning into a global economic crisis.

These few examples remind us that the present — apparent — increase in world prosperity and positive political developments might not be sustainable because they contain destructive mechanisms.

This contribution pursues four aims: first, to demonstrate that the concept of sustainability, well established in the domain of environmental protection, exploitation of natural resources and climate deterioration, is equally powerful as a wide-ranging concept pinpointing the necessary sustainability of political, geo-political, economic, financial and social developments, which are required for world prosperity and peace. Secondly, the contribution would like to show that sustainability is closely linked to the prevention of risks and, thirdly, that universities, in particular research universities, have a great responsibility to promote global sustainability through their triple missions of research, education and engagement. Fourthly — and last, but not least — the contribution will argue that all academic disciplines, i.e. hard sciences, as well as social sciences, the arts and humanities, have to be mobilized towards global sustainability.

TOWARDS HARD AND SOFT SUSTAINABILITY

Sustainable economic development

Following the swift economic development of the Western World since the 1960s and the emergence of huge new economic powers over the past 20 years, as well as the explosive growth of the world's population, the need for sustainable development is rightly becoming at least as important as economic growth itself. The concept of sustainable economic development was based on the observation that economic growth has undesirable secondary effects. Basically, it became apparent that production and consumption were generating pollution, in particular air and water pollution. More than a century ago, economists developed the concept of externalities to analyse this phenomenon. The basic idea is that for many production and consumption activities, decision-makers are not required to take into account all the costs generated by their activity, therefore imposing external costs to other people, without providing compensation for this. The origins of external costs are polluted products dumped into the air or water, diminishing their quality, generating costly damages and/or requiring purification measures. In order to mitigate these market failures, economics and law propose policy instruments to reduce the level of pollution attached to any level of production (or consumption) and/or to force polluters to internalize these costs, contributing to a reduced level of pollution.

Over time, the negative consequences of global economic growth, in particular of industrialization and increased consumption, as well as population growth, became increasingly felt at the global level. The most frequently quoted problem is the constant increase of CO^2 due to burning coal and oil for heating, powering vehicles and planes, and industrial processes. CO^2 is now considered the main cause of climate change due to the greenhouse effect, the source of rising average temperatures in the Earth's atmosphere. Climate change has considerable consequences on living conditions in many areas, in particular desertification and melting of the ice cap and glaciers, and seems to increase the violence of related natural events.

Moreover economic and population growth contributes to a rapid depletion of known available natural resources. It is becoming more and more expensive and risky to the environment to exploit new oil or gas fields and metal deposits, and there is a real danger that the world will face increased scarcity of resources, pushing up prices dramatically. The availability of clean water is at risk in many countries.

As awareness of the need to control pollution has grown since the 1960s, the depletion of non-renewable natural resources and, in particular, the consequences of human activities on the climate have become some of the hottest political issues at world level. They are the focus of both intensive scientific research and important scientific and ideological disputes, as well as of heated political debates, particularly between environmentalists and business leaders who want to maximize short-term productivity and profit. These disputes make it all the more difficult to reach a consensus on policies which look restrictive in the short term, but might well be very positive in the long run. This is not really surprising, considering that the world is composed of 200 nations with different interests and levels of development, with many active international organizations, but no real supra-national government or powerful world body. There is little agreement on the degree of priority that should be given to sustainable development. The question of how to proceed is forever in dispute. The very fact that increased economic prosperity implies not only quantitative, but also qualitative growth, shows why it is so important that development be sustainable.

Sustainable societies

Is the concept of sustainability confined to qualify economic development in relation to the environment, the exploitation of natural resources and the climate? Certainly not! It has become clear today that it can be applied with great benefits to "softer" aspects of sustainability, related to politics and geo-politics, economic, financial and social issues.

The history of political organizations, "clans", feudalism, kingdoms and nations shows again and again that many leaders have been able to build up such enormous power that their regime is not only able to severely restrict the freedom of individuals, but also to impose a transfer of income and wealth in favour of a privileged few who become richer and richer at the expense of the majority. His-tory demonstrates also that such situations cannot last forever. Desperate popu-lations unable to escape poverty are prepared to fight injustice and oppression, and, if an opportunity arises, will rise up to overturn the situation. The same hap-pens to those regimes that aim to extend their sovereignty over other countries and populations. This too generates reactions that generally bring about the defeat of the invader. The history of mankind is littered with examples, and recent events in North Africa and the Middle East demonstrate once more the fragility of political regimes that are unsustainable because the faction in power seeks personal enrichment and authority to the detriment of the rest of the pop-ulation. These situations explain why authentic democracy, according to which citizens can choose their leaders and openly express disagreement with govern-ment, is considered the best, if not the perfect, political system.

The innate weakness of some political regimes demonstrates quite clearly that the problem of sustainability is not limited to natural elements, but can profitably be applied to human and societal questions. The 2008 financial cri-sis and the deficit/public debt crisis that continues today are also striking examples of the consequences of unsustainable. Let us look, at least superfi-cially, at the 2008 (and on-going) banking and public finance crisis to high-light the fact that they too are the result of unsustainable development. The main factors that generated the banking and finance crisis are:

- The development of new investment instruments supposed to better spread risk, but which eventually allowed a dramatic increase in the leverage of bank assets.
- The development of new remuneration practices — at least in mag-nitude if not in concept — by which traders and top bank executives receive huge bonuses, encouraging them to take bigger risks and, in some cases, to behave dishonestly.
- The political strategy, in particular in the U.S., to encourage every-one to become a home-owner, even people with no income, no job and no assets — the so-called NINJNA — thanks to a policy of low interest rates, with the result that many families fell into the trap of buying a house they could not afford.

As soon as the crisis broke out, it became obvious that if one bank failed, many others would follow. This is why both central banks and ministries of finance (treasuries) intervened massively to lend liquidity to banks, take over their bad debts and even nationalize them.

The amounts of money committed to this task, both by the central banks and governments, were unprecedented. In conformity with well-established economic theory, this prevented the financial crisis from spreading deeply into the real economy. Today, the financial markets are still flooded with liquidity, particularly as countries like the U.S. printed money to support the economy.

One consequence of the measures taken to save the bank and finance system is an explosion of the public deficit and, consequently, an enormous increase of the public debt in most developed countries. Many specialists consider that the public deficit should not exceed 3% of GNP. Yet, today, it is more than 10% in many Western countries. Many countries — in particular the U.S. and several European Union countries that have adopted the Euro — are having great difficulties financing their debt at an affordable cost and have to rely on the support of other countries to buy their public bonds.

The disequilibrium in public finance is particularly acute today because many countries had not previously managed their public finances carefully. The simple reason is that democratic regimes create a tendency to spend: it is easier for politicians to win elections if they promise additional programmes than if they threaten tax increases!

And it is impossible to predict how the world will escape from this crisis. The liquidity created to support the economy and the huge disequilibrium between creditors and debtor countries could well bring about many very negative developments, in particular a rapid acceleration of inflation, a currency war, increased protectionism and, finally, an explosion of unemployment.

Global sustainability

These examples highlight the fact that the concept of sustainability is as relevant for human and societal questions as it is for natural ones. It is in this comprehensive, wider sense that we understand the concept of **global** sustainability. In other words, the concept of sustainability has two distinct dimensions: first a natural one, focusing on planet Earth, the environment, the exploitation of natural resources, including air and water, and the climate; second a human and societal one, referring to the well-being of human beings and the economic, political and social organization and development of society. Both "hard" and "soft" sustainability are indispensable for prosperity and resilience to crisis.

In view of the two distinctive natures of global sustainability, it is not surprising that we need different scientific approaches (scholarship) to study them and to make policy recommendations. If the domain of environmental

protection, exploitation of natural resources and climate borrows a lot
— although by far not exclusively — from natural or "hard" sciences, the
other dimension calls mainly for "soft" sciences, that is social sciences, arts
and humanities. Therefore, the traditional approximate distinction between
hard and **soft** sciences has a close correspondence with the two dimensions of
sustainability.

RISKS AND SUSTAINABILITY

An organization or a development can perform reasonably well, but there is
always a risk that, one day, it will seriously dysfunction, causing a disruption,
becoming a source of pain and resulting in the loss of years of progress. This is
why the study of sustainability requires the study of all the risks that could
challenge it in order to imagine measures to mitigate them, therefore securing
a greater sustainability.

A couple of years ago the World Economic Forum (WEF) launched a series
of initiatives on the question of risks, using its close relations with heads of government and high-profile business leaders, as well as its capacity to attract academics (See *Global Risks*, WEF, 2011a, and *The Global Agenda for business government and supra-national governmental organizations*, WEF, 2011b). *Global
Risks* divides risks into five categories — economic, environmental, societal,
geopolitical and technological — and estimates their likelihood and perceived
impact if they occur. An effort has also been made to identify the interconnec-
tion between the different risks. A few comments drawn from the report show
the importance of identifying risks in relation with global sustainability.

- The increasing economic disparity within countries and between
  countries is identified as one of the biggest risks threatening sustainability. An important characteristic of economic development over
  the past 20 years is that the rich have become even richer in all developing countries, despite robust economic growth in some emerging
  countries; many people in many countries remain trapped in a poverty
  circle. This is a serious problem as economic disparity is tightly interconnected with corruption, demographic challenges, fragile states
  and global imbalances, all serious factors affecting sustainability.
- Macroeconomic imbalances that include savings and trade imbalances within and between countries, currency volatility, fiscal crises,
  asset price collapse arising from the tension between the increasing
  wealth and influence of emerging economies and huge debts in
  advanced economies, create increasing risks of unsustainability.
- The rapidly rising global population and growing prosperity are
  putting unsustainable pressures on resources. Demand for water, food

and energy is expected to rise by 30%-50% in the next two decades. Shortages could cause social and political instability.

- A networked world and governance failures, combined with economic disparity, create opportunities for illegal activity to flourish.
- The increased interconnections among risks due to globalization mean a higher level of systemic risk than ever before. Thus there is a greater need for an integrated and more systemic approach to risk management.
- The failure of global governance creates and exacerbates systemic global risks.

These examples drawn from intensive and wide-ranging risk analysis put forward by the WEF reveal the great number and extreme variety of risks and the necessity to identify them and analyse them in order to develop and implement policies capable of mitigating them to secure greater sustainability. This requires a lot of research at a high level and the involvement of all stakeholders, academics, politicians and business leaders.

ROLE OF UNIVERSITIES

The description of the two distinctive dimensions of global sustainability and of the multiple risks that are threatening sustainability reveals the immense complexity of the mechanisms at play and the close interaction between them. It is therefore not surprising that universities and other research or teaching institutions have a key role to play because they offer the right environment for analysing the necessary conditions for sustainability, allowing therefore the formulation of adequate policies. They have at their disposal the research infrastructure and staff with the necessary knowledge, and they are training and educating generations of students.

The ways that universities have been implementing their multiple responsibilities have changed considerably over recent decades. The days when universities served only the elite are over. Now they are a key driver of the knowledge society, having to train and retrain masses of students and to do more and better research to serve the needs of the economy and society. Moreover, they are expected to serve their community and to engage in public debate. This changing position (status) has had a profound impact on their strategy and attitude. The expectation and needs of society force them to be more responsive, that is adapt their output to satisfy the changing demand. However, it is at the same time crucial that universities, in particular research universities, remain responsible institutions (Grin, Harayama & Weber, 2000; and Weber, 2002). The high professional competence of their academic staff and advanced students, their repository of world knowledge, the concentration of sophisticated equipment and the large autonomy they enjoy place them in a unique position to look at events with distance and objectivity, and to analyse them with the most up-to-date methods available. In other words "our institutions are now the leading sources of all three of the most important ingredients for progress and prosperity in modern societies: new discoveries, expert knowledge and highly trained people." (Bok, 2010). Not surprisingly, this is exactly why universities have been given a large degree of autonomy in open and democratic countries.

But, the next question should be: are universities fulfilling their missions in the best way possible? Obviously, like international organizations, governments, firms and not-for-profit organizations, they could do better! The following weaknesses should be addressed with determination:

- Universities are conservative institutions so that it is extremely difficult for the leaders to bring about change.
- Universities are often more a collection of loosely organized individuals rather than an institution pursuing a common goal. They also have an academic organization inherited from the past which is not favourable to the development of interdisciplinary approaches indispensable to study today's societal problems.
- Universities, and in particular public universities, are characterized by a complex web of partly contradictory constraints and incentives set up by governments, parliaments and funding agencies, which makes it more difficult for them to be efficient.
- Most high potential researchers are primarily — if not exclusively — interested in basic, curiosity-driven research. The challenge is, therefore, to persuade them to give part of their attention to research more immediately useful to solving societal problems.
- Teaching programmes do not escape criticism either. The programmes — in particular in research-intensive universities — tend to be conceived on the basis of what the various teachers like to offer. This is perfectly acceptable and even beneficial with regard to the basic intellectual exercise and training of students in ways to learn, but it is not sufficient for preparing students for lifelong learning and for the adaptability needed in fast-developing societies, as well as becoming engaged citizens with strong values.
- The lack of engagement by academics in solving societal problems and in participating in public and political debate is another issue. As members of an institution or beneficiaries of a grant from a research-funding institution, they have also a responsibility to communicate their knowledge and to collaborate with other disciplines and with applied scientists.

The weaknesses identified are not limited to universities, but extend to organizations providing financial supporting to them. Founding agencies are not neutral, first of all because their policy is strongly determined by the scientists themselves. Scientific journals are also a distorting element as they reflect the allocation of resources observed at funding bodies' level. As their policy is also fixed by their reading committees, the same distortions can be observed as in funding bodies. In particular, there is a bias against multidisciplinarity, due mainly to the criteria applied to recruit new professors.

ROLE OF SOCIAL SCIENCES, ARTS AND HUMANITIES

In today's world, largely dominated by markets and performance, the trust put in the capacity of new technologies to solve societal problems is strong, probably too strong. Take the example of energy. No doubt that new technology developed thanks to research in hard sciences and in engineering allows more efficient production of energy and increasing proportions of renewable energies. But what about energy consumption? Again, the demand for energy can be reduced thanks to new technologies allowing for more efficient engines or better insulation. However, consumer behaviour with regard to living, transport, leisure, etc. also plays a very important role; this is clearly observable in the important differences in energy consumption between different world regions with approximately the same standard of living and climate. Therefore, any serious energy policy should also focus on human behaviour in relation to energy consumption and should develop efficient policies in order to bring about a reduction in energy consumption.

The truth is that both hard — that is natural sciences — and soft — that is social sciences, arts and humanities — are equally necessary to contribute to global sustainability. Natural sciences and technology obviously have huge capacity to provide solutions for global sustainability. In addition to the energy question raised above, they offer today numerous new possibilities and great potential for the future. Just a few examples can demonstrate this: bacteria to fight pollution, new technologies to desalinate salty water, new species of corn to secure agriculture production in difficult environments, new vaccines or drugs to fight bacteria immune to antibiotics, etc.

But social sciences, arts and humanities are equally important to better understand the conditions for global sustainability, to support thinking differently and to imagine new policies. The following selective list of a few serious problems for human beings and society puts in evidence the importance of soft sciences and the urgent need to develop them in order to arrive at better solutions and policies:

- What are the causes of the diverging demographic trends, globally and in different regions, and the consequences on the environment, economic development and migration?

- Can our society tolerate an ever-increasing income and wealth inequality between countries, as well as within countries, and, if not, how can income and wealth be redistributed without impacting negatively on economic development?
- Globalization is without doubt contributing to the prosperity of the majority of people on the planet; but should it be pushed to the limit considering the social cost in "old" countries which, for demographic, as well as political and business structural reasons, are slower to adapt?
- How should countries be governed? Is democracy, which took more than 2,000 years to take hold in Europe and North America, necessarily the best political system for all countries, whatever their history, culture, level of education and development?
- What explains the fact that religions can become sources of political power and not simply remain a source of personal faith?
- What is the origin of terrorism and what can be done to eradicate it?
- What can be done to prevent business interests from influencing democratic processes in their favour even when it's against the general interest?

An improved response to such "old" questions and many others would no doubt boost the prosperity of nations and the sustainability of their organization and development. No doubt also that the disciplines most capable of throwing light on these questions in order to better understand the mechanisms and to imagine policies to improve the situation belong to the soft sciences: **the arts and the humanities** which study the human condition and **the social sciences** which study society. Although the arts are not primarily founded on scientific methods, they are complementary to humanities and social sciences, in particular by pursuing beauty, they are contributing to seeing and arranging things differently and to imagining new ways to see reality.

In summary, social sciences, arts and humanities are crucial for two totally different reasons. First, they bring important knowledge about the human condition and society, including its successes and failures, and, second, they develop the capacity of human beings to judge, criticize, argue and envisage things differently, which is essential in complex societies and to ensure sustainability. A society with a poor culture in sciences, social sciences, arts and humanities, lacks the knowledge, aptitude, capacity of critical judgment and intellectual vigour necessary to address challenges with intelligence, rigour, honesty and independence of thoughts. Thus, it risks becoming the victim of unilateral thinking, in particular the sirens of populist/nationalist political movements or religious movements like creationism. The cost of ignorance is huge. There is a great risk today that the power attained by a few states, many corporations and populist political parties in many countries exceeds the professional competences of those who lead them, as well as of their stakeholders who exercise indirect influence. The costs, in terms of prosperity of bad governments, ill-conceived policies and absurd conflicts, are also enormous. With better knowledge and education, better systems, better institutions, etc., the money wasted could be invested in constructive, long-term projects.

Considering the importance of social sciences, arts and humanities for the sustainable development of society, funding agencies and universities should ask themselves why they do not attach a higher priority to these disciplines. It probably has much to do with the methods of investigation and the applicability of results. In hard sciences, the methodologies of investigation, although in general very complex, are better established and more transparent than in soft sciences. The same is true for research results whose applicability to developing practical solutions is generally more immediately visible. On the other hand, soft sciences tackle questions that are often even more complex with research methodologies that are not standardized and do not offer the possibility of creating laboratory conditions. It is therefore not very surprising that hard sciences appear to contribute more to society, in particular thanks to their direct contribution to the country's competitiveness, defence system or energy supply; these are indeed all important in today's world, but nevertheless not sufficient in themselves to secure durable increased prosperity and peace.

The diverging performances between hard and soft sciences are obviously real, but the perspective that leads to such a conclusion can be considered short or medium term. However, it we look at the long term, the contribution of soft sciences is much greater.

NOT TO CONCLUDE: IS GLOBAL SUSTAINABILITY AN ILLUSION?

The message of this chapter is that global sustainability is not only desirable, but should be a high priority for all nations and for society in general. But, is this realistic? All forms of societal organizations from communities to nations, even grouping of nations, have gone through an alternation of successful and difficult periods. Some have even disappeared, which also means that, for whatever reasons, their system was not sustainable or that they were overcome by other, more powerful communities/nations. Does this mean that the fate of our societies is already written or that that the powers at play can lead to an uncontrollable decline, and that, therefore, it is an illusion to be "committed to improving the state of the world", as stated in the World Economic Forum motto? (2011c). Perhaps. Who knows? However, even if this were the case, in any society nobody knows when a downturn is beginning or will begin. As much as most inhabitants of this planet are trying to improve their personal and family situation, it is the responsibility of all political, business and academic leaders to do their utmost to increase the prosperity and peace of the nation, to contribute to the prosperity of other nations and, therefore, to mitigate risks to assure the sustainability of organizations and development. Universities, as well as other research and teaching organizations, social sciences, arts and humanities have more than ever a particular role to play.

REFERENCES

Bok, D. (2010). "Converging for diversity and democracy: a higher education", in Bergan & Damian (Eds), *Higher education for modern societies: competences and values*, Council of Europe higher education series No. 15.

Glion Colloquium (2009). *The Second Glion Declaration*, Association Glion Colloquium, Geneva.

Grin, F., Harayama, Y. & Weber, L. (2000). *Responsiveness, responsibility and accountability: an evaluation of university governance in Switzerland*, Report for the Six-Nation Education Research Project, Office Fédéral de l'Education et de la Science, Berne.

Weber, L. (2002). "Universities' Responsiveness and Responsibilities in an Age of Heightened Competition" in Hirsch & Weber (Eds), *As the Walls of Academia are Tumbling Down*, Economica, Paris.

World Economic Forum (2011a). *Global Risks 2011, Sixth Edition*, Geneva, 56 pp.

World Economic Forum (2011b). *From Risk to Opportunity: Building a Response to the New Reality; Outlook on the Global Agenda 2011*, Geneva, 34 pp.

World Economic Forum Website (2011c). http://www.weforum.org

CHAPTER

Values and Valuation for Sustainability

Jared Cohon

L
ast year, I chaired the U.S. National Academies' Committee that produced the report, "The Hidden Costs of Energy" (2010). Using the most advanced methodology and the best available data, the Committee estimated a lower bound of US$120 billion per year in non-climate damages to Americans from producing and using energy in America. Taking into account impacts of climate change would conservatively double this number. Furthermore, this was just damages *to* Americans from energy use *in* America, and the estimate did not include a wide range of ecological and other impacts. Clearly, the world is incurring enormous uncompensated and largely unrecognized damages from its production, distribution and use of energy.

Sustainability is ill defined, but I think a solid claim, not dependent on a crisp definition of sustainability, is: sustainability in the use of energy, or any other resource, will not and cannot be attained until external effects are internalized. Doing so is relatively straightforward in a conceptual sense, with taxes or other policy measures. I don't know of a single economist who would dispute this; but, I also don't know of a single Republican member of Congress and relatively few Democrats who would publicly support a carbon tax or a policy like a cap and trade system. We clearly have a political and governance problem or at least a disconnect between what we know to be correct and what we're able to achieve in national policy.

Furthermore, while the idea of internalizing externalities is straightforward conceptually, policy prescriptions based on this idea are limited by our assumptions about values. I believe that achieving sustainability will require us to move toward a broader notion of value, one not based solely on human consumption.

THE ECONOMICS OF SUSTAINABILITY

External effects or externalities represent impacts of actions that are not captured by the prices set by markets. In general, whenever an agent (say, a power company) takes actions (say, the generation of electricity from a coal-fired power plant) which produce impacts (health effects of air pollution) on others (people living downwind) that are not reflected in market prices, an externality is said to exist. The existence of an externality is evidence of a market failure which can be corrected through taxes or regulations.

Internalizing externalities or "getting the prices right" is a longstanding idea in environmental policy circles. If the prices that consumers pay, which are reflective of the costs producers incur, are aligned with the "true social costs" of the goods they purchase, then people's choices — consumers and producers — will appropriately reflect the full impact of their actions. This is in some sense a socially optimal state which we fall short of if environmental impacts are not accurately reflected in prices.

Correcting market failures by internalizing externalities is a theoretically non-controversial prescription. It's been a common feature of neoclassical economics theory for a century, and it has been invoked many times in American policy-making and courts. A theoretical justification is one thing; the practical quantification of externalities is quite another. The "Hidden Costs" study cited earlier is the most recent and probably best attempt to date at doing this for energy production, distribution and use. Yet, there were many assumptions that had to be made, and, even putting these aside, quantifying externalities is inherently controversial.

Specific examples are the best way to demonstrate my point. The dominant non-climate external effect (or "damage") of energy use is health effects on humans, primarily excess deaths from air pollution. Putting these in monetary terms requires the valuation of a human life. Although this is well-travelled territory by economists, who have come up with the notion of the "value of a statistical life", this can be treacherous ground. Consider the trouble that the IPCC's social science group got into when, in following common methodology, they produced results that implied higher values for American and European lives than African or Indian lives.

Another example which gives people pause is coal-miner deaths. (The extraction of coal is a part of the life cycle of generating electricity from coal-fired power plants, and, thus, the impacts of mining must be considered in evaluating the impacts of electricity generation.) Coal-mining is among the most dangerous occupations. There is ample evidence that U.S. labour markets capture this risk through higher wages paid to miners. Our committee concluded, therefore, that coal-miner deaths do not represent uninternalized externalities of coal use in America. Try to explain this to the widow of a coal miner or the senator from a coal-mining state.

Some significant effects of energy use are not externalities. A good example is the impact of ethanol production on food prices. Vast amounts of land in the American corn belt are now devoted to producing corn for ethanol rather than for consumption by humans or animals. But this represents a response by farmers to price signals from well-functioning markets and thus higher food prices are not, therefore, an externality.

Other impacts are conceptually very complicated, and it's not clear-cut as to whether they are externalities. For example, the U.S. undoubtedly maintains a larger military and has been involved in more military operations because of the nation's dependence on oil from foreign sources. Is this an externality of oil use in America? It would seem to represent a subsidy to the oil industry, but declaring it an externality is not straightforward, nor is quantifying it.

Consider ethanol from corn again. Would the conversion of the Amazon rain forest into corn fields to produce ethanol for cars in the U.S. be an externality? We've already decided that high food prices from conversion of U.S. farmland to corn ethanol was a market impact, not an externality. What's different about a Brazilian jungle?

This last example leads to another important set of issues which are, in my view, the most significant if we are to "get the prices right" and achieve sustainability. The Amazon *is* different from an Iowa farm, but why? And, if it is, how do we capture, measure and monetize the difference?

The rain forest of the Amazon is different for at least three reasons. It plays a crucial role as a carbon sink, the "lungs of the world". It is a place of ecological distinctiveness and unique biodiversity. And, some would argue, it has value just by being there in its present, "undisturbed" state. Each of these three reasons represents a challenge for economics and our ability to value natural resources and environmental assets.

The notion of the Amazon as a carbon sink raises the question of how we value climate change and its impacts. The fact is we are at a very early stage of understanding any of the consequences of climate change, let alone assigning monetary value to them. In addition to the physical and biological complexity of predicting consequences, there is tremendous uncertainty due especially to the long time periods into the future over which climate changes will occur. Economists have a very long way to go before they can produce reliable estimates of impacts from climate change.

The second and third dimensions of the value of the Amazon, or any environmental asset, get into basic questions of what do we mean by "value"? Attempts by economists to deal with this have tended to cast environmental values in terms of the human benefit derived from the "services" an ecosystem provides. Thus, the ecosystem services approach would associate a value with, for example, the high-quality water that downstream Amazon communities enjoy. The quality of the water depends to an extent on the integrity of the ecosystem, so, in valuing the water, which humans use, we are capturing some of the value of the ecosystem. The implication of this approach is that something has value only if humans use it. But, doesn't the Amazon have a value just by virtue of being there, so-called "existence value"? There is a philosophical question here, not unlike "what is the sound of a tree falling in a forest with no humans around to hear it?"

A BROADER NOTION OF VALUE

I believe that sustainability will be illusive so long as we value everything only in terms of human consumption. The ecosystem services concept basically implies that if I can't reduce an environmental asset into a service that produces a benefit for humans, it necessarily must have a value of zero.

Economics, as it's generally understood and practised in free-market societies, is predicated on the notion that each of us is "rational". This means that each of us seeks to maximize our utility, which is generally taken to mean our consumption, i.e. consuming and acquiring more things increases our utility. However, there have been those who have argued that this view of human behaviour and decision-making is too narrow and unrealistic. One of the most prominent proponents of this broader and more realistic view was Herbert Simon, a long-time Carnegie Mellon faculty member, (see, for example, Simon, 1955; and Simon, 1957.) In fact, this broader, more realistic view of human behaviour goes back to the origins of neoclassical economics. In two beautiful papers (Loewenstein, 1999, and Ashraf et al., 2005), another colleague at Carnegie Mellon, George Loewenstein, has argued persuasively that Jeremy Bentham and Adam Smith themselves were what we would call today "behavioural economists". We've basically simplified and assumed away what they first conceived as a much more complicated view of human decision-making. As Loewenstein put it (Loewenstein, 1999, p. 335): "The issue is not whether economics will be based on psychology or not, but whether it will be ground in good psychology or bad psychology."

The broader view of what makes people tick has emerged in some recent national policy discussions. Recently, Prime Minister David Cameron called for the U.K. to adopt the notion of "General Well-Being" as a broader measure of national prosperity than Gross National Product. This is not a new idea — it's been around for more than 20 years (see, for example, Repetto et al. 1989) — but it's getting talked about more and more in the popular press (see, for example, Friedman, 2011). It's an uphill battle, especially in a global culture that firmly believes that you can't manage what you can't measure, but surely a broader view of human satisfaction and happiness will be necessary. I don't think GNP-driven efficiency-based prices — even if they're "right" in an orthodox economic sense — will take us to sustainability. I think they inevitably undervalue nature, because all value is framed by direct contributions to human consumption.

I don't believe it's an unthinkable leap to imagine an economic response to more than the instrumental value of nature. Elsewhere (Cohon, 2011), I noted the dramatic shift in the drivers of the American economy. Google, which didn't exist ten years ago, is much bigger in market capitalization and revenues than almost all of the major companies of 20 years ago (if they even exist today.) Of course, Google doesn't "make" anything; it provides information. I acknowledge that the company's main revenue source is still advertising, a conventional and even depressing observation from the perspective of social value. But, does Google's success say something about a shift in what we value? And, if it does, what might be coming in the future? As I queried in the other paper: "Might it be that consumers in 2050 will value natural resources in a way that allows companies to make money without exploiting them? Will there be a Google of 2050 — maybe Google itself — that converts the existence value of a resource into monetary value for its shareholders?"

VALUES AND POLITICS

Dealing with the value of natural resources and the environment and related public actions is necessarily and appropriately a political matter. But, there is a real and serious question as to whether America's political system is up to the challenge of sustainability. As Bocking (2004, p. 13) put it: "Environmentalists and some environmental scholars argue that the environment cannot survive democracy."

In America today we see gridlock in Washington on almost all environmental issues including and especially climate change and energy policy. Recent survey results suggest, however, that this is not just an "inside-the-Beltway" issue; in fact, Washington's posture matches that of the American public.

In a recent publication, Matthew Nisbet (2011, available on-line) reproduces a graph which shows a strong negative correlation between the unemployment rate and the portion of the American population for which environment, including global warming, is a top priority. Nisbet cites the social psychological notion of a "finite pool of worry" (p. 62) to explain this. "As one perceived risk gains attention, other risks are bumped from concern." We only have so much worry to go around, and when you don't have a job or you're worried about keeping one, everything else gets pushed aside.

In addition, there is a strong ideological element to people's views of environmental issues, the consequence of which is that our current highly partisan politics become a roadblock to action. We've become used to ideological and political disputes, but Nisbet (2011) provides some survey results which are sobering if not downright shocking. He uses data from the Pew Center for People and the Press to show that members of the American Association for the Advancement of Science (AAAS), the publisher of *Science*, are similarly ideological and partisan about science issues as the American public. When asked whether the Earth is getting warmer due to human activities, AAAS members said yes depending on their ideological leanings to a surprising degree.

Strong Liberals	95%
Liberals	94%
Moderates	80%
Conservatives	44%

When asked if global warming is a very serious problem, the spread was even larger:

Strong Liberals	88%
Liberals	83%
Moderates	62%
Conservatives	26%

Similar spreads were observed in the general public, most of whom were presumably not scientists.

All of this can make one despair about our capacity to achieve or move toward sustainability, and sometimes I do. But, I'm an engineer, trained to solve problems. The solution to this problem, it seems to me, will come only when our values shift.

CHANGING OUR VALUES: THE ROLE OF UNIVERSITIES

I don't know how people's values are shaped, or when in one's life that happens. I am certain there is a large literature on the topic. However, while I am ignorant about the origin of values, I do know this: virtually every member of almost all governments and almost all CEOs and leaders of every sort spent some part of his or her life in our universities. Surely, we, the academic community, have contributed to the way society values nature, for good or ill, and we can help to shape how it will view nature in the future.

It is controversial to suggest that universities should dictate values to their students. We have to be careful to distinguish between values and ideology. I think we're all comfortable with promoting, for example, good citizenship and community service, while we would all be opposed to preaching liberalism to our students (even though we in America are routinely accused of doing so.) As a starting point, we can make environmental literacy a basic requirement or goal of our curricula. Being sure that every student has some basic understanding of environmental issues and phenomena seems desirable. Interestingly, however, ecology is one of those fields in which it can be hard to avoid ideology, an issue explored by Bocking (2004, especially Chapter 3.) He notes, for example, that Aldo Leopold, one of the great pioneers of ecology, wrote in *Sand County Almanac* (probably second only to Rachel Carson's *Silent Spring* among the great popular works of ecology): "A thing is right when it tends to preserve the integrity, stability and beauty of the biotic community. It is wrong when it tends otherwise."

I believe one can separate out value judgments from the facts of ecology, i.e. the impacts on ecosystems of a disturbance like destroying habitat from the question of whether it's "right" to destroy the habitat in the first place, but it's fair to ask: Should we? This is a basic question that we need to debate.

CONCLUSION

Achieving sustainability is possible only if the decisions we make and the actions we take reflect the true value of the natural resources we use. Current markets don't do that. Correcting these market failures — as difficult as that is — would move us in the right direction, but not enough, for current ideas of value capture only consumption. We need both a broader notion of the value of natural resources and mechanisms for communicating appropriate signals. Universities have a crucial role to play through their research and as the educational institutions in which future decision-makers are formed.

REFERENCES

Ashraf, Nava, Camerer, Colin F. & Loewenstein, George (2003). "Adam Smith, Behavioral Economist", *Journal of Economic Perspectives*, 19 (3), 2003, pp. 131-145.

Bocking, Stephen (2004). *Nature's Experts: Science, Politics and the Environment*, Rutgers University Press, Chapel Hill NC.

Cohon, Jared L. (2011). "Two Big Issues for Water Resource Systems: Advances in Educational Technology and Changes in Valuation," Chapter 22 in *Toward a Sustainable Water Future: Visions for 2050*, Grayman, Walter & Loucks, Daniel P. (editors), American Society of Civil Engineers (forthcoming).

Friedman, Thomas L. (2011). "The Earth is Full," *New York Times*, 8 June.

Loewenstein, George (1999). "Because it is There: The Challenge of Mountaineering… for Utility Theory," *KYKLOS*, 52, pp. 315-344.

Nisbet, Matthew C. (2011) "Climate Shift: Clear Vision for the Next Decade of Public Debate", School of Communication, American University. (available online at ClimateShiftProject.org)

Repetto, Robert *et al.* (1989). *Wasting Assets: Natural Resources in the National Income Accounts*, World Resources Institute.

Simon, Herbert A. (1955). "A Behavioral Model of Rational Choice," *Quarterly Journal of Economics*, vol. 69.

Simon, Herbert A. (1957). *Models of Man*, Wiley.

U.S. National Academies Committee (2010). "The Hidden Costs of Energy". The National Academies Press, Washington DC.

CHAPTER 3

Global Governance, the Sustainability of International Institutions and the Potential Role of University-based Research Institutes

Thomas Biersteker

INTRODUCTION

Given the complex interdependence of our contemporary world, the challenges of global governance are exceedingly daunting. The task is made all the more difficult because most of the international institutions we still rely upon to manage contemporary global challenges were originally created and designed more than 60 years ago. They were profoundly state-centric in their governance and design, and they were created with very specific purposes in mind. Although they have constantly adapted themselves to maintain their relevance and enhance their activities, institutional change and reform are highly uneven and rarely follow a linear or coherent pattern. Some institutions have proven more adaptable than others.

In the sections that follow, I will first define what I mean by global governance (and articulate criteria for evaluating the quality of governance). Second, I will describe the differential capacity of leading economic and political institutions to adapt to core institutional challenges and sustainably reform their governance. I will conclude with some reflections on the potential role of the university-based, policy-oriented research institutes in both governance and sustainable institutional reform.

CONTEMPORARY GLOBAL GOVERNANCE

Global governance is a permissive concept. Like globalization, with which it is often associated, the frequency with which global governance is invoked in the scholarly literature and in policy practice far exceeds the number of times it is precisely, carefully, or consistently defined. As a result, the term "global governance" is applied to a wide variety of different practices of order, regulation, systems of rule, and even to simple patterned regularity in the international arena. The term "global governance" is permissive in the sense that it gives one licence to speak or write about many different things, from any pattern of order or deviation from anarchy (which also has multiple meanings) to normative preferences about how the world should ideally be organized.

Scholars and policy-makers alike make frequent references to global governance without specifying precisely what they mean, so to add focus to these important discussions, I would like to make four general observations about the nature and meaning of contemporary global governance. This is done not to foreclose debate and discussion about global governance, but to clarify some basic terms, specify their conceptual scope and identify their most appropriate application and implications.

First, we should not think about global governance in the singular or talk about it as a unitary phenomenon. *There is no single, unitary or dominant form of governance in today's world.* The way the global financial system is governed — whether by the G-2, the G-7, the G-8, the G-20, the international financial institutions, or the Basel accords — is profoundly different from the way international security is governed. Security is arguably governed by regional spheres of influence, a variety of different forms of political security community, and the predominance of, and ongoing negotiations among, the Permanent Five (P-5) members of the U.N. Security Council when it comes to the determination of what constitutes a contemporary threat to international peace and security. Global environmental and global health issues are governed by a complex variety of governmental, intergovernmental, and nongovernmental actors (including a number of important private sector actors). Indeed, the governance of domain names in the Internet is largely provided by private, non-state actors, though this is increasingly being contested by states and intergovernmental organizations.

Thus, when we talk about the concept of governance in the global domain, we should not think about global governance as if it were a single or unitary system. There are multiple, overlapping, and at times, even contradictory *systems of governance* operating in different issue domains across the globe today. Even within a single issue domain — such as international security, international political economy or the global environment — there are multiple systems of governance in operation. Consider, for example, the nature of governance in contemporary global counter-terrorism efforts. There are different governance arrangements for countering the financing of terrorism, for intelligence sharing, and for strengthening efforts to keep nuclear materials out of the hands of groups engaged in committing acts of terrorism. In some ways these efforts are mutually reinforcing. In other ways, they are duplicative, offer opportunities for forum shopping (where individual actors can select the forum most conducive to their narrow self-interests), or are sometimes even contradictory of one another.

Even in the period of most significant U.S. hegemony immediately following the end of World War II, there were a variety of alternative forms and players in (as well as resistances to) the governance of different issue domains. The Soviet Union and the Eastern bloc opted out of the system of governance established under the auspices of the Bretton Woods institutions following the end of World War II, just as they stayed out of the European regional security system and resisted efforts to engage in collective action under U.N. auspices. Today there are simultaneously many different forms of governance co-existing with one another, with different institutions, different operational bases and different participants for different issue domains.

Contemporary governance arrangements are overlapping and interpenetrating, but at the same time, they can also be fragmented and diffused. One of the contemporary challenges to global governance is determining whether the density of governance arrangements facilitates or inhibits the purposes of (sometimes defined in terms of the collective goods provided by) different governance arrangements (Busch, 2007). The different worlds of global governance often tend to be relatively "small" worlds of specialized practitioners operating trans-governmentally (Slaughter, 2005), and working in certain instances to form transnational policy networks in conjunction with dedicated NGO activists and highly specialized, policy engaged (and informed) scholars. As discussed below, this can create both opportunities and challenges for University-based, policy-oriented research institutes.

Second, *it is important to try to define precisely what we mean when we invoke the term "global governance"*. Global governance is often defined in terms of what it is not — neither a unitary world government or world state nor the disorderly chaos and anarchy associated with a Hobbesian "state of war of all against all". It is constructive to think about global governance as an inter-subjectively recognized, purposive order at the global level (Biersteker, 2009). It is a purposive order which defines, constrains and shapes actor expectations and conduct in an issue domain. Its varied purposes might be to manage conflict, to facilitate cooperation, to reduce uncertainty, to procure resources, and/or to address widely perceived collective goods problems.

Governance connotes a *system of rule* or rules that operate on a global level. These rules can either be formal and embodied within formal institutions or they can be informal and reside inter-subjectively among a population or a set of key institutional actors. Global governance entails decisions that shape and define expectations ("controlling, directing, or regulating influence") at the global level. There can be different degrees of institutionalization associated with different forms of governance, and there is much debate about whether formal or informal institutions (or some combination of the two) are necessary for governance. It is not required, however, that these rules be universally recognized as legitimate, but only that they be widely shared, recognized and practised on a global scale (on multiple continents) by relevant and important actors. Most actors tend to be norm takers, rather than norm makers.

There are two elements of this conception of global governance that should be emphasized. One is that global governance entails a social relationship between some authority and some relevant population that recognizes and acknowledges that authority as possessing a certain degree of legitimacy. Governments can persist without widespread popular support, but governance requires the performance of functions necessary for systemic persistence. Governance should not be equated with government, but with the functions of government (Rosenau, 1992). The other element is that governance can exist in the absence of an easily identifiable agent deliberately governing. The word "governance" is derived from the Latin word *gubernare* (which means both "to steer" and "to regulate") (OED, 1971:1182). While governance typically connotes some agent who *steers* the process in most of the scholarly discourse and much of the popular discussion of the phenomenon, it also allows for *self-regulation*. In this sense, a market or set of market mechanisms can be said to govern, be allowed to govern, or be relied upon to govern in some domains. The market can be constituted as authoritative by the public statements (speech acts) of leaders of important states and private institutions when they suggest that they are "governed" by its behaviour.

Third, *not all systems of governance are necessarily "good" or normatively desirable*. A great deal of discussion of global governance implicitly assumes that governance is normatively a good thing. This is, at least in part, because there has been so much attention to "good governance" in the domestic realm. The global governance literature in general (for reasons already cited above) often assumes that governance and order, as opposed to anarchy and chaos, must inherently be normatively a good or desirable thing. But this is not necessarily the case. An issue domain can be governed poorly, but it is governed nonetheless. Thus we should turn our attention to articulating normative criteria for evaluating the quality of governance.

Global governance can and should be evaluated according to a number of different normatively derived, defended and distinguishable criteria. First, how *inclusive* is a particular system of governance? Are all significant populations of the world included in the system of governance? The United Nations provides an institutional venue for an inclusive system of governance, with participation of 192 Member States. The emergence of G-20 as an institutional venue is an improvement over the G-7 or G-8, but it is still far less inclusive than the U.N.

Second, and related to the first criterion, how *representative* is the system of governance operating in a particular domain? It is one thing to be inclusive, but quite another to be genuinely representative, something which has significance for the broader legitimacy of the system of governance. Whether different populations are able to express themselves and influence the core agenda is an important basis for determining how representative a particular governance arrangement turns out to be. The quality of the U.N. as a venue for security governance is more limited than it is for other issue domains, since the U.N. Security Council (which has the power to determine what constitutes a threat to international peace and security) is dominated by the five permanent Member States who possess a veto in its deliberations.

Third, a system of governance can be evaluated on the basis of its *adaptability*. That is, can it accommodate changes of power distribution and/or normative developments over time? The system of global security governance under the U.N.'s auspices has not proven to be particularly adaptable, given the fact that Security Council membership reform remains deadlocked over ways to accommodate significant changes in the global distribution of economic, financial and military power of Member States. The U.N. Security Council has done a relatively better job in adapting to normative change, as it has altered its conception of threats to international peace and security over time to accommodate post-Cold War challenges to peace. It also joined the U.N. General Assembly in altering the operational meaning of state sovereignty, by including the contested norm of the "responsibility to protect" among the rights and responsibilities of sovereign states. It has also added transnational crime, violence against women and environmental degradation to its growing list of contemporary threats to international peace and security. More generally, the U.N. system has served as an important arena for the articulation of new normative concerns, from the rights of women and children to concerns about the global environment. It is somewhat ironic, but important to note, that international organizations tend to be more adaptable (concerned, as they are, with their own institutional survival) than many prevailing global governance arrangements.

Fourth, governance can and should be evaluated according to its *efficiency*. Whether a particular governance arrangement is able to provide public goods that cannot be delivered at the domestic level or by other institutions at the regional, transnational, or global level is an important consideration, as is whether they do so at a relatively minimal, or sustainable, cost to participants and potential beneficiaries of a system of governance. The efficiency of a governance arrangement is important, because as defined above, governance requires the performance of functions for its continuation and persistence in order to maintain its legitimacy. Greater efficiency is associated with greater public legitimacy.

Fifth and finally, the *fairness* of a governance arrangement is a critically important aspect of the quality of governance in a particular domain. The extent to which a particular governance arrangement is equitable in terms of the distribution of goods and services, and/or the extent to which it is equally accessible in terms of due process for those who are affected by, or who might wish to challenge the governance arrangement, are both key aspects of fairness and thus important for assessing the quality of governance overall.

At a minimum, different global governance arrangements can (and should) be compared and evaluated over time according to these five (and possibly other) criteria. Not all governance is good governance. Indeed, there may be some instances in which poor governance may be worse than no governance at all.

Fourth and finally, although the realm of global governance has traditionally been occupied predominantly by states and intergovernmental organizations, *a variety of different institutional actors, particularly non-state actors, are increasingly playing a salient role in contemporary global governance.* They articulate alternative forms of governance, play active roles in formulating agendas, create spaces where a purposive order of authoritative sets of rules can be articulated and established, and generate ideas that governmental and intergovernmental actors act upon.

At times, the "authority of expertise" of some of these actors enables them to play an active role in governance itself (Hall & Biersteker, 2002:14). The independent assessments of non-governmental human rights organizations are important for evaluating (and potentially challenging) existing inter-governmental governance arrangements routinely conducted largely by states. The "good cops" of the U.N.'s Human Rights Council (peer Member States) are able to counter the "bad cops" of human rights NGOs in their assessments of human rights violations, sometimes softening the assessments and facilitating face-saving negotiated reforms. The evaluations of private bond rating agencies are also significant, as indicated by the 2011 down-grading of U.S. debt by Standard and Poors.

Non-governmental actors also participate in a variety of different transnational policy networks. They are not found in the form of governance provided by "the international society of states" and are largely invisible in the governance arrangements provided by an individual state's hegemony or by many international regimes, but they are often principal players in the production of international norms and institutions. It is here, as discussed below, that research university-based research institutes can occasionally play a role in contemporary global governance.

THE SUSTAINABILITY OF EXISTING GLOBAL INSTITUTIONS

Most of the international institutions that participate prominently in contemporary global governance were created in the middle of the last century, at the conclusion of World War II. The United Nations, the IMF and the World Bank were all formed during this period and accordingly reflect the ideas, the interests, the concerns and the identity of the Great Powers that emerged victorious in 1945 (particularly the U.S., U.K. and to a lesser degree, France). The U.S. tried to engage the former Soviet Union in the post-war order, but the Soviets largely opted out of active participation in any but the principal security organization, the U.N. Security Council. The world, however, has changed dramatically in the last 65 years, and one of the principal challenges facing these institutions today is their sustainability — namely, whether and how they will be able to adapt to and accommodate the emergence of new powers.

A widely cited Goldman Sachs International report in 2003 estimated that "over the next 50 years, Brazil, Russia, India and China — the BRIC economies — could become a much larger force in the world economy" and that, by 2025, could equal over half the size of the G6. Adaptability was identified above as one of the criteria for evaluating the quality of global governance, and how the international system and international organisations are able to accommodate the emergence of these four countries will indicate a great deal about the sustainability of these organizations, about the governance role they continue to provide, and about the order(s) they reinforce.

Three or four decades ago, an essay on the geopolitics of the emergence of new powers would invariably have focused on power transition and hegemonic succession, with a search for which among the emerging powers would likely be the single country to challenge the continuation of U.S. hegemony, namely the former Soviet Union, Europe or Japan. The analysis would be couched in state-centric terms, and a principal concern would have been whether major inter-state war could be avoided. Two decades ago, a comparably themed essay would have focused on the temporality and sustainability of American unipolarity. The military expenditures gap between the U.S. and any potential challenger today remains extremely large and has even expanded technologically in recent years. At the same time, however, the global security agenda has been complicated with the inclusion of a variety of transnational threats from non-state actors — from terrorism, piracy and transnational criminal organisations to global climate change and the potential spread of pandemic disease — many of them emanating from the developing world.

With regard to global security governance, the U.N. Security Council (UNSC) continues to reflect the distribution of power in 1945, and, as a result, faces a growing crisis of legitimacy and sustainability. Fortunately for the organization, two of the four BRIC countries (Russia and China) are permanent members, so the gap in legitimacy is not as great as it might have been. Nonetheless, despite widespread calls for Security Council membership reform in recent years, changes in UNSC permanent membership remain unlikely. India and Brazil were joined by the dramatically transformed former Axis powers, Germany and Japan, in a campaign to join the Security Council as permanent members (with or without a veto). Despite widespread consensus about the undemocratic nature of the Council, however, opposition to their permanent membership on the U.N. Security Council remains somewhat over-determined, largely due to the articulation of a variety of different regional power concerns against the candidacy of each of the leading contenders, along with the notable absence of any African permanent members. Three of the four leading contenders served on the Security Council in 2011, but the role they played and the positions they took on a number of contentious issues (from Libya and Iran to Syria) led some observers (not only among the P-5 but in their own countries) to question whether they were actually ready for "prime time" in global security governance.

The international financial institutions have ironically shown an ability to adapt more flexibly to changing power configurations, in part, because the share of voting power in the organisations is linked to their members' financial contributions. They accommodated the rapid financial accumulation of the oil-rich Middle East countries during the last quarter of the 20th century, and have the potential to accommodate China as well, as it continues to build up huge financial reserves in other countries. Whether this flexibility can be applied to the selection of the leadership of the IMF remains to be seen, since the opportunity was not taken up when the Directorship came open in 2011.

The G-8 was central to informal economic governance, at least until the global financial crisis of 2008, and previously illustrated some ability to adapt, by adding Russia to the former G-7. It conducted routine side meetings with China, India and Brazil, among others, and was largely superseded by the G-20 in the immediate aftermath of the global financial crisis. That body remains a location for high-level meetings and conversations, and for the broaching of new ideas, and there is currently a great deal of discussion about whether it should retain that role or create more of an institutional infrastructure to reinforce the initiatives floated at the meetings.

Reform of political institutions remains more challenging than reform of economic organizations and may have been complicated by the formation and use of "coalitions of the willing" on different issues. While changing coalitions might be able to address pressing challenges (like the humanitarian crisis in Darfur or responses to the Arab Spring), in the end, they are likely to undermine existing institutions and create new crises of legitimacy of their own. It remains to be seen whether the threat of their formation might prompt, rather than delay, genuine Security Council reform. Hence the sustainability of existing global security institutions remains very much in doubt.

THE POTENTIAL ROLE OF POLICY-ORIENTED, UNIVERSITY-BASED, RESEARCH INSTITUTES

Research University institutes and centres participate in contemporary global governance and can sometimes even play a modest role in the reform and sustainability of existing international institutions. They play a role through the independent studies they conduct (both of contemporary global challenges and the performance of existing institutions and forms of governance), through the opportunities they provide for sabbaticals for current policy officials (or retirement opportunities for reflection from former policy leaders), and through semi-independent reviews and analyses of contemporary policy options and alternatives. They participate in either reinforcing or challenging contemporary global governance through a number of different practices.

First, they can play an important *convening* function, bringing together different groups who otherwise would not interact with one another. Research universities offer a neutral space to ask a different set of questions than those defined within the confines of the day-to-day policy arena. They can also provide a basis for the formation of new networks or the extension of existing ones.

Second, university-based institutes and centres can also perform an important *training* function. Many are engaged in diplomatic training for graduate students or in the design of specialized courses for mid-career professionals. They can conduct simulations of potential crises with the direct participation of policy practitioners, and they can also serve as a repository of historical information about a given issue domain (particularly in instances where there is a high turnover in specialized policy staff).

Third, they can play a *legitimating* function, assessing, for example, the quality of existing governance arrangements, the need for reform, or the sustainability of existing institutions. University-based researchers can also participate in transnational policy networks, an institutional form that is broadly analogous to Pierre Bourdieu's concept of a specialized "field" of expertise (Bourdieu, 1990, 1980) and are constituted by a group of individuals who share a common expertise, a common technical language to communicate that expertise, broadly shared normative concerns, but not necessarily agreement on specific policy alternatives. They include trans-governmental networks (Slaughter, 2005), but transcend them to include actors other than state officials — actors from the private sector, from international organizations, from international legal practice, and sometimes from research universities. Scholarly participants in transnational policy networks might be asked for legitimating support of initiatives taken by policy practitioners or for pubic (supportive) commentaries on proposals from groups of states.

Fourth, university-based institutes and centres perform an important *research* function. They can undertake research that policy practitioners have an interest in, but lack the time, the resources, or the technical ability to engage in on their own. Scholars occasionally engage in forms of Track II/III *diplomacy* and can also be drawn upon for an historical exploration of major international crises (such as in the critical oral history conferences conducted by James Blight on the Cuban Missile crisis and the Vietnam war (McNamara *et al.*, 1999)).

Fifth, scholars can occasionally *serve as agents* of policy principals, testing ideas those principals could not risk articulating themselves within their own institutions. Scholars are free to pose hypothetical propositions or "out of the box" ideas that a career civil servant would be loathe to propose (even though they might wish to). Members of the U.N. Secretariat have on occasion used simulations involving U.N. Security Council Member States sponsored by university-based research institutes to test out the use of different policy instruments for peace enforcement.

Sixth and finally, university-based scholars can *articulate an alternative framework* or way of thinking about an issue domain. This requires careful translation into a language recognizable and usable by policy practitioners. Once they do so, university institutes can become known as a place for a particular view, vantage point or school of thought (either to be shunned or to be placated by policy practitioners).

There are important, ethical and practical implications associated with the policy engagement of university-based research institutes and their faculty members. Not only is it important that they maintain a certain degree of political independence and distance from the world of policy, but they also have to be careful about potential donor interference (or getting too close to their subjects). In practical terms, they will also have to rethink their criteria for tenure and promotion, if they wish to become engaged in the social world in this manner. The Glion Colloquium is a unique forum for pursuing these kinds of issues — issues that have important implications not only to the future of global governance, but for the sustainability of existing international institutions of governance.

REFERENCES

Biersteker, Thomas (2009). "Global Governance" in Cavelty, Myriam Dunn & Mauer, Victor (eds.) *Routledge Companion to Security*, New York and London: Routledge. (The definitional section of the current chapter has been partly adapted by the author from this article).

Bourdieu, Pierre (1990, 1980). *The Logic of Practice (Le sens practique)*, Stanford: Stanford University Press.

Busch, Marc L. (2007). "Overlapping Institutions, Forum Shopping, and Dispute Settlement in International Trade", *International Organization*, Vol. 61, pp. 735-61.

Hall, Rodney Bruce & Biersteker, Thomas J. (2002). *The Emergence of Private Authority in Global Governance*, Cambridge: Cambridge University Press.

McNamara, Robert S., Blight, James G. & Brigham, Robert K., with Schandler, Herbert Y. & Biersteker, Thomas J. (1999). *Argument without End: In Search of Answers to the Vietnam Tragedy*, New York: PublicAffairs Press.

Oxford English Dictionary, Complete Text, Volume I (A-O) (1971) Oxford: Oxford University Press.

Rosenau, James (1992). "Governance, order and change in world politics", in Rosenau, James & Czempiel, Ernst-Otto, (eds) *Governance without Government: Order and Change in World Politics*, Cambridge: Cambridge University Press.

Slaughter, Anne-Marie (2005). *A New World Order*, Princeton: Princeton University Press.

CHAPTER 4

Responsibility of Business Schools to train Leaders sensitive to Global Sustainability

Pascal Morand

Business Schools have been seriously challenged in recent years and have sometimes accused of contributing directly to the financial and economic crisis that has deeply shaken the world and has not been yet overcome. Different types of arguments have been used against BS, including the setting up and use of financial tools and products that turned out to be to be catastrophic; greedy behaviour at such a level that moral hazard negative effects are hugely amplified; a constant preference for short- and even very short-term decisions, forgetting any long-term vision; more globally, a kind of contempt for global sustainability, despite a light painting of courses and research giving no more than an insufficient flavour.

These criticisms are clearly largely exaggerated and reflect the common bitterness emerging from the subprime and financial crisis. In fact, Business Schools are more and more concerned with sustainability in every aspect including environmental, economic and social matters. Still, a lot more needs to be done.

A MAJOR CHALLENGE FOR BUSINESS SCHOOLS

An important factor is the strong demand expressed in this direction by students. There has been surely a real move in recent years. The most important aspects of this strong demand are environmental aspects, on one side, and corporate social responsibility, on the other. Students are less and less involved in politics in the classical sense (right/left, etc.), even in the countries in which they used to be, and are developing a broader sense of politics (which future for the "cité" and for the world?) linked to an extended sense of responsibility. They also themselves undertake pragmatic action to bring a direct contribution or wish they could. The World of NGOs is also becoming more and more familiar to BS students, an emerging trend being that young alumni can easily decide to work in an NGO for some time and then have a more "classical" job, and conversely.

It is also a fact that the vision of Global Sustainability can vary depending on cultures and nationalities. I have in mind the strong difference between German and French student perceptions one could observe at School in a debate on nuclear industry (which indeed took place before the Fukushima drama), where the French considered it as a clean and sustainable development contribution, whereas the Germans were totally and vigorously opposed to this vision (the BS students' vision reflecting here global different national perceptions).

On the BS Executives and professors side, there is an imperative need for global sustainability. In a classical way, we see the emergence of a specific industry in this field, meaning jobs, demand, development and profit opportunities. The different kinds of sustainability issues are spreading in all businesses and regard Business Schools core activities in any aspect.

GLOBALIZATION AND SUSTAINABILITY

What characterizes the current wave of globalisation is the move generated by the technologies of information and communication, which started in the 1980s in a limited number of industries such as textiles, spread out in the economy in the 1990s and continues breaking on the global economy. Competition does not take place only between countries and companies any more, but within companies themselves, which are now permanently confronted with choices linked to the optimization of their supply chain. How to manage outsourcing and offshoring at the lowest cost? How to reduce, as much as possible, transport and inventory costs? How to be less dependent on cost/price competition through an active innovation and a business model preserving global competitiveness? This leads to what Richard Baldwin (2006) calls the *Unbundling of the value chain*, which generates a general climate of uncertainty and suddenness. It clearly strongly interacts with sustainability. On economic and social aspects, the instability of sub-contracting and buying policies mechanically induced by this process goes against sustainability. Optimizing supply chain policies in the context of the global village implies increasing volatility. Though the challenge of green supply chain is getting more and more important.

Under another angle and following here a classical scheme, globalization fosters the sustainability imperative, since it accelerates the intensive exploitation of natural resources and raw materials. This is linked to the former parameter, since it directly impacts the cost and flexibility of transportation, the prices of products and services, more globally the whole supply chain process. It also confers a greater awareness of the limited resources of the planet. Still, the extensive use of information systems, computers and smartphones in the context of professional/private life is not very ecological, while not generating much guilt among consumers and citizens.

CULTURAL CAPITALISM AND SUSTAINABILITY

Some years ago, Jeremy Rifkin (2000) shed light on the cultural nature of contemporary capitalism. "Cultural" is here meant in its broad sense: the power of brands, of design, story-telling and creativity. This matters for the quick rise of the so-called cultural or creative industries (fashion, luxury, communication, medias, cinema, music, architecture, design, etc.), but also for consumer goods and services in a more general sense, from Disneyland to the Urban culture, from Nike to Starbucks Coffee. Cultural capitalism questions the classical "think globally, act locally" motto: the reverse proposal, "think locally, act globally", sounds very true as well. Globalization facilitates the diffusion of products and brands with a local identity, the image of which reflects a given culture and background. What makes these products/brands attractive is also that they embrace the codes of globalization, avoiding remaining strictly "ethnical" which would prevent them from having a high market power and potential. Preventing the consumer from getting bored supposes to largely amplify the immaterial content proposed to him or her. The immaterial/intangible economy concept is linked to the one of knowledge economy, which tends to be sometimes too much linked to Research and R&D challenges, eclipsing the fundamental idea that it deeply concerns too the relationship towards design in the broad sense, imagination, sensitivity, contemporary mythology. This looks a priori very favourable to sustainability, since it emphasizes non material aspects of consumption in an environment marked by brands constituting the pillars of our immaterial landscape. Nevertheless, it does not affect the tendency to accelerate over and over again consumption of new products and services. The life cycles of products and services keep on getting shorter. Searching for growth and development results in the renewal of products, "surprises" and "solutions" offered to the consumers.

This of course contradicts the consumers' demand for sustainability. In this ambiguous context, new consuming paths emerge along with new lifestyles. As an illustration, the 100 miles challenge, according to which only consuming products which have been manufactured at a distance less than 100 miles should be encouraged and even allowed, at least in the case of food, lies in the forefront of these emerging trends. Other patterns appear, such as second-hand markets, as well as vintage consumption. This is a mechanically endogenous process which is sustainability-compatible. The question is to know how far these trends will structurally transform consuming patterns.

FINANCIAL CRISIS AND SUSTAINABILITY

As well as for production and consumption, technologies of information and communication have largely contributed to financial globalization, since they have facilitated the mobility of capital. The current financial crisis of developed economies is usually described in terms of macroeconomics referring to the debt of nations, budgetary deficits, the regulating and also noxious power of speculation, etc. It needs to be emphasized here that, as for the other aspects, this is also strongly linked to microeconomic parameters, therefore as expertise fields coming somehow under Business Schools. This is indeed not denied, but in general evoked in quite superficial terms, for instance as regards excessive bonuses allocated by Banks to traders. The important factor is that this question is related to a broader and more fundamental one: the right way to measure the value of assets, bonuses being correlated to the gains in values and also to their variability. This is strictly linked to the accounting standards conditioning the assessment of values. The traditional method consisted in referring to "historical costs", which tended to be sometimes disconnected from the economic reality, when the real value of assets was diverging from their historical one. What is called "fair value" means in fact market value, which indeed sounds "fair", but raises considerable problems when there is no or no more market, that is no sellers and buyers. In the absence of a market, the use of models can enable the measurement of the value of assets ("mark-to-model"). But the scientific nature of these models, how sophisticated they are, can be easily questioned and is incidentally more and more so. All these elements favour a high level of volatility.

Financial volatility, adding to consumers' volatility and industrial volatility: all this creates an environment full of uncertainties and of general instability, which clearly enters into contradiction with the idea and quest of sustainable development.

THE DIFFERENT APPROACHES OF BUSINESS SCHOOLS

Sustainability concepts are now perfectly and largely integrated within Business Schools. Corporate Social Responsibility (CSR) has become a kind of common name, and this has been reinforced after the recent financial crisis; it is the same with environmental matters. This does not mean that there is only one way to deal with sustainability in Business Schools. Although each BS wishes to plough its own way, two models can be clearly identified, with a global distinction between the American and the European approaches. Let us add that this dichotomy is used for giving here a clear-cut analysis, knowing of course that the reality is more subtle; in particular the British approach is somehow quite close to the American one, and there are frequent differences between the BS themselves in the United States and in Europe. Still a dichotomy exists, referring to a more general one: the belief of the virtues of the market economy and its capacity to manage any challenge including sustainability (American approach), on one side; the conviction that the market economy needs regulatory long-term oriented measures to be compatible with sustainable development, on the other side (European approach). Asian Business Schools enter more and more into the debate. It is premature to identify a specific approach at this moment, although the influence of American methods tends to outdo approaches which would exhale specific cultural influences (ex: the concept of harmony in the Chinese culture, etc.)

The market-economy oriented American approach does not by far exclude the idea that rules should be elaborated, well thought out and respected. On the contrary, guidelines given to decision-makers are most useful in this perspective. This is what we can call a compliance approach. Another important factor is the expression of the philanthropic culture inherent in the American culture. Generosity and giving do matter. They are conditioned by the commitment of Business leaders and managers at any level, who can and must (in the moral sense) participate in sustainable development by giving money and time to honourable purposes, which is also true for companies themselves. This favouring of philanthropic practices takes place not only within courses but also with the development of students' philanthropic projects through participation in NGOs. This policy never questions the freedom to decide what needs to be done, which depends on the responsibility of people themselves.

European Business Schools also teach the compliance approach and encourage philanthropy in student awareness, probably in less a systematic way. But they rather explore new sustainable social models, the tensions between business models and the ecological and social challenges, new ways for regulation to make the market economic system compatible with the sustainable challenges (role of the State or of independent Authorities; Environmental accounting, etc.).

Both approaches also foster "social entrepreneurship", but sometimes laying stress on different backgrounds (profit opportunity on one side; socially responsible investment on the other). Of course, this can be de facto fully convergent. Besides, all BS tend to develop partnerships with institutions reinforcing their expertise and visibility in sustainable development.

THE ENVIRONMENTAL PREREQUISITE

The substantial importance of the environmental approach is taken into account in BS. In particular, the Green economy is considered as a new area for developing business activities. More globally, BS are ready to play more important a role. The difficulty notwithstanding remains in finding the right way to do it, and this is true for American as well as for European Business Schools. We are here in the heart of a paradox: Economic science is supposed to be the science of scarce resources, but environmental matters (the most typical example of scarce resources) are not taken much into account in the models in a deeper way than as being considered as "externalities". And this is also true in management sciences. So there are a number of courses, majors and master degrees referring to this subject, but there is a crude reality: Ecology does not really belong to the core of Business theories, models and teaching.

Another important point is the challenge to align the evolution of the market and of competences. Jobs in this industry are not so numerous, at least at this moment, and it would be fallacious to orientate the students in this field in an excessive manner. But it is also sane that all the students have a real awareness and analytical understanding of the subject, so as to be innovative players once they are in a position to make strategic and operational decisions.

MORALS AND ETHICS

The crisis has generated intense questioning of ethics and moral behaviour as a condition for a healthy and sustainable development in the coming decades. Amoral behaviour is said to have harmed economics and society. Indubitably the financial crisis can be interpreted as an effect of a moral hazard syndrome, as it was defined by Adam Smith: those who have made the bad decisions were in fact not responsible for the effects of these decisions. This has created a global irresponsible environment, leading the world to a dead end. Reducing moral hazard certainly is a key sustainability factor for the future. However and out of this primordial question, a certain confusion arose in BS and around them about the significance of ethics. Ethics are often supposed to be introduced or extended as a specific course and also diffused in all disciplines. A first problem deals with a harmful confusion between morals and ethics. If we refer to Max Weber, morals consist in acting by duty, whereas ethics consists in acting according to duty. Should we educate people so as they do things because they must or because they naturally feel like doing it? It is indeed not necessarily incompatible. To behave can be supported by both principles, but the two types of behaviours are not however identical. Ethics look better and stronger than morals, but it also opens the true question of duty.

"Truth on one side of the Pyrenees, error beyond," said Montaigne. As an example, a Confucian understanding of ethics can be different from a Christian one, and examples could be multiplied, in function of the diversity of cultures.

Besides, it looks quite strange to remark that these types of debates surprisingly tend to forget that there is a discipline, the core of which is anchored on a question such as ethics, which is philosophy. BS would gain in referring to thought elaborated over numerous centuries by Plato and Cicero, Kant and Spinoza, among many thinkers. How to reach sapience could be an appropriate motto for decision-makers' Education.

RESEARCH AS AN ASSET OR A HANDICAP?

This title seems to be provocative, since Research by definition aims at exploring the ways of reason and deepening knowledge, for the good of society. So research about sustainability is appropriate for correcting the present and preparing the future. However, the nature of Research in BS can paradoxically turn away — at least sometimes — from the real challenges of sustainability. So the positive impact of Research, which should be substantial, is unshakable but also partially ambiguous. The question here is not to deny the excellent works done in many aspects, such as the seminal works in strategy in the early 1980s about the transformation of the value chain and externalization, ten years before the economists really did tackle the subject; the flourishing works dealing with Corporate Social Responsibility; the consideration of environmental factors in management control, etc. But the problem is that Research is more and more specialized and scientific, at the expense of transversal and systemic approaches, anthropological and cultural analysis. As in many fields, Research is certainly more rigorous and scientific than it used to be, since it is codified by high-level publications criteria. But this can also carry on visions which are not large enough, whereas working on sustainability would benefit associating different and complementary visions and paradigms. We can think of a line by T.S. Eliot, saying that "a specialist is one who has sacrificed too much for too little". But the problem here is more specifically linked to epistemological foundations of soft sciences, with a dose of hard sciences on ecological questions. Sustainability is a global questioning, and it necessitates a strong collaboration between different disciplines, which supposes overcoming the focusing on different axes of research progressing in parallel. Even in strict management/economic science, mixing economics and finance and accounting can appear perfectly opportune and useful for understanding the foundations of economic sustainability, but nothing in the scientific publication criteria tend to encourage this kind of meeting. In a nutshell, Sustainability requires holism, but this simple and natural principle is far from being applied in BS academic circles, because it can be eventually discredited by the "rating agencies" (accreditors/rankings) impacting the career objectives of researches.

THE CONTEMPORARY PARADOX OF TIME

Many companies and people are now in search of sustainability, starting with their own durability. Softening the struggle to stay alive appears like a kind of shared and legitimate aspiration, with a deeper consciousness of the effects of generalized moral hazard. Simultaneously time keeps on accelerating and seems impossible to slow down, as is the unceasing flood of emails in the mailbox of decision-makers. Life cycles of products and even services are accelerating. Slow motion is difficult to bear because it is boring, unless it is the fruit of a deliberate project, such as the slow food movement. And meanwhile the need for greater stability reinforces and the planet is exhausted. The French writer Henry de Montherlant said last century that there would come a time when "slowness will be the only way to express a certain delicacy". Contributing to finding a new and sustainable balance between short-term and long-term perception and action needs to be an at least implicit orientation of Business Schools for the Future.

REFERENCES

Acquier, A. (2010). "CSR in search of a management model: A case of marginalization of a CSR initiative", in Smith, C., Bhattacharya, C.B., Vogel, D., & Levine, D., *Global Challenges in Responsible Business*, Cambridge University Press.

Baldwin, R. (2006). *Globalisation: the Great Unbundling*, Prime Minister's Office, Economic Council of Finland.

Brown, L. (2011). *World on the Edge: How to Prevent Environmental and Economic Collapse*, Earthscan Ltd.

Delbard, O. (2009). *Pour une entreprise responsable — Comment concilier profits et développement durable?* Editions le Cavalier bleu.

Hawken, P., Lovins, A. & Lovins, H. (2000). *Natural Capitalism: Creating the Next Industrial Revolution*, Back Bay Books.

Morand, P. (2007). *Mondialisation: changeons de posture*, Documentation Française.

Morand, P. & Marteau, D. (2010). *Normes comptables et crise financière: Propositions pour une réforme du système de régulation comptable*, Documentation Française.

Porter, M. & Kramer, M. (2006). "Strategy and Society, The Link between competitive advantage and CSR", *Harvard Business Review*.

Rifkin, J. (2000). *The Age Of Access: The New Culture of Hypercapitalism, Where All of Life is a Paid-For Experience*, Putnam Publishing Group.

Stiglitz, J. (2002). *Globalization and its discontents*, W.W. Norton & Company.

Viveret, P. (2002). *Reconsidérer la Richesse*, Editions de l'Aube.

CHAPTER

How can Research Universities Contribute to Fostering Sustainable Societies in Developing Countries?

Anne-Marie Leroy

INTRODUCTORY REMARKS

Although law is hardly a science, rather an intellectual discipline, it is at the heart of many of the issues discussed in this Colloquium: it shapes the functioning of democracy; it regulates markets; contributes to protecting the environment, to fighting corruption and crime; it avoids or solves conflicts, translates the ethical values of society into concrete rules, and sanctions violations. Yet, it does not lend itself to a one-size-fits-all approach and must be tailored, not just to fit the specific values of a society even for the values that mankind regards as universal, but also the very capacity of a country to implement it, and that capacity varies widely.

I have structured my presentation into three key themes. I will start by considering what I perceive as the key dimensions of the multifaceted challenge of achieving "societal" and "global" sustainability. In doing so, I will pay particular attention to the place of the law in the process, and emphasize that we need to look beyond the pure mechanics of the law in order to forge a more creative approach in the service of development. Second, I will dwell on the theme of the role of research and universities in helping the development community. I will highlight a number of challenges pertaining to law and development where universities can play a critical role in helping to generate innovative solutions. The third and last theme will focus on possible avenues

43

of collaboration between the World Bank and research universities. Here, I will show how a new initiative we are trying to launch at the World Bank called the *Global Forum on Law, Justice and Development*, which relies on advances in information and communication technologies, may provide an adequate platform for knowledge sharing, exchange and collaboration in order to better tackle development challenges.

THE MULTIFACETED CHALLENGE OF ACHIEVING SOCIETAL AND GLOBAL SUSTAINABILITY

Understanding the Problem

The theme of global sustainability with the multiplicity of disciplines and interventions it implies is one that we, at the World Bank, identify with and strive towards in our work. In addition to our vantage point as a global development institution focused on the big picture in terms of global challenges, many of our interventions are country and, often, sector specific. This means that we often deal directly with communities and beneficiaries of World Bank financing. As such, I think it is safe to say that we have accumulated a wealth of experience in working for instance with rural communities and with other development partners. In short, we have had a very direct and hands-on engagement in forging "sustainable societies" and in contributing towards "global sustainability".

What then do we mean by a "sustainable society" and what do we understand by "global sustainability"? At this point, I should perhaps point out that I view "global sustainability" as being the end point along the continuum from "environmental sustainability" to "sustainable development" to a "sustainable society" and ultimately, "global sustainability". In the simplest sense, the common strand that runs through them is that goal of wanting to meet the needs of the present, without compromising the ability of those who come after us to meet theirs.

In one sense, therefore, "global sustainability" entails the involvement of various stakeholders in ensuring that the world is a cleaner, healthier and safer place to live in. As an interdisciplinary and multidisciplinary concept, "global sustainability" involves, inter alia, the promotion of economic progress whilst strengthening environmental stewardship and social responsibility of all stakeholders. In another sense, global sustainability encompasses the concept of a "sustainable society" in which the rule of law, fairness and equity are given greater primacy. This view of a sustainable society is in accord with Nobel Laureate Amartya Sen's (1999) thesis on "development as freedom" where he postulates that all individuals are endowed with a certain set of capabilities, and that it is a matter of realizing those capabilities that will permit an individual to escape from poverty and their state of "un-freedom".

In essence, a sustainable society is one that continues to thrive overtime, developing progressive social cohesion through sustained human and social capital, and offering a high quality of life to its citizens without harming, destroying or depleting the various resources in the internal and external environments.

It is common knowledge now that unsustainable patterns of production, consumption and population growth are challenging the resilience of the planet to support human activity. More than ever before, we live the reality of those stresses. The spectre of global poverty still haunts us. Nearly a billion people are still hungry. Many more are excluded from the mainstream economy and the chance to earn a decent living. A large cross-section of others have only limited access to basic services and live in a state of heightened vulnerability. This exclusion and vulnerability may be attributed to different causes, including conflicts, poor governance and corruption, discrimination, disease, vagaries of the weather, poor or lack of infrastructure, poor economic management, weak property rights regimes and inattention to the rule of law.

In a speech marking his first 100 days in office back in 2007, the World Bank President, Robert Zoellick, eloquently captured these concerns in a manner that still rings true today, perhaps with even greater urgency. In his speech, President Zoellick acknowledged the incredible opportunity that globalization has offered, but asked us to re-envision an "inclusive and sustainable globalization". By this he meant that we must leverage the opportunities that increased global interconnectedness offers, to overcome poverty, enhance growth with care for the environment and create individual opportunity and hope. In working towards this vision of an "inclusive and sustainable globalization", President Zoellick identified a number of strategic themes, one of which I would like to pay particular attention to here. That is the theme of fostering "global knowledge and learning" within the context of the World Bank's mandate and taking into account its unique and inter-disciplinary "brain trust", varied experience throughout the world, and, very importantly, meaningful partnerships and networks.

A threshold question that I would therefore like to pose, and reflect upon paraphrased from the World Bank's *World Development Report 2011* (2011) is: how do we find ourselves in this situation in the modern world, with all the tools we have at our disposal, with all the technological and human advancement? How does an ancient problem like piracy continue to be a problem to global commerce off the coast of Somalia? How does violence persist in Afghanistan? How do the threats of drug and human trafficking continue to be a major source of national instability in the Americas and elsewhere? And who could have imagined social upheaval at the scale we are witnessing in the

Arab world? More than anything else, any answer should demonstrate that short-term solutions will not work. As the *World Development Report 2011* notes, what is needed are solutions that generate the institutions capable of providing people with a stake in security, in justice and economic prospects. In sum, what is needed is "societal sustainability", and I dare say, "global sustainability" in its multifaceted nature.

Law as a Tool to Respond to the Challenge of Building Societal and Global Sustainability

Now, what then would one say is the place of the law in the effort to meet the challenge of "global sustainability"? At its core, the theme of "global sustainability" implies a sense of equity. It implies a levelling of the playing field. It also implies broad-based longer-term prosperity and increased opportunities for the most vulnerable be they indigenous peoples, women in developing countries, the rural poor particularly in Africa, or children. Clearly therefore, inherent in the theme of "global sustainability" is a prominent role for the mediating power of the law.

Law must be grounded in the societal context in which it applies: The law cannot, and does not, exist in a vacuum. It derives from the overall values of society. Indeed this is the philosophical basis of legal legitimacy. Nevertheless, without delving too deeply into jurisprudential abstractions, we must acknowledge that different legal traditions have different interpretations of the role of law in society. But the law, with its venerated traditions, proposes at least one set of answers to fundamental societal sustainability questions, such as on distributive justice and by distributive justice here what is meant are those normative principles designed to guide the allocation of the benefits and burdens of economic activity. From my standpoint, in debating how to best approach distributive justice, theorists often forget the realities and enormous complexities of translating abstract theories into working statutes and legitimate legal principles. Knowing more about the law, and the social context in which it operates, would clearly be helpful to understanding peoples' real commitments to distributive justice and thereby craft policies that have a chance of being implementable.

Lawyers must work differently, not shy away from asking the difficult questions and help find answers to them: Given the natural grounding of the law in social values and social experiences, we must move away from the perception of the law as just a set of pedantic rules that are best left to lawyers. We must learn to appreciate the law in its proper socio-economic context, and allow it to become a key and meaningful element in the development imperative. That, in my view, is the only way through which we can achieve "sustainable societies". It is the only way we can do justice to the intrinsic equity implied in the concept of global sustainability.

Not too long ago, President Zoellick (2010) threw a major challenge to the economics profession, in an important speech at Georgetown University. In his view, "…*economics, and in particular development economics, must broaden the scope of the questions it asks thereby also becoming more relevant to today's challenges. It must help policymakers facing complex, multi-faceted problems.*" I think the law can and must be put through the same test. That means it must help broaden the boundaries of social enquiry, and it must be responsive to the mitations, capacities, values and priorities of each society.

I do know, from my own experience and that of my colleagues, that in order for legal research to play its rightful role in development, lawyers must be more pragmatic, without necessarily sacrificing their role as the custodians of process in their respective professional environments. They must be willing to look beyond the pure mechanics of the law and its interpretation and forge a more creative approach in the service of development.

Moving past old assumptions: In the past, there have been approaches and assumptions made that stood in the way of meaningful and lasting solutions to development challenges. Some of these, such as the over-emphasis on cookie-cutter solutions, which are often easier to develop, have proven ineffective and have been discredited. As a "global society" therefore, the World Bank also has to face down the power of such assumptions and the challenges they pose, which also include understanding how developing countries can better foster the development of sound laws and effective institutions to reflect the needs of their societies.

Different contexts require different emphasis. It is against this background that the development of legal tools that are suitable to a particular society or community should take into account the specific socio-economic and political context and the purposes for which they are developed. A contingency and holistic approach should be favoured over a one-size-fits-all prototype. We at the World Bank are certainly fully cognizant of the pitfalls of assuming that one size fits all. To be candid, that is something we were heavily criticized for in the past. But our experience thus far is that the potential for longer-term impact and real success is much more enhanced when solutions are tailor-made and reflective of the particularities of the societies which they aim to improve.

To illustrate, the recent events in the Middle East have shown us that societies in that part of the world demand and believe as strongly as others in justice, as well as laws that are fair, predictable and transparent. This evidence is in accord with the idea of the rule of law to which I will turn later. Here, suffice it to say, a related argument why the transplant of foreign or international legal models to developing countries has sometimes failed is that there is inadequate attention given to the issue of legal cultural diversity. As Louise Arbour, the former U.N. High Commissioner for Human Rights and former

Supreme Court Judge in Canada, observes: "[t]he resistance to the exportation of 'Western values' might be no more than the rejection of a foreign way of expressing a particular norm, rather than a rejection of the norm itself."

Criticality of respect by all for the rule of law: Another challenge is how to promote adherence by international global actors to the rule of law at the international level within a globalized world. Clearly, the last two decades or so have seen a major affront to the Westphalian system. The concept of Westphalian sovereignty, holding sacred the sanctity of nation-state sovereignty, based on two fundamental principles, territoriality and the exclusion of external actors from domestic authority structures, has suffered an affront from globalization. The Westphalian system is being challenged by the increasing growth of international global standards in areas such as economic regulation and trade. In addition, various regional integration groups and public international bodies, such as the European Union and the World Trade Organization, respectively, are promulgating regional and international standards that superimpose and prevail over national standards. But how does this all relate to, or fit into, the concept of the rule of law?

It is not uncommon to find international or regional norms being contested as unconstitutional or offending the rule of law in a Member State of a concerned regional integration scheme. While legal rules alone may be straightforward in determining the order of precedence and/or legal validity between regional and national laws, the legitimacy of such rules goes beyond mere legality. The United Nations has defined the concept of the rule of law as: "...a principle of governance in which all persons, institutions and entities, public and private, including the State itself, are accountable to laws that are publicly promulgated, equally enforced and independently adjudicated, and which are consistent with international human rights norms and standards. It requires, as well, measures to ensure adherence to the principles of supremacy of law, equality before the law, accountability to the law, fairness in the application of the law, separation of powers, participation in decision-making, legal certainty, avoidance of arbitrariness and procedural and legal transparency."

But, we know that discussions on what the "rule of law" means are marked by disagreements and that its meaning, key elements, requirements, benefits and limitations all vary between different nations and legal traditions.

So, while an action may be deemed legal in one sense, it may be offensive to the rule of law in another sense. For example, the enactment of laws that have retroactive effect or laws that discriminate against certain minorities could offend the rule of law, albeit these laws seeming somewhat valid under the law of the enacting State. It is such issues that legal scholars need to explore further in order to help shape the discourse of a constitutionally globalized world. Together with the legal scholars, we should all be moving away from a reactive, descriptive approach to a more proactive approach in developing legal tools to fight poverty. And through scientific inquiry and research, the academic community can help identify proactively critical legal problems, as well as fill the gaps where there are lacunas in the law, without having to wait until the legislature enacts a new law or the judiciary passes a new judgment.

THE ROLE OF RESEARCH UNIVERSITIES IN HELPING TO ADDRESS DEVELOPMENT CHALLENGES AND FORGING SUSTAINABLE SOCIETIES

In discussing the role of research universities towards fostering global sustainability, there are three issues I would like to focus on. The first is related to the undeniable potential for creating synergies between the development community and research universities in finding innovative solutions to the development challenge. Second, I would like to zero in on some of the challenges that the World Bank has faced in its development interventions, that I offer as avenues for potential collaboration in the search for answers, albeit, from a legal perspective. And third, I will highlight the role of partnerships and knowledge networks in the development process as a vehicle for responding to the said challenges.

Universities and Sustainable Societies: Creating Synergies to Find Innovative Solutions

There are several areas of development where our cooperating partners can provide effective leadership. These areas include examining, from a rule of law perspective, some of the challenges faced by a global organization such as the World Bank in contributing to the development of sustainable societies. It would be beneficial to the international community if we can all draw on each other's strengths as cooperating partners. Such synergies could help, for example, to inform us how the World Bank can assist some of its Member States to develop effective and sound legal systems when faced with weak or low institutional capacity pertaining to rule-making, compliance and enforcement.

Challenges Faced by the World Bank as a "Global Society"

While the World Bank has its own experts and specialists, it is always helpful to draw synergies with external partners in order to develop more concrete solutions to a number of these problems. As such, we in the Legal Vice-Presidency of the World Bank seek contributions from partnering institutions on how we can make our interventions more effective on both conceptual and methodological, as well as substantive issues and questions.

Conceptual and methodological issues: Together, we must find ways of developing viable methods of analysing the law through different lenses to determine its adequacy and effectiveness, taking into account the political, economic, social and cultural contexts in which it operates. In addition, our experience is that it is often worthwhile to critically examine the impact of legal reform initiatives and how they correlate with the objectives and needs of end-users of the law. In developing legal reform proposals, we must avoid an overly theoretical approach, which ignores political constraints and does not often translate well into implementable legislative proposals. We should always carefully look into developing legal tools and solutions that take on board implications on both the internal and external environments, the issues of legitimacy and sustainability of the law, the role of other stakeholders in adopting or using these legal tools, the available dispute resolution mechanisms, the amendment procedures, the compatibility of the legal tools with general principles of law and societal values, and the flexibility in implementing new or revised laws. The process of developing such legal tools requires broad participation of different stakeholders in order to retain legitimacy and acceptability.

We also invite academic input in helping development practitioners to develop effective tools for measuring the rule of law and its development effectiveness. A particularly urgent area is, for example, how to develop useful and impartial indicators to measure the development effectiveness of *justice* and good governance.

My call is here for legal research to move away from two frequent weaknesses in the papers it publishes: (i) a mere description of existing legal framework and of innovations made by practitioners (indeed law must be the only discipline where innovation comes more often from practice than from research); and (ii) an advocacy for drastic reforms that ignores the social and political realities in which any legal action must be founded, if it is to pass into actual implementation. Instead, my call is for research to be anchored in the day today, concrete issues that we face in developing countries.

Substantive issues: Some of the substantive questions we grapple with include the following:

- How do we help build legitimate and effective legal and judicial institutions in post-conflict and fragile situations, considering the low institutional capacity, infrastructural and other limitations? In these often difficult circumstances, how do we focus attention on the criminal justice sector and balance due process issues, citizen rights and security concerns?
- With regard to environmental challenges, how do we design appropriate legal frameworks to deal with environmental crimes such as illegal exploitation of marine resources, wildlife poaching, deforestation,

pollution and so on? What kind of regulatory frameworks should be put in place in order to ensure that carbon finance realizes the twin objectives of reducing Green-House Gas emissions and providing a stream of income to communities and businesses involved?

- How can we design legal and policy responses to the development challenge that are better adapted to the economic, social and cultural contexts of developing countries? And how do we take account of the legal pluralism that prevails in many of these societies, whereby customary law has almost as much influence as formal legal systems?

- How do we harness international law in order to provide answers to situations where new States are emerging (for example South Sudan) and the so-called "failed States" (such as Somalia) become fertile ground for regional instability? How can we develop a better understanding of the interrelationship between human rights, as well as international human rights law and development?

- How do we respond to the global financial crisis through domestic and international legal and regulatory reforms? How can we develop sustainable systems of financial sector regulation in middle-income countries in the aftermath of the recent financial crisis?

- How can we ensure that land and property rights systems (including intellectual property rights) provide adequate protections for the most vulnerable and do not hinder meaningful economic development? How do we ensure that the increasingly common large-scale international investments in land, particularly in food insecure countries, do not exacerbate the precarious situation in these countries and undermine their long-term ability to provide for and feed themselves, and on the contrary help improve agricultural productivity and the diffusion of more efficient techniques?

- How can the law contribute to enhance transparency, citizenship involvement and accountability? How can we help civil society to play a meaningful and constructive role in this process? In short, how do we help build a better informed citizenry?

- How do we fight corruption in the judicial system, which undermines all legal frameworks and can annihilate reform efforts?

- How can we help women effectively access equality of rights and opportunities?

In addressing these kinds of questions, we are inviting all our cooperating partners, including legal scholars and the academic community, to work collaboratively with the World Bank.

CREATIVITY AND PARTNERSHIPS AS KEY TOOLS
IN THE DEVELOPMENT PROCESS

The World Bank has the experience of partnering successfully with many different institutions and agencies in the delivery of development programs. For example, different donor agencies and institutions have partnered up with the World Bank for the latter to administer trust funds provided by these donors. Also, the World Bank is partnering up with different co-financiers on some of its lending programs. That different situations require different emphases explains why the World Bank continues to adapt to the changing business environment. We are learning from others in as much as we are also sharing with them our own experiences. For example, there are lessons to be learned from pioneering initiatives such as the "Scholarship in Action" approach at Syracuse University (2011) which emphasizes cross-disciplinary community outreach and collaboration with stakeholders beyond the University community. One could also mention the "Law in Context" (2011) approach pursued by institutions such as the University of Warwick, the University of Wisconsin and the University of Baltimore, through which legal education emphasizes the context, realities and the need to find solutions to social problems. Similarly, other leading initiatives, such as the Global Administrative Law Project (2011) spearheaded by New York University Law School, have helped to shape the debate on how to approach and better address issues related to global legal governance.

Many of our cooperating partners from academia and think-tank institutions continue to provide intellectual leadership in developing new concepts and theories based on a deep understanding of the challenges in the real world, including developing theoretical tools and frameworks for better understanding of complex reality. As such, the World Bank is keen on involving research universities and think-tank institutions to find solutions to real world challenges. We need their input and participation to find lasting solutions to some of the world's most pressing problems.

GOING FORWARD: POSSIBLE AVENUES
FOR COLLABORATION

Going forward, in order to build sustainable societies, legal scholars and the academic community should be participating more actively in the identification of cutting-edge legal and justice challenges at the country, regional and global levels, respectively, focusing their research at developing creative solutions through inter- and multi-disciplinary approaches. And since we know that one size does not fit all, our joint research efforts should focus more on developing legal tools that support optimal customization of legal solutions, while, of course, not neglecting the important role played by international best practices. We at the World Bank are eager to forge strategic partnerships and alliances with various stakeholders, including those from the practitioner world, in order to address all these areas. After all, our work at the World Bank involves significantly "development in practice".

Therefore, the inclusion of development practitioners, governmental and private sector institutions is unavoidable for us as much as is working with practitioners to help develop customized practical solutions to real world challenges. Ideally, the overall goal of these partnerships should include shaping the development policy agenda with other institutions in anticipation of future challenges, as well as to help educate the next generation in matters pertaining to global sustainability and sustainable societies.

We are actively pursuing knowledge and learning partnerships. In 2010, for example, the Legal Vice Presidency of the World Bank hosted a major international conference during the *Law, Justice and Development Week* in close collaboration with a number of Universities and International Financial Institutions from around the world. A number of these key partnering institutions and persons attended to share their experiences and knowledge on many of the issues highlighted above. We hope to convene a similar forum this year in close collaboration with all World Bank institutions, as well as outside partners. We also hope that we can do it on an annual basis going forward. We remain open to new ideas and initiatives that can better inform our global fight against poverty. And, internally, within the World Bank, our lawyers are also playing a significant role in developing and promoting the enforcement of governance structures and frameworks that can help to promote the rule of law and transparency in our work. In general, the fidelity of the World Bank to the rule of law and transparency remains unshaken.

That said, a major challenge facing the World Bank in the field of global sustainability and sustainable societies lies in the fact that many members of the public expect the institution to take leadership in almost all areas of human and social endeavour. But we can only do so much within the context of the resources available and in accordance with our mandate. However, through strategic partnerships and related alliances, the World Bank can make a much stronger and more effective contribution to promoting global sustainability and sustainable societies.

We are continually looking at ways in which we can better combat and prevent poverty in the world. To this end, we have not only enhanced the degree of transparency in our work at the World Bank through the adoption of the new World Bank *Policy on Access to Information*, but are also stepping forward to invite cooperating partners to work with us in developing useful legal tools to fight and prevent poverty. I am therefore extending an invitation to all of you, institutions and specifically their law schools, to consider partnering with the

World Bank through a major initiative spearheaded by the World Bank's Legal Vice-Presidency, namely, the *Global Forum on Law, Justice and Development*.

The *Global Forum on Law, Justice and Development* is both a South-South and North-South collaboration on law, justice and development issues. It is a Platform for knowledge exchange and sharing through access, exchange and dissemination of knowledge products, both raw data and value-added knowledge. Indeed, the *Forum* will contribute to:

- generating innovative and customized legal solutions to development and scaling-up of any successful solutions;
- better integrating law and justice considerations in the development process to increase development effectiveness;
- better sharing of legal solutions to development challenges among development practitioners around the world; and
- better collaboration with academic and research institutions to help solve legal development challenges. It also encourages communication and exchange of knowledge among partners and stakeholders.

The Forum is not a new institution. It will be a network of hundreds of already existing networks of law practitioners and law schools, fostering innovation, dissemination and multi-disciplinary cross-fertilization. It will use a web portal: a portal of portals, a repository of knowledge and database of databases, a networking tool and will host sub-portals for communities of practice. It will also host online training activities.

In closing…

There is no doubt that forging societal and global sustainability, and realizing the development imperative is a major challenge that can be overcome only through synergizing our efforts. In addition, the legal community, in particular, needs to step up to the challenge of re-invigorating legal responses aimed at building sustainable societies as I mentioned earlier. In forging this re-envisioned paradigm of law as a critical instrumentality of development, legal knowledge and solutions must build upon past successes and studiously avoid mistakes of the past. Legal research and practice should therefore identify and make full use of the law's potential for innovation in the development process and in empowering otherwise marginalized groups and thereby enabling them to be a core part of development interventions. Needless to say, Universities as engines for human resource generation and as they push the frontiers of knowledge creation and dissemination have a central role to play in this re-envisioned paradigm.

Our hope is that the proposed *Global Forum* will help to fill a gap in development practice. It will also provide several benefits to World Bank Member

States as well as to other cooperating partners through the creation and sharing of innovative knowledge and the partnering with a wide range of stakeholders. Through such joint efforts, we can draw greater synergies and strengths to overcome the challenges that we face today. Everyone here has a vital role to play. We cannot minimize or overlook the role of any stakeholder. We are all bound by the same destiny: to ensure that the world we live in now and the world we handover to posterity is a more just, fair, equitable and sustainable one.

A world free of poverty.

REFERENCES

Law in context (2011). See University of Warwick, www.warwick.ac.uk/fac/soc/law/lawinthecommunity; University of Wisconsin Law School, www.law.wis.edu/ils; and University of Baltimore, www.ubalt.edu/law.

New York University Law School Global Administrative Law Project (2011). See www.iilj.org/GAL/GALworkingdefinition.asp.

Sen, Amartya (1999). *Development as Freedom*, Oxford University Press.

Syracuse University Vision (2011). See www.syr.edu/about/vision.html.

The World Bank (2011). *World Development Report 2011: Conflict, Security and Development*, Washington DC.

United Nations (2004). *Report of the Secretary General: The rule of lay and transitional justice in conflict and post-conflict societies*.

Zoellick, R. B. (2010). *Democratizing Development Economics*, a paper presented at Georgetown University, Washington DC, 29 September.

PART II

•••••••••••••

The Challenges of Global Sustainability

CHAPTER 6

Strategy in the Face of Uncertainty and Unpredictability: The Research University Role

Charles M. Vest

UNCERTAINTY, RISK AND POLICY-MAKING

One of the most vexing problems we face today in moving toward a more sustainable society is the problem of uncertainty and imperfect predictability of complex physical and biological phenomena. Such states of knowledge cause havoc when scientific and technological knowledge, projections and predictions feed into social and political decision-making systems. It appears that democratic systems have particular difficulty dealing with strategic issues to begin with, and these difficulties are greatly compounded when the forcing functions that need to be recognized by strategies have nontrivial uncertainty. This may not be strictly inherent in democracy, because there are democracies, especially in Europe, that seem to have dealt better with such uncertainties than has the United States. Nonetheless, decision-making is much more difficult when it must be based on factors that are not deterministic and predictable.

The most obvious example, which is directly associated with our theme of sustainability, is the role of human activity in disrupting the stability of the earth's climate. But this is not the only such area of concern. It also appears in consideration of humankind's ability to rapidly alter biological processes, as in the case of genetically modified foods. It even arises in the context of selecting treatment options for various human diseases.

Although the theme here is *uncertainty*, one is quickly drawn into the related concept of *risk*.

In seeking certainty, we are trying to answer some seemingly simple questions:

- What will happen?
- Where will it happen?
- When will it happen?
- Why will it happen?
- What will be the consequence of it happening?

If I throw a rock at a tin can sitting on a wall, assuming I have good aim, I know from experience more or less what will happen. And indeed, if a scientist knows the initial conditions and physical parameters of the rock, the can, etc., and applies Newton's Laws, he or she can predict exactly what will happen, where it will happen, when it will happen, why it will happen and what the physical consequences will be.

What most citizens know about scientific and technical matters is based explicitly or implicitly on such classical deterministic science as Newton's laws of motion. Whether we formally learn such science or simply build intuition through experience, most of us have a mindset that if we do A, then B will predictably follow, and C will be the consequence. Furthermore, citizens think of science and engineering as producing deterministic knowledge or predictable devices. If a scientist is asked a question, we expect an answer that we can count on. Ask an engineer how a device will react to a certain input, and we expect an equally clear answer.

Unfortunately, many of the phenomena we need to consider today are not inherently certain, and to make matters worse, we usually have incomplete information to begin with. Ask a scientist whether it will rain in a certain location tomorrow and she will only be able to assign an approximate probability to the importance of you carrying an umbrella. This is largely because of complexity and insufficient data. Interestingly, many human-made devices are now so complex that engineers cannot always predict their responses with full certainty either. In both cases, the public and policy-makers probably feel that the scientists and engineers have let them down, or that they do not know what they are talking about.

To navigate the shoals of uncertainty regarding phenomena that can have bad consequences, we apply *risk analysis*. Basically, this means that we attempt through modelling, simulation or analysis of historical data to describe the probabilities of various outcomes and then to connect them to the consequences of those possible outcomes. This may apply to engineered devices or systems, e.g. a nuclear power plant; or it may apply to natural biological systems such as a disease. Decision-makers, such as government officials or business leaders, usually think about these matters in a way that can be made explicit by simple slider bars (Ropeik & Gray, 2002). Ropeik and Gray introduce two slider bars representing the probability of occurrence and the severity of the consequence of that occurrence:

Figure 1: Slider bar to display risk (high probability, low consequence)

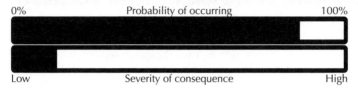

This clearly represents the way most of us think about risk. The event that is shown above has a rather high probability of occurring, but its negative consequence is fairly low. For example, the weather prediction may be an 85% chance of rain, but if you walk to work without your umbrella, the chance that you will be significantly damaged by getting wet is very small.

The situation that causes more consternation is one that has a very low probability of occurrence but has potentially disastrous consequences.

Figure 2: Slider bar to display risk (low probability, high consequence)

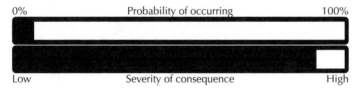

The probability that an earthquake of magnitude 9.0 would occur with an epicentre near Fukushima Japan was undoubtedly very low, and the probability that it would launch a tsunami with a wall of water 128 ft high (39 metres) was even lower, yet the consequences were horrible when both events actually occurred simultaneously on 11 March 2011. As a consequence, approximately 25,000 people died. In addition, a complex of nuclear power plants and their spent fuel repositories were seriously affected, causing great physical damage and small leaks of radiation. Furthermore, the economic, psychological and even political consequences were very large.

Whether or not policy-makers and business leaders make the right decisions regarding such low-probability/severe-consequence scenarios, most of them would readily understand this discussion and see it as the starting point for decision-making or regulation. Why? Because events such as earthquakes and tsunamis are understood to be natural physical phenomena that occur from time to time and they know experientially that the force of nature can be enormous. They do not expect scientists to be able to predict these occurrences accurately, especially well in advance. Furthermore, the occurrence of an earthquake and the launching of a tsunami are understood to be relatively *straightforward* physical phenomena, in the sense that they have occurred many times before and to some extent their causes can be explained.

Global warming and climate change, on the other hand, are far more complex. Their prediction is inherently probabilistic. Even our understanding of the past and present is incomplete and statistical. Indeed, a key finding of the recently released U.S. National Research Council report (National Research Council, 2011) is stated as follows:

*The **preponderance** of the scientific evidence **points to** human activity — especially the release of CO_2 and other heat-trapping greenhouse gases (GHGs) into the atmosphere — as the **most likely** cause for **most** of the global warming that has occurred in the last 50 years **or so**. [Underlining mine.]*

Climate change depends on nonlinear interactions of many subsystems of the climate and on various forcing functions that are complicated to understand. The impact of human activities on global warming was scientifically controversial in the early years of studying this phenomenon because our understanding was largely based on computer modelling with insufficiently fine computational grids and on a large number of simplifying assumptions and sub-models. Most of all, however, the long time scales involved and the nonlinearity of the phenomena make it really hard to for many people to relate to.

In order to move toward consideration of roles universities might play in improving understanding and policy in support of sustainability, we might benefit from examining a few cases of past reaction to global challenges.

CFCs and the Ozone Layer: Getting it Right in the Face of "Certainty"

In the 1970s, scientists determined that depletion of the stratospheric ozone layer due to widespread human use of chlorofluorocarbons (CFCs) was a threat to life on earth. The trace gas ozone that resides in the stratosphere establishes one of the many delicate balances that make life possible, because in its natural state it protects organic life, including human beings, from harmful levels of ultraviolet radiation.

CFCs were developed in the 1930s and were considered to be *wonder chemicals* because they are nontoxic, noncorrosive, nonflammable and very useful, e.g. as refrigerants, as propellants in pressure cans, and in the production of

Styrofoam. But in 1973, Molina and Rowland hypothesized a complex chemical process by which man-made CFCs were depleting stratospheric ozone (Molina & Rowland, 1974). Considerable controversy ensued in government and industry circles that was not unlike that surrounding global climate change today. In 1977, the United Nations Environmental Programme (UNEP) established a Coordinating Commission on the Ozone Layer.

In 1978 CFC spray cans were banned in the U.S. and in Scandinavian countries. In 1985, the UNEP *Vienna Convention on the Protection of the Ozone Layer* was signed. This convention pledged several countries to cooperate on research into the effects of CFCs and into alternative industrial and consumer technologies. They further agreed to cooperate on legal and policy matters and in facilitating the development of knowledge and the transfer of relevant technologies to industry.

In 1987, 24 countries signed the *Montreal Protocol on Substances that Deplete the Ozone Layer*. This now famous international protocol froze consumption of key CFCs at 1986 levels, and committed the signing countries to reduce consumption by 50% within ten years. Importantly, developing countries were given an additional grace period before they were required to phase out the use of CFCs. Interestingly, once the process got rolling, worldwide CFC consumption was phased out far more rapidly than was committed to in the protocol.

The story of CFCs and the Ozone Layer as outlined above seems remarkably smooth, certainly as compared with climate change matters in the present era. But to an extent, this is misleading. There were plenty of rocks along the road. There were loud political arguments and some countries were adamantly opposed to the phase-out in the early stages of discussion. So why was the plan successful on a reasonably short time frame?

I think that the relationship of CFCs to ozone depletion and the fact of major depletion were more or less considered as "certainties". The ozone hole above the South Pole was graphically and dramatically presented in satellite images for all to see. Although the science was still considered to be speculative during the negotiations of the Montreal Protocol, in due course scientists at DuPont and other companies that had manufactured most of the CFCs studied the science thoroughly and concluded that Molina, Rowland and others were correct.

Nonetheless, the global community, with deep engagement by scientists and leadership of the United Nations came to grips with a complex environmental threat of global dimension that would play out over the long residence time of the relevant chemicals in the stratosphere.

Industry coming proactively on board once the science became clear would seem to be an important factor, and perhaps *the* key factor, in the successful phasing out of CFCs. The immediate economic consequences, while certainly not trivial, were much smaller than those posited in the current debates about global climate disruption. It undoubtedly was extremely relevant that industrial chemists developed economical alternatives to CFCs.

A different, though pertinent, example comes from the rapid advance of life science a few decades ago.

Recombinant DNA Safeguards: Getting It Right in the Face of Uncertainty

In the early 1970s, the public read in the newspapers and heard on radio and television that scientists had developed something called *recombinant DNA technology*. This involved transplanting genes from one species into the cells of a different species. The ability to do this emerged rather rapidly in the late 1960s and early 1970s from several laboratories across the U.S. and Europe. The public, and indeed many scientists, worried that application of this new technology might pose fundamental risks to life on our planet.

Although the immediate consequences of such gene transplantation were well understood by biologists and molecular chemists, there was deep concern that unforeseen negative consequences for health and the environment might be on the horizon. For example, rapidly propagating diseases with no known treatments might inadvertently be launched, or newly created modified organisms might interact with other organisms in ways that had unpredicted, dire consequences.

These concerns were very deep among much of the lay public and were made even stronger by those who saw it primarily as a moral issue. Leaders of the biology community took these concerns about unpredictable consequences seriously; indeed a few of the scientists held these worries themselves. The key group of scientists engaged in recombinant DNA research was fairly small by today's standards, and after discussion they decided in 1974 to establish a voluntary moratorium on certain recombinant DNA work. They then decided to convene a conference to discuss the issues with other scientists and concerned parties.

This conference was held at Asilomar, California, in February 1975. There were 140 participants. Most were scientists, but physicians, lawyers, government officials, journalists, philosophers and religious leaders also participated. The purpose of the conference was to decide whether to lift the moratorium and, if so, to define the conditions for safely conducting recombinant DNA research.

The group assembled at Asilomar came to a strong, though not unanimous, consensus that the moratorium should be lifted; however, they also spelled out in some detail strict biosafety guidelines for safely conducting such work. These specifications for research facilities and procedures were subsequently adopted by the U.S. National Institutes of Health (NIH) and ultimately in many other countries as well.

So here we have an example of explicitly coming to grips with a type of scientific uncertainty. The leaders of the scientific community drove this solution through a nongovernmental consensus process. It appears to have been successful. It led directly to subsequent governmental regulation, and it engendered considerable public trust. Nonetheless, it should be noted that some have criticized this process for having given insufficient weight to ethical and legal discussion and for failure to consider in depth implications for biological warfare.

In my view, the temporary, self-imposed moratorium on recombinant DNA research and the deliberations of the subsequent Asilomar Conference comprise a high point in setting policy and strategy in the face of uncertainties that might hold serious, negative consequences for life on earth. However, it was simple to deal with in the sense that the solution involved straightforward technology and protocols for containment of any biohazards that might occur. Furthermore, only highly trained scientists and technicians in small facilities conducted the work involved.

Nonetheless, it is an instance of us having "gotten it right".

GLOBAL CLIMATE DISRUPTION: GETTING IT WRONG?

A Complex, Nonlinear, Probabilistic Phenomenon

As we think about moving aggressively toward a more sustainable global society in the face of rapid development in large populations and an inexorable march toward a world population of nine billion people, the world's inability to take action against climate change is a major problem. The poster child for paralysis in this regard is the United States, although they are joined in it by many other countries. What keeps the U.S., and perhaps other countries, from setting a firm course in the face of enormous risk to life on earth in the context of considerable real or apparent uncertainty?

There seems to be a clue to the problem in the use of language. Both politicians and scientists discuss whether or not they *believe* that climate change is real and if so, whether or not they *believe* that it is caused in large measure by human actions. In far too much of the discourse in the U.S., *belief* has taken on a connotation of a religious-like or ideological belief, rather than implying whether or not scientific observation and analysis are sufficient to form a basis for policy.

Climate science is complex because the earth's environment and energy systems are complicated and held in delicate balance. Climate science is not easily reduced to a few simple observations and explanations immediately

Figure 3: Notional immediate, linear response to an action: Easy to understand

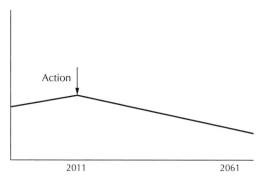

Figure 4: Nonlinear, Delayed Response: Not So Easy to Understand

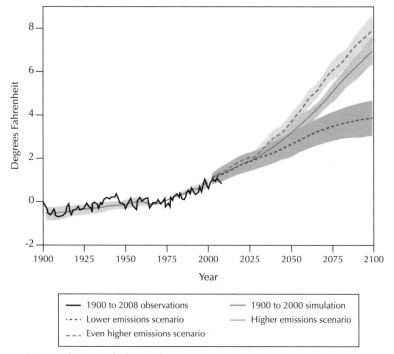

Source: National Research Council, 2011. Figure 2.4, p. 22.

accessible to lay persons. While images of polar bears on melting ice are dramatic, their significance is not crisp, static and obvious in the same sense as were the images of the ozone hole in the stratosphere. The analysis of what we face going forward is probabilistic in nature, and that is always a problem in public policy formulation. The time frame for major damage is not immediate. The necessary risk mitigation, however, requires near-term action to stem problems that would occur many years into the future. The nonlinearity, i.e. future acceleration of the processes, is a particularly vexing issue to put before the public and policy-makers who are used to thinking linearly.

Cultural Impediments and Mindset

Because we are dealing with our earth and its ability to sustain life, the mindsets and belief systems of individuals and groups frequently come into play. The very successful history of the United States is quite recent by world standards. Its narrative is one of a continual, individualistic, westward movement. The pioneers *tamed* nature and harvested bountiful crops, minerals, animal life and energy resources. The industrial age amplified this taming and harvesting to a massive scale. Resources were readily available. Nature provided. It is ingrained in our mindset.

Americans, based on experience, are predisposed to think of resources as limitless on the time scale of a human lifetime, and by extrapolation, much longer. For many, a religious belief system also underlies the way they think about long-term issues like climate change. Indeed, one Congressman who holds a key position with regard to national policy in energy and environment has stated that he does not believe that humans will be responsible for catastrophic climate change and cites the "infallible word of God" in the Bible's Book of Matthew as the source of his belief (Rudolf, 2010).

Another issue that arises clearly in America, and in a different guise in other nations, is a lack of true global view. Americans of previous generations, and even of my own generation, lived very insular lives. Except for the military experience of the World Wars and international travel by the wealthy, we lived very much apart from the rest of the world. A huge swathe of the American public lived in small, relatively self-sufficient towns and came to view the rest of the world as something exotic. Although America, its business, economy and culture are now highly integrated into the world, this reality remains at odds with the national narrative deep within the psyche of many citizens. So national interests are often seen apart from the interests existing in other countries.

In a not altogether different way, many in the developing world, who actually have an opportunity to build their infrastructure and economy in a more *green* manner, also seem to perceive their national interests to be independent of those of the rest of the world. They may believe that they are starting up the economic ladder from the bottom and have a right to develop, at least for a period, without carrying the additional costs of green technologies. This argument is understandable, and possibly one that could be accepted as valid if the developing nations were a small part of the world's population. But the fact is that they comprise a huge part of the world's population and the rapid industrialization of countries like China and India will soon dominate the world scene.

Many Americans and others in the developed world have been fortunate to have a comfortable life. These lives have been built by individuals or by the preceding generation, and they include mobility, physical comfort and access to a wide variety of food and products that make their lives enjoyable, but that use large amounts of energy and other resources. There is an understandable instinct that if the environment is to be improved, and if our climate is to be rendered more stable, they will have to give up these things, i.e. to make great sacrifices. Undoubtedly some sacrifice is required to achieve a more sustainable economy and lifestyle, but there are huge possibilities that through focused innovation we can dramatically lessen the actual *sacrifice* required. The most obvious case is that by increasing the efficiency of buildings, appliances and other systems that use large parts of our energy budget, we can realize very large reductions in emission of greenhouse gases and still live and work comfortably.

Finally, there seems to be a substantial part of the American population that believes that science and technological innovation will be able to conquer the challenges ahead to our environment and climate. This, we hope, is true; however, there must be a starting point, a strategy and a political will. An optimist can see the beginnings of such movement, especially in the viewpoint and passions of the younger generation. But somehow, the American "can do" spirit has not yet been tapped on a broad scale.

All of the factors discussed in this section lead to a tendency to say *mañana* and take slow action or no action. And if we add to this stew uncertainty and nonlinearity, two things happen. First, the danger of inaction or slow action is greatly amplified, as are the ultimate costs of coming to grips with climate change. Second, the necessary extent of action required, and its near-term and long-term economic consequences, are difficult to measure.

But there is one last thing that may be at work here: *scale*. In a recent interview on NPR (National Public Radio in the U.S.), *New York Times* columnist Nicholas Kristof discussed what he viewed as his failure to motivate the public to take action against the horrible human suffering in Darfur. He cited social science research that suggests that individuals tend to simply tune out information that seems to portray issues of a scale that they cannot really comprehend and intuitively do not believe they can impact. He described experiments in which a group of potential philanthropic donors were presented with an exposition of extreme hunger among 21 million people in West Africa. This group was subsequently solicited for contributions to aid these starving people, but they pledged almost no money for this purpose. A second group was shown a photo of a single starving girl from Mali. This group pledged very generous support. This suggests that it is human nature to turn away from problems of large scale with which we do not emotionally connect or think we cannot effectively confront as individuals. (Kristof, 2010)

So, among the factors that may be leading to a lack of political will in the U.S. and elsewhere to set serious strategies toward sustainability and toward combating global climate disruption are:

- Belief systems, including religion
- Complexity
- The American narrative of the preceding three centuries
- The "right" of developing nations to climb the economic ladder unencumbered by costs of sustainability
- Sacrifice
- Science and technology will solve it (without investment and political will)
- *Mañana*; it's in the distant future
- Being overwhelmed by scale.

When these factors are combined with uncertainty, risk and nonlinearity, it becomes quite difficult to achieve the breadth of understanding and commitment to develop the political will required in a democracy.

What Can Universities Do to Help?

In the face of these and other realities, what should the university community do? What should be our goals? Possible goals include:

- Reduce the uncertainty?
- Concentrate on understanding risk?
- Develop better social/political means of discussing uncertainty and risk?

Universities could play major roles in addressing all three of these possible goals.

It is in everyone's interest to reduce the uncertainty associated with phenomena associated with sustainability and especially climate change. Part of the political controversy about climate change stems from the fact that early discussions were indeed based on computer modelling that was restricted by the technology of the day to grid sizes and time steps that were really insufficient. More recently, the computational capabilities have improved dramatically, and much of the scientific evidence and understanding now come from direct *observation*. Of course, the nature of most scientific progress means moving down a path, usually an iterative one of observation, experimentation and simulation that continually reduce uncertainty. Even though our core understandings of climate change are now accepted as scientifically solid by most of the scientific community, continued work to reduce uncertainty in what we know and what we project forward in time remains an extremely important role for university researchers.

It certainly appears that movement toward a more sustainable future is one of many important domains in which democracies could make better decisions if citizens had a better, imbedded understanding of risk. They would also need to view risk assessment and cost-benefit ratios as natural elements of decision-making. All too frequently, the public and many policy-makers think of risk in a binary fashion. Things are either required to be absolutely free of risk, or else they are assumed to be unacceptably dangerous. This human instinct is fully understandable, but in a modern, complex society, we must do better. It seems to me that universities, in their research and education in the social sciences, could contribute greatly to understanding risk, understanding the cognitive responses to risk, and enhancing our ability to communicate effectively about risk. If society is handed more effective means of analysing, considering, communicating and utilizing risk as a more natural part of our discourse, wiser decisions might be made about areas such as sustainability and priority setting.

Uncertainty generally is well understood by people with education and training in science, medicine or engineering. But uncertainty of the type discussed here often is not handled well in public discourse and political decision-making. There may be a very productive role for the humanities and arts in ameliorating this. After all, the humanities largely evolve around understanding and communicating about deep human challenges, motivations and reactions, including the role of luck, complexity and human nature. Humanistic inquiry ranges over vast periods of time and from global truths to the narrowest spaces of human thought and motivation. Surely there is room here to contribute to our progress toward a more sustainable future. After all, in the first instance, sustainability is largely a mindset.

Similarly, the arts help us to understand big themes and the interplay of individuals and ideas with the larger society. Indeed, it is sometimes said that artists see the future before the rest of us. There should be a productive common cause of artists with scientists, engineers, economists, business scholars and others on our campuses for moving toward the understandings necessary to deal effectively with challenges like sustainability in the face of uncertainty.

SUMMARY

In summary, challenges like sustainability that must be addressed in the context of uncertainty, risk and complexity, are daunting because of many easily identified factors. These factors have their origin in history, belief systems, personal experience and the popular expectation of scientific certainty. There would seem to be very important roles for virtually every corner of research universities — natural science and engineering, social science, humanities and arts — to bring their research, scholarship, analysis and especially education to bear on the challenge of creating a citizenry, a policy community and political system better able to join together to move toward a more sustainable future in a context that is inherently uncertain.

REFERENCES

Kristof, N. (2010). Interviewed by Krista Tippett on National Public Radio program *Being*. 23 September 2010. Transcript retrieved from: http://being.publicradio.org/programs/2010/journalism-and-compassion/transcript.shtml

Molina, Mario & Rowland, F. S. (1974). "Stratospheric Sink for Chlorofluoromethanes: Chlorine-Catalysed Destruction of Ozone," *Nature*, 249, pp. 810-812.

National Research Council. (2011a). *America's Climate Choices*. Washington, DC: National Academies Press.

National Research Council. (2011b). *America's Climate Choices*. Washington, DC: National Academies Press.

Ropeik, D. & Gray, G. (2002). *Risk: A Practical Guide for Deciding What's Really Safe and What's Really Dangerous in the World Around You*. New York: Houghton Mifflin.

Rudolf, J. C. (16 November 2010). Climate Skeptic Seeks Energy Committee Chairmanship. Green: A Blog About Energy and Environment. *The New York Times*. Retrieved from: http://green.blogs.nytimes.com/2010/11/16/god-man-and-congress-on-climate-change/

CHAPTER 7

Global Sustainability: Timescales, Magnitudes, Paradigms and Black Swans

James J. Duderstadt

We live in a time of great change, an increasingly global society, driven by the exponential growth of new knowledge and knitted together by rapidly evolving information and communication technologies. It is a time of challenge and contradiction, as an ever-increasing human population and invasive activities of humankind are now altering the fragile balance of our planet. The concerns are both multiplying in number and intensifying in severity: the destruction of forests, wetlands and other natural habitats by human activities leading to the extinction of millions of biological species and the loss of biodiversity; the buildup of greenhouse gases such as carbon dioxide and their possible impact on global climates; the pollution of our air, water and land. A global, knowledge-driven economy places a new premium on technological workforce skills as governments place increasing confidence in market forces to reflect public priorities, despite the evidence that they have become increasingly unstable. Shifting geopolitical tensions are driven by the great disparity in wealth and power about the globe, manifested in the current threat to homeland security by terrorism. We are challenged to find new ways to provide for a human society that presently has outstripped the limits of global sustainability.

Yet, as the declaration of the Glion VII conference, drafted by Frank Rhodes, reassures us (Rhodes, 2009):

"The daunting complexity of the challenges that confront us would be overwhelming if we were to depend only on existing knowledge, traditional resources and conventional approaches. But universities have the capacity to remove that dependence by

the innovations they create. Universities exist to liberate the unlimited creativity of the human species and to celebrate the unbounded resilience of the human spirit. In a world of foreboding problems and looming threats, it is the high privilege of universities to nurture that creativity, to rekindle that resilience and so provide hope for all of Earth's peoples."

Today's challenges presented by global sustainability differ from those faced in earlier eras, and these will require major changes in educational, research and service activities of our universities. This is the topic of this paper. Yet here, there are many things that puzzle me.

SOME PUZZLES

There is ample evidence that the world's climate is changing — and quite rapidly in fact, e.g., the shrinking of the Artic ice cap, the melting of glaciers around the world, shifting climates and more intense storms. Furthermore, the fact that the only thing that has changed in a massive way over the last thousand years is the doubling of carbon-dioxide concentrations in the atmosphere produced by the burning of fossil fuels and land-use practices. This strongly suggests this climate change is due to the activities of humankind. The increasing confidence on the part of the vast majority of the scientific community that the activities of humankind are changing the climate of the planet is illustrated by the most recent conclusion of the International Panel on Climate Change: "Warming of the climate system is unequivocal... Most of the observed increase in globally-averaged temperatures since the mid-20th century is very likely due to the observed increase in anthropogenic greenhouse gas concentrations" (IPCC, 2007). Yet, not only have we made rather feeble attempts to address this, but a substantial part of our population denies the reality of both climate change and human impact.

It is also puzzling that, despite the growing evidence that our current energy infrastructure based largely on fossil fuels is no longer sustainable, whether because of limited reserves of oil and gas, the rising costs driven by the imbalance between supply and demand or environmental impact, we continue on with business as usual — drilling more wells, fracturing more shale deposits for gas, building more coal-fired power plants and producing more gasoline-guzzling automobiles. Of course, we do hear suggestions that perhaps renewables such as wind or solar power are the answer, if only we would just invest in them — although another carbon-free technology, nuclear power, is rarely mentioned as an option.

The past several years has also clearly established the vulnerability of our financial markets, dependent as they are on poorly understood instruments such as derivatives and credit default swaps, guided by abstract theories developed by renegade theoretical physicists, driven by the insatiable greed of traders and gigantic banks, and linked tightly together through computers and networks into highly unstable, nonlinear and poorly understood systems. Yet, despite the loss of many trillions of dollars and the livelihood of millions of people as these systems collapsed in 2008, pulling down our economies with them, we seem unwilling to take steps to regulate these dangerously unstable markets or discipline those who have made billions from speculative activities. Any engineer could warn that removing constraints (e.g., friction) from an intrinsically unstable system will lead to catastrophe!

Finally, I remain puzzled by how our society views the great tragedy this past year in Japan, hit by a massive tsunami triggered by one of the largest earthquakes in history. Although this natural disaster has destroyed cities and claimed tens of thousands of lives, we instead seem more concerned by the impact the tsunami caused to a 40-year-old nuclear power plant, that while seriously damaged, has yet to have a measureable impact on public health, although it seems likely to have thrown seriously off course the global effort to expand nuclear power as the only currently viable major source of carbon-free electricity generation.

Of course, there are a lot of explanations to these puzzles. To be sure, people tend to believe what they want to believe. They tend to seek simple solutions to complex problems such as global climate change. So too, greed can be a very powerful destabilizing force, and the wrong incentives can stimulate taking excessive risks, whether in financial markets or the design of complex technology (e.g., BP's deepwater drilling). There are also problems in the way that experts describe these issues to the lay public (Bierbaum, 2011). Of course, it is not surprising that people do not believe what scientists try to tell them. Climate change can be both complicated and counterintuitive, for example, explaining why global warming could lead to major snowstorms. Furthermore, the scientific community can appear arrogant and cavalier at times (e.g., the "Climategate" scandal that led to cries of conspiracy and hoax). But to disregard Mother Nature is another matter.

We should have learned the dangers of benign neglect from a 20th century characterized by two world wars, the threat of nuclear holocaust, the impact of global pandemics (e.g., the influenza pandemic of 1918), the havoc caused by dictators and failed states, and the list goes on. The forces we face today are somewhat different, but no less threatening and challenging. Our current inability to generate sufficient concern and action to address the challenge of global sustainability may suggest that something more fundamental may be involved: the difficulty we have in comprehending the timescales, magnitudes, and paradigm shifts characterizing the challenges threatening global sustainability. There is one more characteristic that complicates this even further: the degree to which our world is being reshaped by "Black Swan" events (a term to be explained later).

TIMESCALES

We usually think in terms of the timescales characterizing our own experiences. For example, businesses tend to function on timescales determined by quarterly earnings statements — little wonder here, since this is how Wall Street estimates the value of their stock. Public policy evolves on timescales of election cycles, in the U.S. typically two-year cycles corresponding to state and federal elections. (Of course, dictatorships tend to function on timescales determined by the lifetimes of their leaders, as vividly being demonstrated today in the Middle East and Africa.) We tend to think of natural phenomena, such as climate change or biological evolution operating on very long timescales, thousands or even millions of years. But all of this is changing, with serious implications for global sustainability.

As we have noted, evidence of global warming is now incontrovertible — increasing global surface and air temperatures, receding glaciers and polar ice caps, rising sea levels and increasingly powerful weather disruptions — all confirm that unless the utilization of fossil fuels is sharply curtailed, humankind could be seriously threatened. There are several timescale issues here. In the near term (meaning decades), if the current rate of growth of fossil fuel combustion continues, atmospheric carbon dioxide concentrations that have been in the range of 200 to 300 ppm by volume for 400,000 years and have already increased to current levels of 390 ppm are projected to rise even further to 550 ppm by 2050 (Lewis, 2007). Although human adaptation could probably occur at this level, it would be in a radically different world in which biodiversity would be seriously threatened (e.g., the coral reefs would die), and the seas would rise by 1-2 metres, flooding much of the world's lowlands. A world that continued to be primarily dependent upon fossil fuels could see carbon dioxide concentrations of 800 ppm by 2100, approaching the point at which even more serious events, such as the melting of the ice masses in Greenland or Antarctica could raise sea levels by several metres, or the methane in the Artic tundra could be released, triggering a possible runaway greenhouse process (think Venus).

Unfortunately, the lifetime of carbon dioxide in the atmosphere is very long. Even if current emissions could be eliminated, it would take thousands of years for concentrations to decay back to acceptable levels. Hence, we have only a few decades to address this problem before reaching the point of no return. As Nate Lewis of Caltech suggests, we are currently conducting the biggest experiment with Planet Earth that humankind has ever performed by tinkering with our climate: "We get to do this experiment exactly once. And there is no tomorrow, because in 20 years that experiment will be cast in stone. Within the next 20 years, we either solve this problem or the world will never be the same!" (Lewis, 2007).

However, the success of this "experiment" depends on facing up to a second challenge: Our current energy infrastructure, heavily dependent upon fossil fuels, is unsustainable, particularly within the context of global climate change, but also because of possible mismatch between supply and demand (particularly for oil that may already have reached a peak in production). Clearly, if nations are to meet their responsibilities for national security, economic prosperity and environmental impact, the world must move rapidly and aggressively to address the need for a sustainable energy future. Yet, time is not on our side.

The energy industry and its markets are the world's most massive, most indispensable, most expensive and most complex, in which major technological change occurs on a timescale measured in decades, not years (Smil, 2010). As Lewis points out, new energy sources, such as renewable energy technologies, are a "substitution" product that require first, fostering a marketplace where the technology can come to scale and compete (Lewis, 2007). Hence, even with strong government involvement in developing new energy technologies and intervention in the marketplace, it will take decades for sustainable technologies to have major impact. Yet, the clock continues to tick, carbon dioxide levels continue to rise, and the climate continues to change.

As yet another example of shifting timescales, we might consider the recent experiences of our financial markets, now not only coupled together electronically about the world, but with supercomputers instantaneously solving the complex equations developed by mathematicians and physicists ("quants") to determine key trading decisions, rather than the more deliberate decisions of analysts and brokers on the trading floor. Here the timescale issue involves new technologies driving such profound changes in our world, such as information technology, are characterized by an exponential pace of evolution in which characteristics such as computing speed, memory and network transmission speeds for a given price increase by a factor of 100 to 1000 every decade. Scientists and engineers today believe that the exponential evolution of these technologies is not only likely to continue for the conceivable future, but, in fact, the pace may be accelerating.

MAGNITUDES

In sharp contrast to the rapidly contracting timescales characterizing exponential technologies such as computers and networks, other activities critical for determining global sustainability are more constrained by their scale or magnitude. For example, producing energy, distributing it to society and transforming it into useful functions requires a massive and expensive infrastructure. The scale of the necessary transformation of our energy infrastructure is immense. It is estimated that over $16 trillion in capital investments over the next two decades will be necessary just to expand energy supply to meet growing global energy demand driven by the energy needs of developing economies (compared to a global GDP of $44 trillion and a U.S. GDP of $14 trillion). Put another way, to track the projected growth in electricity demand, the world would need to bring online a new 1,000 MWe powerplant every day for the next 20 years! (Lewis, 2007) Moreover, the International Energy Agency estimates that to keep carbon dioxide emissions below 450 ppm (and global temperature increases below 2°C) would require an investment of $12 trillion in low-carbon energy technologies and energy efficiency by 2030 (Smil, 2011).

Yet, there is another important magnitude issue here. Unfortunately, most renewable energy sources, such as wind, biofuels and solar, are very dilute. MacKay demonstrates this by comparing the land mass requirements for each energy source by comparing power densities: windpower: 2.5 watts/m^2; biofuels: 1.5 watts/m^2 (in Brazil); solar: 6 watts/m^2 to meet the needs of the UK population, 1.5 watts/m^2, concluding that a renewable energy economy would take most of the UK land mass. He goes on to note that to meet the needs of Europe with solar energy would take a region of solar collectors about the size of Germany (MacKay, 2009).

A second example of just how magnitudes influence global sustainability is demographics. The United Nations has recently updated its projection of world population growth to 9.3 billion by 2050 and to over 10 billion by 2100 (United Nations, 2011). This raises the logical question: Can we sustain a population of such magnitude on Spaceship Earth? In fact, the basic premise of the free market system, which relies on steady growth in productivity and profits, based in part on similar growth in consumption and population, must be challenged by the very serious problems that will result from a ballooning global population, such as energy shortages, global climate change, and dwindling resources. The stark fact is that our planet simply cannot sustain a projected population of 10 billion with a lifestyle characterizing the United States and other developed nations with consumption-dominated economies.

To be sure, there are some signs of optimism here: a slowing population growth in much of the world (although not in Africa), the degree to which extreme poverty appears to be receding, both as a percentage of the population and in absolute numbers, and the rapid economic growth of developing economies in Asia and Latin America. During the past several decades, technological advances, such as the "green revolution" in agriculture, have lifted a substantial portion of the world's population from the ravages of extreme poverty. In fact, some nations once burdened by overpopulation and widespread poverty, such as India and China, now are viewed as economic leaders in the 21st century.

Yet today, there remain substantial and widening differences in the prosperity and quality of life of developed, developing and underdeveloped regions; between the North and South Hemisphere; and within many nations (including the deplorable level of poverty tolerated in my own country, the richest on the planet). It is estimated that roughly one-sixth of the world's population, 1.5 billion people, still live in extreme poverty — defined by Jeffrey Sachs as "being so poor you could die tomorrow", mostly in sub-Saharan Africa, parts of South America, and much of central Asia. Sachs states this in even stronger terms: "More than 8 million people around the world die each year because they are too poor to stay alive. Malaria, tuberculosis, AIDS, diarrhea, respiratory inflections, and other diseases prey on bodies weakened by chronic hunger, claiming more than 20,000 lives each day". (Sachs, 2005).

PARADIGM SHIFTS

Looking back over history, one can identify certain abrupt changes, discontinuities in the nature, the fabric, of our civilization. Clearly, we live in just such a time of very rapid and profound social transformation, a transition from a century in which the dominant human activities involved the exploitation of natural resources to manufacture and transport goods to one in which communication technology has become paramount, from economies based upon cars, planes, and trains to one dependent upon computers and networks. We are shifting from an emphasis on creating and transporting physical objects such as materials and energy to knowledge itself; from atoms to bits; from societies based upon the geopolitics of the nation-state to those based on diverse cultures and local traditions; and from a dependence on government policy to an increasing confidence in the marketplace to establish public priorities. A radically new system for creating wealth has evolved that depends upon the creation and application of new knowledge and hence, upon educated people and their ideas and institutions such as research universities, corporate R&D laboratories and national research agencies where advanced education, research, innovation and entrepreneurial energy are found (Drucker, 1999).

Whether through travel and communication, through the arts and culture, or through the internationalization of commerce, capital and labour, or our interconnectedness through common environmental concerns, the globally community is becoming increasingly integrated. The liberalization of trade and investment policies, along with the revolution in information and communications technologies, has vastly increased the flow of capital, goods and services, dramatically changing the world and our place in it (National Intelligence Council, 2005). Today, globalization determines not only regional prosperity, but also national and homeland security. Our economies and our companies are international, spanning the globe and interdependent with other nations and other peoples.

It is also becoming increasingly clear that we are approaching an inflection point in the potential of information and communications technologies to radically transform knowledge work. When we think of digitally mediated human interactions, we generally think of the awkwardness of e-mail or televideo conferences or the instantaneous interaction with text messaging or video Skype. More recently, we have seen the power of social networking through software, such as Facebook and Twitter, to link together millions of people, not only building new communities, but empowering social movements, such as the Arab Spring of 2011.

Beyond acknowledging the extraordinary and unrelenting pace of evolution of such technologies, it is equally important to recognize their disruptive nature. The impact on social institutions such as corporations, governments and learning institutions is profound, rapid, and quite unpredictable. As Clayton Christensen explains in *The Innovators Dilemma*, while many of these new technologies are, at first, inadequate to displace today's technology in existing applications, they later explosively displace the application as they enable a new way of satisfying the underlying need (Christensen, 1997). If change is gradual, there will be time to adapt gracefully, but that is not the history of disruptive technologies.

BLACK SWANS

During the past year, the world has been rocked by unanticipated events such as the failure of the BP Deepwater Horizon drilling platform in the Gulf of Mexico and the Fukushima Daiichi nuclear power plant accident resulting from a massive tsunami hitting the coast of Japan. It seems appropriate here to adopt the terminology of "black swan" introduced by Nassim Taleb to refer to an event that is "outside of regular expectations; carries an extreme impact; and makes us concoct explanations for its occurrence after the fact, making it explainable and predictable" (Taleb, 2007). The name arises from a 16th century conjecture that since all swans were presumed at that time to be white, and black swans were then presumed not to exist, if one were found it would disprove the impossibility of this presumption. (Actually, black swans did exist, but in Australia. Today they have also been imported into Europe.)

Taleb suggests that Black Swan events are increasing as our world becomes more complex and integrated, and today they may be more important than ordinary events in determining issues like global sustainability. "Black Swan logic makes what you don't know far more relevant that what you do know. Since Black Swans are unpredictable, we need to adjust to their existence (rather than naively trying to predict them). We need to consider the extremes, improbable or not, particularly if they carry an extraordinary cumulative effect. We need to invest more in prevention than in treatment." (Taleb, 2007).

The tsunami-driven accident at the Fukushima Daiichi nuclear plant in Japan was just such an event. Here the driving cause was a gigantic tsunami, over 35 m in height, created by a massive 9.0 quake that was several times the size of the maximum event deemed possible in the design of the Fukushima nuclear power plant. So what was the consequence? To be sure, there was catastrophic damage to the plant as it lost all electrical power and cooling for an extended period of time, allowing the fuel to overheat and partially melt and releasing radioactivity to the environment. Yet, the impact on public health has been minimal (at least to this point). As noted by *The Economist*, despite being hit by a natural disaster of biblical proportions causing immense damage to the plant, there was little damage to the environment beyond the plant's immediate vicinity or to public health (*Economist*, 2011).

In fact, the most serious impact is likely to be the erosion of public confidence in nuclear power, ironically a carbon-free technology that today provides 14% of the world's electricity with a 50-year safety record in which only one nuclear plant accident has occurred with a major consequence for public safety (Chernobyl). As observed by *The Economist*: "Fear and uncertainty spread faster and farther than any nuclear fallout" (*Economist*, 2011).

A second example is the failure of the BP Deepwater Horizon drilling platform in the Gulf of Mexico last year. Unlike Fukushima, the BP accident has caused many deaths and vast damage to the Gulf environment. And unlike the Japan incident, which was triggered by a natural disaster of biblical proportions, the BP Deepwater Horizon accident was clearly the result of human error — inadequate design, operation and response. Yet, it was also a Black Swan event, thought to be impossible, of major consequence, yet clearly understandable and explainable in retrospect.

Clearly, such Black Swan events threaten global sustainability. The impact of major environmental events, such as the melting of the Arctic tundra and release of massive amounts of methane could trigger runaway global greenhouse instability. The rapid melting of the ice sheets in Greenland or the Antarctic could raise sea levels by several metres inundating coastal cities and populations. In fact, one can imagine Black Swan events that today seem of such remote possibility that they currently exist only in science fiction. Clearly, phenomena such as machine consciousness, contact by extraterrestrial intelligence, or cosmic extinction from a wandering asteroid are Black Swan "possibilities" for our civilization, but just as clearly they should neither dominate our attention nor our near-term actions. Indeed, the most effective way to prepare for such unanticipated events is to make certain that our descendants are equipped with education, wisdom and foresight of the highest possible quality.

THE ROLES OF UNIVERSITIES IN ADDRESSING THE CHALLENGES OF GLOBAL SUSTAINABILITY

In summary then, the forces driving change in our world — anthropogenic driven changes in our environment (climate change, declining biodiversity), changing demographics (aging populations, migration, increasing ethnic

diversity), environmental impact (climate change, biodiversity), globalization (economic, geopolitical, cultural) and disruptive technologies (info-bio-
nano technologies) — are likely to require very major changes in post-secondary education as a global knowledge economy demands a new level of knowledge, skills and abilities on the part of our citizens. It will also require research
universities capable of discovering new knowledge, to develop innovative
applications of these discoveries, transfer them into society through entrepreneurial activities, and educate those capable of working at the frontiers of
knowledge and the professions.

Yet, there are broader responsibilities beyond national interests
— particularly for developed nations — in an ever more interconnected and
interdependent world. Global challenges, such as crippling poverty, health
pandemics, terrorism and global climate change, require both commitment
and leadership. So, what are the implications of these shifting timescales,
magnitudes, paradigms, and emerging Black Swans characterizing a rapidly
changing world for the future of the university? To be sure, the traditional
roles of the university will continue to be important. But our educational programs must be characterized by both the depth and breadth to prepare our
graduates for a world of constant and ever accelerating change. For example,
an increasingly complex and rapidly changing world requires "T" graduates,
capable of both depth in a particular discipline as well as intellectual breadth
(Donofrio, 2005). Our research activities must evolve to develop the intellectual tools to address the challenges of a world increasingly threatened by
humankind. And we must become more engaged with society beyond our
campus to shape both public understanding and action. Whether motivated
by the economic desire to create new markets or the more altruistic motives
of human welfare, our universities have a responsibility to address global
issues. Globalization requires thoughtful, interdependent and globally identified citizens. Educational institutions must think more concertedly about
their role in promoting both individual and civic development.

But we must also recognize that a changing world demands a change in the
university itself. Social computing will empower and extend learning communities beyond the constraints of space and time. Open knowledge and education resources will clearly expand enormously the knowledge resources available to our institutions. Immersive environments will enable the mastery of not
only simply conventional academic knowledge, but as well tacit knowledge,
enabling our students to learn not only how "to know" and "to do", but actually
how "to be" — whether scholars, professionals, or leaders — but above all,
contributing citizens of the emerging global community (Thomas, 2011).

But there is a possibility even beyond these. Imagine what might be possible
if all of these elements merge, i.e., Internet-based access to all recorded and
then digitized human knowledge, augmented by powerful search engines;

open source software, open learning resources, and open learning institutions (open universities); new collaboratively developed tools (Wikipedia II, Web 3.0); immersive environments (World of Warcraft, Second Life); social networking (Facebook, Twitter); and ubiquitous information and communications technology (digital appliances such as smart phones and iPads). In the near future, it could be possible that anyone with even a modest Internet or cellular phone connection will have access to the cyberspace cloud containing all recorded knowledge of our civilization, along with ubiquitous learning opportunities and social networking communities throughout the world.

Imagine still further the linking together of billions of people with limitless access to knowledge and learning tools enabled by a rapidly evolving scaffolding of cyberinfrastructure, which increases in power one-hundred to one thousand-fold every decade. This hive-like culture will not only challenge existing social institutions-corporations, universities, nation states — that have depended upon the constraints of space, time, laws, and monopoly but it will also enable the spontaneous emergence of new social structures as yet unimagined. Just think of the early denizens of the Internet such as Google, Wikipedia, Facebook, Twitter …and, unfortunately, Al Qaeda. In fact, we may be on the threshold of the emergence of a new form of civilization, as billions of world citizens interact together, unconstrained by today's monopolies on knowledge or learning opportunities.

Perhaps this, then, is the most compelling vision for the future of knowledge and learning organizations such as the university, no longer constrained by space, time, monopoly or archaic laws, but rather responsive to the needs of a global, knowledge society and unleashed by technology to empower and serve all of humankind.

REFERENCES

Bierbaum, Rosina (2011). "Science, Policy, and Politics". Powerpoint Presentation, University of Michigan.

Christenson, Clayton (1997). *The Innovator's Dilemma*. Cambridge, MA: Harvard Business School Press.

Donofrio, Nicholas (2005). "Innovation that Matters", Remarks at New York State Education Summit, Albany, NY, 2 November 2005.

Drucker, Peter (1999). "Beyond the Information Revolution". *Atlantic Monthly*, 284: 4, October, 1999.

The Economist (2011). "When the Steam Clears", March 24, 2011; "In Place of Safety Nets", 23 April 2011.

Goodstein, David (2004). *Out of Gas: The End of the Age of Oil*. New York: W.W. Norton.

IPCC, Intergovernmental Panel on Climate Change (2007). "Climate Change 2007", Cambridge: Cambridge University Press.

Lewis, Nathan S (2007). "Powering the Planet". *Engineering and Science*, No. 2, pp. 13-23.

MacKay, David (2009). *Sustainable Energy — Without the Hot Air*. UIT Cambridge Ltd.

National Intelligence Council (2004). *Mapping the Global Future, Project 2020*. Government Printing Office: Washington, DC.

Rhodes, Frank (2009). Universities and the Innovative Spirit. The Second Glion Declaration, Geneva: Glion Colloquium.

Sachs, Jeffrey (2005). *The End of Poverty: Economic Possibilities of Our Times*. New York, NY: Penguin Press.

Smil, Vaclav (2009). "U.S. Energy Policy: The Need for Radical Departures". *Issues in Science and Technology*. National Academies, Washington, DC: National Academy Press, Summer 2009.

Smil, Vaclav (2011). "Global Energy: The Latest Infatuations". *American Scientist*, Vol. 99, pp. 212-219.

Taleb, Nassim Nicholas (2007). "The Black Swan: The Impact of the Highly Improbable". *New York Times*, 22 April 2007.

Taleb, Nassim Nicholas (2010). *The Black Swan: The Impact of the Highly Improbable*, Second Edition. NewYork: Random House.

Thomas, Douglas & Seely Brown, John (2011). *A New Culture of Learning: Cultivating the Imagination for a World of Constant Change*. San Francisco: Thomas and Brown.

United Nations (2011), *2010 Revision of the World Population Prospects*. Population Division. New York: United Nations.

Vest, Charles M., Chair (2003). *Critical Choices: Science, Energy, and Security*. Advisory Committee to the Secretary of Energy. Washington, DC: U.S. Department of Energy.

CHAPTER 8

Addressing global
and social Challenges
and the Role of University

Yuko Harayama and René Carraz

INTRODUCTION

The world today is experiencing drastic transformations of its functioning and its underlying systems, driven by entrepreneurial individuals,
institutions and States, characterized by increasing interdependency,
and multi-dimensional and global nature. This creates new economic opportunities and entails social progress, but can also have negative consequences
that may induce the spread of instability and a domino-like effect of a particular crisis worldwide. More generally, it is becoming apparent that the
progress of our society generates unintended impacts on global welfare. Being
embedded with a somehow limited rationality, economic agents do not foresee all the consequences of their acts and therefore do not bear the full cost of
their actions. We are confronting global challenges, such as climate change,
loss of biodiversity, food scarcity and hunger, shortages of energy, water and
other natural resources, all of them having the characteristics of "global" public good (or "public bad") and they are evolving and interlinked. In economic
terms, a public good has three particular properties. The first one is non-rival
possession, or the fact that a good is not depleted by its use. The second is its
low marginal cost of reproduction and distribution, which makes it difficult to
exclude others from accessing it. Third, there is a substantial fixed cost of original production. Because of these properties, it is argued that the producers
cannot capture the benefits stemming from the production and therefore market forces remain inadequate in delivering the socially optimal level of the

desired good. For instance, the fight against global warming is the problem of all and of no one at the same time. The solution has to be global, as it would be difficult to exclude a country, which did not participate in halving it, to benefit from a solution to the problem. Therefore, there is a need for collaboration and co-operation in solving these issues.

How do we tackle these global challenges, while increasing the quality of life and leaving room for development? To deal with these market failures, traditional policy tools — incentive taxes, subsidies or regulation — may be mobilized in theory. In the case of climate changes, economic solutions can be used to create incentives to move forward a decarbonised economy, such as carbon taxes and emissions trading systems. But a genuine solution would need to involve more dimensions such as widespread political recognition, a better scientific knowledge of the process, sociological understanding and public awareness among others. Indeed the reality is often more complex than economic models predict: the premises of underlying economic models, notably information asymmetry, are not fully fulfilled; a solution for static optimality is not necessarily optimal in an evolving context; each of the challenges being multi-dimensional, and at the same time being interlinked with other challenges, difficulty and tension may arise when defining political and operational objective and targeting actors, and identifying an appropriate policy tool, and even more, the solution, the result of a trade-off, would be partial, far from an overall solution; these challenges call for a choice of certain values to society, but the consensus making on social choice is often out of the scope of policy actions.

However, pressed by the urgency and severity of the problems, we should take action, despite these constraints and our limited capacity to foresee the future, while remaining humble by addressing global challenges. Our approach should be also pragmatic, at least try out some solution, while being aware of sustainability in terms of economic, social and environmental perspectives. Here, experience sharing and policy learning at a global level, based on credible information and mutual trust among actors, prevail. In our view, however, the existing framework for policy making, basically confined within national borders, is not appropriate to induce a move in this direction. How to prepare the ground for a more global and co-operative approach? This paper attempts to respond to this question, focusing on the eventual role that universities may play. We will discuss whether it would be appropriate to talk about "University Social Responsibility (USR)", paraphrasing the concept of Corporate Social Responsibility (CSR). Broadly speaking, CSR could be defined as actions that favour social goods beyond the pure economic interest of the firm and that required by law. Some examples of CSR actions include going beyond legal requirements in recycling, banning animal-testing, abating pollution, supporting local ventures, developing products with social attributes or characteristics. More to the point of our analysis, CSR not only takes into consideration shareholder values and returns, it also encourages and is mindful of co-operation through the evaluation of the firm's activities on the environment, consumers, employees, communities and all stakeholders. In that sense, this paper argues that universities could embrace social responsibility in tackling global challenges by not only providing scientific and technical expertise, but by actively targeting potential stakeholders, facilitating the sharing of ideas and solutions, and playing the role of a catalyst in multi-actor initiatives. In that way, it could increase the rate of solutions to global issues, without being consumed by the reaction itself.

The structure of this paper is as follows. The first section analyses the role of science, technology and innovation in addressing global challenges and underlines the importance of international co-ordination, based on an OECD project "Governance of International Co-operation on Science, Technology and Innovation for Global Challenges (STIG)", launched in 2010. The second section focuses more specifically on the social dimension, referring to the OECD works on "Fostering Innovation to Address Social Challenges". Based on the discussion developed in the first two sections, the role of universities addressing global challenges is highlighted in the third section, followed by the concluding section.

THE ROLE OF SCIENCE, TECHNOLOGY AND INNOVATION, AND THE NEED FOR AN INTERNATIONAL CO-OPERATION

Science, technology and innovation (STI) play a key role in understanding global challenges and the interaction between various environmental, technological and social factors framing these challenges, in the assessment of risks and the development of solutions. Gaining scientific knowledge of the phenomena is essential to understand the root of the problem and the mechanism through which key determinants interact; technological solutions may be envisaged and tested to mitigate damage or to propose an alternative to the existing technologies; once proven, these technological solutions would be implemented and adapted in the real context of social system, thereby transforming the functioning of our society. It is worth noting that the process through which science, technology and innovation are mobilized on the ground is rarely in a linear manner: most of the time, actions are undertaken by diverse actors at different parts of STI with possible interactions among them.

To enhance our capacity to react to global challenges, recognizing the role that STI could play, government may initiate and co-ordinate these actions. The presence of double externalities — first one engendered by the nature of global challenges and second one by the public good characteristics of STI —

supports government intervention. Governments may give incentives to speed up scientific and technological progress, or facilitate the implementation of new technologies by changing the regulatory framework.

However, as we have already remarked, these problems do not stop at national borders, thus there is a need to address these challenges collectively. Then arises the question of who should initiate, how to make this initiative operational, how to support its cost and how to assess its effectiveness?

We recognize that several international STI co-operations initiated by a certain number of lead countries or decided by an international organization have been implemented in the past, e.g. the Group on Earth Observation (GEO), the Consultative Group on International Agricultural Research (CGIAR) or the Inter-American Institute for Global Research (IAI). But existing policy frameworks and governance mechanisms seem to fall short of adequately supporting broad-based collaborative action of the scale and intensity required to tackle the global challenges we face today.

Given the importance of governance dimension for the success of collective actions in STI for global challenges, the OECD has launched a project with the aim to provide a space for discussion and sharing good practices on governance, named "Governance of International Co-operation on Science, Technology and Innovation for Global Challenges (STIG)" in 2010. This project focuses on five key spheres of governance as follow:

- Institutional arrangements, agenda and priority setting: Strong and inclusive agenda and priority setting mechanisms and models that ensure optimal outreach and stakeholder involvement, while keeping co-operation effective and efficient.
- Funding and spending arrangements: Models that lead to a significant up-scaling of funds, flexible and responsive spending arrangements, monitoring and evaluation that impact the funding and spending cycle.
- Knowledge-sharing and intellectual property: Mechanisms for improved access to and utilization of knowledge generated from international collaborative STI activities; institutional arrangements for benefit sharing.
- Capacity-building and technology transfer: Mechanisms that factor the different levels of STI capacity in countries into the conceptualization of co-operation, including technology transfer, build-up of absorptive capacities, joint laboratories.
- Delivering benefits — putting STI into practice: Arrangements which ensure that innovation is rolled out in a timely and dynamic manner and that the outcomes of international collaborative STI efforts are delivered into practice.

It is too early to extract policy implication from this on-going project, but, given the interest expressed by the OECD member countries and non-member countries, including China and South Africa, there is a need to frame appropriately an international setting, enabling participating countries to take concrete actions in a co-ordinated manner, which in turn would trigger not only technological but also social innovation within the national context.

SOCIAL INNOVATION TO ADDRESS GLOBAL CHALLENGES

Making efforts in science and technology may be a first step to address global challenges, but if we want to move ahead towards global sustainability — taking account of environmental, economic and social dimensions — not only the co-ordination and co-operation problems, as discussed in the previous section, but also problems of implementation and social acceptances should be tackled.

In recent years, most OECD member countries have increased the weight of target-driven research funding, aiming at bringing scientific and technological insight to the problems recognized as critical by the government and more generally responding to societal needs, but rarely have the outputs of this funding been translated in terms of social practices; or else we have to wait for a long time to perceive their impact on society. How is it possible to trigger or accelerate this process?

In order to explore these issues, an OECD project was initiated in 2009, resulting in two workshops on "Fostering Innovation to Address Social Challenges". This project contributed to clarify key concepts — such as "social innovation" or "social entrepreneur" — assess needs for and barriers to social innovation and review a range of local and national initiatives to promote STI with a view to address social challenges. This project did not refer explicitly to "global" challenges, while it recognizes the "global dimension" of the problems we face today. The preference for "Social Challenges" came from the fact that this project focuses on the "social" responsiveness, which could be localized actions, rather than on the capacity to bring response "globally" (OECD, 2011).

The key findings of this project are the following:

- Addressing social challenges by means of innovation requires setting clear and agreed definitions and the creation of a new framework to better understand the changing nature of innovation and the multiplicity of economic, social and technical drivers.

Box. Toward the conceptualization of social innovation

The most pervasive definition of social innovation encompasses all social impacts of STI activities and progress. Indeed, regardless of their objectives, all STI activities have direct or indirect social impacts. Evaluations of research and innovation policies and programmes aim to assess these impacts, along with other effects (scientific progress, economic and policy impacts). The significant methodological issues to be tackled as to best assess social impacts (imputation, timescale of effects) are not the only limitations of this definition of social innovation. It is far too narrow as it relates to the understanding of social progress as an unintentional by-product — not as strategic driver — of STI activities. A more comprehensive definition of social innovation is therefore needed. Social innovation refers to a group of strategies, concepts, ideas and organizational patterns with a view to expand and strengthen the role of civil society in response to the diversity of social needs (education, culture, health). The term covers, inter alia: new products and services, new organizational patterns (e.g., management methods, work organization), new institutional forms (e.g., mechanisms of power distribution by assignment, positive discrimination quotas), new roles and new functions, or new coordinating and governance mechanisms. The OECD LEED Forum on Social Innovations has endeavoured to clarify the situation and provide a common understanding of innovation to address social challenges. The key principle of this definition is that social well-being is a goal, not a consequence. Thus, *"there is social innovation wherever new mechanisms and norms consolidate and improve the well-being of individuals, communities and territories in terms of social inclusion, creation of employment, quality of life."*.

Key actors in this early period where social innovation is still weakly institutionalized are so-called "social entrepreneurs". A social entrepreneur is someone who:

- Intends to create systemic changes and sustainable improvements with a view to sustain the impact.
- Assesses success in terms of the impact s/he has on society.
- Identifies a social challenge and has stepped up to make social change with social mission, to find innovative, immediate, small-scale and large-scale solutions that produce sweeping and long-term change, transforming the system, spreading the solution and persuading entire societies to take new leaps. Is encouraged to produce social impact with a selfless, entrepreneurial intelligence and innovative drive.
- Can simply manage to apply an existing idea in a new way or to a new situation, simply needs to be creative in applying what others have invented (designed?) On the funding side, social entrepreneurs look for ways to ensure that their ventures will have access to resources as long as they are creating social value.

Intends to provide real social improvements to their beneficiaries and communities, as well as attractive (social and/or financial) returns to their investors.

- Social innovations are by nature multidimensional insofar as a variety of issues are addressed as social challenges, which entails a significant degree of diversity in terms of knowledge basis in science and technology. The complexity derives from the wide scope covered by "social innovations", as social challenges are related to demographic changes, climate change, poverty, employment, health care, education. The multidimensional package of existing social challenges and the systemic failure in fostering social innovation clearly call for a reform of the research and innovation system governance.

- Social challenges are also multi-stakeholders (e.g. universities, research institutes, private companies, government, civil society, citizens). This calls for more research activities on multi-disciplinarity and promoting stakeholders' involvement, in particular by favouring the implementation process of research priorities (while avoiding lobbyism). To do so, the development of a new governance system, in particular participative tools aiming at facilitating partnerships, is still to be strengthened in order to be effective. Moreover, new actors have emerged and challenge the current established innovation support institutions and instruments. These actors range from social entrepreneurs and enterprises to amateur scientists, International Organizations, NGOs and private foundations, and new ways to establish proper and fruitful cooperation between them have to be found. Their respective role in the social innovation system has to be reshaped so that they become an effective driving force of technical and social progress. In particular, as a new actor, social entrepreneurship proves to be more and more essential to promote this trend but still has to be fully recognized and supported by governments.

- Social challenges have a public-good nature. Market processes and the "invisible hand" are, even more than in other innovation activities, inefficient to coordinate these activities that directly address social challenges. Prospects of large, private profits in the social area are limited, which hinders incentives to invest and commit resources to these activities. As a consequence, specific processes and mechanisms should be specifically established to support innovation activities that aim to address social challenges.

- These barriers result in governance and coordination inefficiency, lack of incentives to invest in social innovations, uncertainty, which hinder the development and dissemination of social innovation. As social challenges are growing, the cost for failing to solve them is increasing dramatically. Innovative solutions to address these social challenges are clearly not adequately exploited. New solutions, new collective initiatives, new instruments, as well as new modes of public support and management, are required to allow STI to address social challenges.

These findings led to a set of policy proposals, which are:

Policy response to conceptual barrier

- Launch an international initiative to agree upon a common definition of social innovation.
- Continue research and reflection on the definitions and measurement of innovation based on the Oslo Manual definition, in order to better take into account social innovation efforts and results.

Policy support to social innovators

- Design information systems (e.g. through technology scanning and foresight) to be able to detect, characterize and diffuse knowledge on cases of social innovation.
- Design support scheme dedicated to social entrepreneurs and, more generally, social innovation.
- Support interdisciplinary research on social innovations, provide incentives for linkages between research and social innovators.
- Provide incentives for corporate firms to address social challenges.

Creating the framework conditions that are conducive to social innovation

- Favour cross-sectoral, inter-ministerial initiatives to foster social innovation.
- Seek a more inclusive and forward-looking policy-making process.
- Explore rationale and need for specific training.
- Encourage new forms of evaluation.

ROLE OF UNIVERSITIES

In our view, universities are expected to play a key role in search of global sustainability.

Through their research function, they may contribute to a better understanding of the phenomena and underlying mechanisms of the global challenges we mentioned. Aware of their social responsibility, certain universities are already strongly committed by setting their own agenda, and mobilizing their expertise and knowledge in different fields, including social sciences and humanities. By doing so, universities may create scientific basis to better formulate the "perceived" global challenges and to identify key issues to be tackled, and this would help the policy-makers to move a step further in the direction of evidence-based policy making.

Also, universities are largely responsive to government incentives and actively participating in target-driven research projects aiming at addressing global challenges, and some projects in cooperation with private companies focusing on particular technologies are already in a phase of prototyping or testing. Technological advancement initiated by universities is becoming perceptible in some fields, while implementation and diffusion are still slow to come. It is worth noting that here we face not only well-known problems of innovation cycle and management of technology, but also and precisely the underlying problems of social innovation we identified earlier. This, in turn, raises the problems of co-ordination of interests among stakeholders and identification and allocation of responsibility. Should or would universities take the lead to induce social change beyond their accustomed role of proposing technological solutions? This remains an open question, but what is certain is that universities are a key stakeholder in this framework.

Putting this question another way, we may ask what are the comparative advantages of universities relative to other existing institutions with respect to attempts at gaining sustainability in our society?

Universities may contribute to increase awareness of the public of sustainability, by framing the problems as objectively as possible, providing state-of-the-art information in an appropriate way at the same time as signalling the limits of a scientific approach, offering a place to debate on the evolution of social values. In this perspective, universities, while mobilizing their competencies and experiences in research, teaching and training, could offer a "learning space" to society, and by acting so, they would prepare eventual future "globally conscious citizens".

Gaining the awareness of the people is one side of the coin. To mark a step forward in moving society toward more sustainability, this awareness should be translated in terms of concrete actions, including policy action. Here, universities may play the role of catalyst. Universities, throughout their development as a social institution, acquired their own social capital, which could be mobilized to identify potential key stakeholders, to facilitate sharing their ideas, working together and formulating an eventual action plan. The comparative advantage of universities in this task resides in their neutrality — prerequisite of any scientific approach — vis-à-vis particular private interests, together with their expertise in a wide variety of disciplines, propitious for multi-disciplinary approach.

It could be a consequence of the exercise of their missions, and/or a deliberate choice, nonetheless, the fact is that universities have the potential to play a role in promoting global sustainability. By exploiting this potential to serve society, universities could exercise what we may call "University Social Responsibility" (USR). Universities could be encouraged in their actions that favour social goods beyond their pure academic interests and missions.

Until recently, universities have been preoccupied with two missions: research, mainly of a fundamental nature, and teaching. These two activities have been beneficial to society as a whole by providing human capital and basic knowledge to society. On top of that, recent developments have moved forward a third mission for universities: contributing to innovation. Indeed, universities play an important role as a source of new knowledge, and, on occasion, industrially relevant technologies. Since the 1970s, governments have pushed to increase the rate of transfer of academic research to industry and facilitate its utilization by national firms as part of a broader effort to improve national economic performance in a "knowledge-based" society.

Within the boundaries of these three missions, universities could easily engage themselves in proactively promoting public interest and solutions to global problems by encouraging the diffusion of best practices and information, favouring the development and education of social entrepreneurs, and be part of an innovation eco-system which promotes international, cross-sectorial and interdisciplinary solutions to global challenges. All capabilities that universities possess and could push forward in the direction of a USR.

CONCLUSION

STI are certainly key elements to consider while trying addressing global challenges, as they are involved in many parts of the process of recognizing, analysing and finding ways to alleviate them. Recognizing the increasing scope of the scientific inquiry, the physicist and historian of science, Silvan S. Schweber, (1993) noticed that:

"[...] the goals of most of the scientific enterprise are no longer solely determined internally; other interests come into play. The scientific enterprise is now largely involved in the creation of novelty — in the design of objects that never existed before and in the creation of conceptual frameworks to understand the complexity and novelty that can emerge from the known foundations and ontologies. And precisely because we create those objects and representations we must assume moral responsibility for them."

Moral consideration, or we might say responsibility, is bound to play an increasing place in STI issues. Scientists, certainly, should freely decide the path of research they decide to follow and pursing them in the light of their own judgment as put forward by Michael Polanyi. They should also embrace, especially when working in university, wider goals to tackle social challenges that are to some extent the results of their quest for novelty.

REFERENCES

OCDE (2011). *Fostering Innovation to Address Social Challenges*, Workshop Proceedings, Paris.

Schweber, S.S. (1993). "Physics, community and the crisis in physical theory." *Physics today*, November 1993, pp. 34-40.

CHAPTER

Action is what counts: Sustainability at ETH Zurich and EPFL

Ralph Eichler and Patrick Aebischer

Tackling the challenges of sustainable development requires critical thinking, innovative technologies and an open dialogue between science, industry, and society. As Swiss-based universities that are consistently high in the leading international university rankings, the Swiss Federal Institute of Technology Zurich (ETH Zurich) and the Ecole Polytechnique Fédérale de Lausanne (EPFL) are committed to playing a key role in addressing these challenges on a national, European and global scale. Sustainability must be at the core of the main areas of academics: research, education and knowledge transfer. The following article illustrates the general commitment of EPFL and ETH Zurich to improve their sustainability performances.

THE COMMITMENT TO ETH ZURICH AND EPFL SUSTAINABILITY

Integrating sustainability into the institutional mindset

In research, EPFL and ETH Zurich stress inter- and transdisciplinary collaborations, as these are particularly fruitful for generating ground-breaking innovations. In education, the two technical universities focus on teaching methods that are tightly integrated with cutting-edge research projects in order to enable the leaders of tomorrow to make real world change. Between 2009 and 2010, ETH Zurich and EPFL were also successful in supporting the foundation of 44 and 34 spin-off companies respectively, not only to transfer research results into marketable products, but also to create qualified jobs for agents of change with regard to sustainability.

In addition, EPFL and ETH Zurich recognize that addressing complex environmental problems requires an ongoing exchange between science, stakeholder groups and decision-makers. Therefore, both schools support public policy debates as an "honest broker", providing impartial scientific information to all parties concerned, with due emphasis on the assumptions and uncertainties that are unavoidable in all scientific studies.

ETH Zurich and EPFL also act as role models for the decarbonization of society by sharing their own operation management techniques and fostering a sustainable campus environment for working and living. For instance, ETH Zurich has developed an energy strategy based on three pillars: energy efficiency, renewable energy and electrification. To underline the commitment to low carbon emissions, ETH Zurich is currently constructing underground storage fields to dynamically store and circulate energy from geothermal and waste sources across the Science City campus, both for heating in winter and cooling in summer. In 2009, EPFL received the International Sustainable Campus Award for its efforts regarding criteria like heating (thermopump), sustainable architecture and mobility. At present, the largest photovoltaic power station in Switzerland is under construction on the flat roofs of the EPFL buildings.

ISCN/GULF network: Linking strong partners to make a change

EPFL and ETH Zurich are aware that sustainability encompasses more than just environmental issues. Both universities are working towards a sustainable workplace in other ways, such as by placing strong emphasis on diversity in the student body, faculty and staff. This is not only an issue of equal opportunity, but is also essential for creating the dynamic mix of ideas and people crucial for generating innovation. For this reason, the two universities have taken a leading role in setting up, funding and supporting the ISCN/GULF Sustainable Campus Charter.

The Charter is a joint initiative of the Global University Leaders Forum (GULF), which convenes higher education representatives within the World Economic Forum (WEF) and the International Sustainable Campus Network (ISCN), a global organization that brings together sustainability managers, academics and senior administrators from universities around the world.

The aim of the ISCN/GULF network is to pool global knowledge on how universities can best support sustainable development through their research and education, and by walking the talk in their own operations in order to inspire future leaders. ETH Zurich and EPFL jointly host the ISCN secretariat, which magnifies the conviction that organizations of research and higher education have a particular responsibility in our society's journey towards a sustainable future.

Sharing a common vision: 30 world leading universities take action for sustainability

In January 2010, after four years of preparation, the partnership between ISCN and GULF led to the development and dissemination of the ISCN/ GULF Sustainable Campus Charter. The Charter asks endorsing organizations to acknowledge shared principles regarding the sustainability impacts of their buildings, their campus-wide planning and target-setting processes, and their integration of research, teaching, outreach and facilities into a "living laboratory" for sustainable development. Each Charter member commits to setting its own concrete goals related to these shared principles, and to report publicly on its progress in realizing these goals.

Since the endorsement ceremony in 2010, 30 universities have committed to the ISCN-GULF Charter as members (an alphabetic list of all members is attached at the end of this text).

Three principles, measurable goals and regular reporting for improving campus performance

The signatories of the ISCN/GULF Sustainable Campus Charter acknowledge that organizations of research and higher education have a unique role to play in developing the technologies, strategies, citizens and leaders required for a more sustainable future. Signing on as a Charter member represents an organization's public commitment to aligning its operations, research and teaching with the goal of sustainability. The signatories commit to:

- implement the three ISCN/GULF sustainable campus principles described below;
- set concrete and measurable goals for each of the three principles and strive to achieve them;
- and report regularly and publicly on their organizations' performance in this regard.

Charter principle 1

The signatories of the ISCN/GULF Sustainable Campus Charter demonstrate respect for nature and society, and agree that sustainability considerations should be an integral part of planning, construction, renovation and operation of buildings on campus.

A sustainable campus infrastructure is governed by respect for natural resources and social responsibility, and embraces the principle of a low carbon economy. Concrete goals embodied in individual buildings can include minimizing environmental impacts (such as energy and water consumption or waste), furthering equal access (such as nondiscrimination of the disabled), and optimizing the integration of the built and natural environments. To ensure buildings on campus can meet these goals in the long term and in a flexible manner, useful processes include participatory planning (integrating end-users such as faculty, staff and students) and life cycle cost analysis (taking into account future cost-savings from sustainable construction).

Charter principle 2

The signatories of the ISCN/GULF Sustainable Campus Charter ensure long-term sustainable campus development, and that campus-wide master planning and target-setting should include environmental and social goals.

Sustainable campus development needs to rely on forward-looking planning processes that consider the campus as a whole, not just individual buildings. These processes can include comprehensive master planning with goals for impact management (for example, limiting use of land and other natural resources and protecting ecosystems), responsible operation (such as encouraging environmentally compatible transport modes and efficiently managing urban flows), and social integration (ensuring user diversity, creating indoor and outdoor spaces for social exchange and shared learning, and supporting ease of access to commerce and services). Integrated planning can benefit from including users and neighbours, and can be strengthened by organization-wide goals (for example, reducing greenhouse gas emissions). Existing low-carbon lifestyles and practices within individual campuses that foster sustainability, such as easy access for pedestrians, grey water recycling and low levels of resource use and waste generation, need to be identified, expanded and disseminated widely.

Charter principle 3

The signatories of the "ISCN/GULF Sustainable Campus Charter" align the organization's core mission with sustainable development, facilities, research, and education should be linked to create a "living laboratory" for sustainability.

On a sustainable campus, the built environment, operational systems, research, scholarship and education are linked as a "living laboratory" for sustainability. Users (such as students, faculty and staff) have access to research, teaching and learning opportunities on the connections between environmental, social, and economic issues. Campus sustainability programs have

concrete goals and can bring together campus residents with external partners, such as industry, government and organized civil society. Beyond exploring a sustainable future in general, such programs can address issues pertinent
to research and higher education (such as environmental impacts of research
facilities), participatory teaching, and interdisciplinary research. Institutional
commitments (such as a sustainability policy) and dedicated resources (such
as a person or team in the administration focused on this task) contribute to
success.

"Walk the talk" of sustainability

As signatories of the ISCN/GULF Sustainable Campus Charter, EPFL and
ETH Zurich strive to share the goals and experiences on sustainable campus
initiatives among peers and other stakeholders. A key instrument for this is
the regular reporting on progress under the Charter. At the last GULF meeting, which took place during the 2011 WEF Davos event, ETH Zurich and
EPFL were among the first to submit their reports in order to disseminate best
practices among the GULF members.

Final or draft reports were also available from more than half of the other
GULF members that endorse the Charter: Brown University, Georgetown
University, Harvard University, Indian Institute of Technology Madras,
Johns Hopkins University, Massachusetts Institute of Technology, National
University of Singapore, University of Cambridge, University of Oxford, Uni-
versity of Pennsylvania, and Yale University. In addition to these GULF
schools, further Charter members that have already reported include Carnegie
Mellon University and the University of Luxembourg.

ISCN/GULF Charter offers option for comprehensive sustainability reports

The ISCN-GULF Charter Reporting Guidelines provide not only the option
of short, freestanding Charter Reports with goal and performance tables, but
also more comprehensive sustainability reports for example following the
guidelines of the Global Reporting Initiative (GRI). The GRI "is a network-
based organization that pioneered the world's most widely used sustainability
reporting framework. [...] GRI's core goals include the mainstreaming of disclosure on environmental, social, and governance performance" (www.global-
reporting.org, May 2011). The GRI-framework for sustainability reporting
receives wide acceptance as a standard for high quality, independency and
confidence, particularly within the corporate sector. Since the first idea of a
disclosure framework for sustainability information was conceived in 1997,
the GRI-framework has become the most widely used standard for sustainably
reporting. Today, more than 2,700 organizations apply the GRI reporting

framework worldwide. Among them, however, only two dozen pioneer universities have committed to disclosing their sustainability performance according to this independent standard.

By referencing the GRI framework for sustainability reporting, the ISCN/GULF Charter Reporting Guidelines offer a format that enables more intense experience exchange on sustainability between universities and corporations, which often choose this framework for their ongoing reporting on corporate sustainability.

Outlook

After the GULF meeting in January 2011, all ISCN-GULF Charter Reports were finalized and published on the ISCN website (www.isc-network.org), including that of EPFL and ETH Zurich. Since that time, Charter membership has opened to all organizations of research and higher education, including corporations with research and development campuses.

The two technical universities in Switzerland, ETH Zurich and EPFL, are convinced that the ISCN/GULF Charter process will help enhance the reputation of each charter member as an international centre of excellence in the field of sustainability. Therefore, EPFL and ETH Zurich will continue to support the ISCN network strategically, financially and logistically over the next two years.

With their interdisciplinary expertise in natural, engineering and applied sciences, ETH Zurich and EPFL are in an excellent position to play a pioneering role in the development of sustainable technologies, but also with practical actions towards sustainability. Commitment to the ISCN/GULF network illustrates that EPFL and ETH Zurich aim not only to be leading academic institutions, but to contribute significantly to solving some of the world's most pressing environmental and social problems.

PRACTICAL EXPERIENCES FROM ETH ZURICH

In the first year of ISCN/GULF reporting, ETH Zurich produced a comprehensive GRI-standard report to meet the requirements of the ISCN/GULF Sustainable Campus Charter. First experiences gained with the new reporting format and selected results are illustrated below.

ETH Zurich as pioneer: Benchmarking standard for sustainability performance in academia

ETH Zurich sees sustainable development as a central issue for society, and is committed to contributing to this goal through its research, education and knowledge transfer, as well as through its own operations. Therefore, the president of ETH Zurich decided to apply a more comprehensive sustainability report for the reporting period of 2009 to 2010. In order to increase transparency for all stakeholders, this ETH-sustainability report combines the annual ISCN-GULF Charter Report with an overview of ETH Zurich's sustainability goals, initiatives and achievements (see attachment).

In May 2011, ETH Zurich received its first approval of the GRI Application Level Check (B-Level). This report includes detailed information on research, education and knowledge transfer related to sustainability. It comprises facts about students, faculty and staff. It refers to ETH Zurich's sustainability performance in terms of facility management and environmental issues. Finally, the report illustrates ETH Zurich's commitment as an "honest broker", and its role to inform society and decision-makers is demonstrated in detail. Aspects of funding and governance are also discussed in the context of sustainability.

Selected results from ETH Zurich's Sustainably Report 2009 to 2010

The following chapter illustrates ETH Zurich's reporting standard by means of environmental parameters. It provides insight into aspects such as energy demand, greenhouse gas emissions, paper use and waste management.

Savings in relative energy demand

ETH Zurich's total direct energy use (defined as fuels like natural gas burned in own facilities) was 39.6GWh in 2009 and 41.7GWh in 2010. Indirect energy use (mainly electricity and district heating from outside providers) was 123GWh (2009) and 122.5GWh (2010). Thereof, almost 28GWh in 2009 and 31GWh in 2010 were sold as heating energy to third parties in the district heating networks around the two campuses of ETH Zurich. Electricity consumption at ETH Zurich has increased over the last few years due to several reasons: expansion of the building portfolio, increased use of highly electricity demanding instruments and facilities (which are essential to ensure cutting-edge research at a technical university), and the shift from heating with fossil fuels to electricity (which requires the use of heat pumps). The increase of ETH's electricity consumption does not, however, cause significantly higher greenhouse gas emissions, as electricity in Switzerland is mostly generated by hydropower (55.8%) and nuclear production (39.8%). In addition, relative energy demand expressed per person (full-time equivalent, or FTE, campus users) and per floor area has steadily fallen. As new and renovated high efficiency buildings will be added to the energy budget over the coming years, relative energy use figures are expected to drop. Also, a focus on more efficient use of floor area will allow ETH Zurich to limit further needs of work space, even as student and staff numbers grow.

Waste heat recovery

ETH Zurich owns and operates seven large central cooling plants. In addition to cooling, each of their chillers produces waste heat. By optimizing the waste heat recovery units (WHRC) over the last few years, ETH Zurich was able to use 10.6 GWh of waste heat in 2009 and 10.9 GWh in 2010 that would otherwise have been lost. In addition to environmental benefits, waste heat recovery led to energy cost savings that allow the university to amortize the investment in the optimization of the WHRCs in less than two years.

Closely monitoring greenhouse gas emissions

ETH Zurich has a strong tradition of measuring and managing its carbon emissions. In 2009/2010, direct or "Scope 1" carbon emissions, mainly from fossil fuels like natural gas burned at in-house facilities, were 8,240t/7,868t expressed in CO_2-equivalents. Indirect or "Scope 2" emissions caused by ETH Zurich's consumption of electricity were 1,445t/1,462t. In order to address the overall carbon footprint of ETH Zurich, further "Scope 3" emissions outside the organization's boundaries are considered, for example emissions from students and staff commuting, and from business travel. This part is responsible for more than 14,200t/15,900t expressed in CO_2-equivalents.

Carbon reduction as a key goal

Comparing emission contributions and options for improvement, key areas for action have been identified. More than 50% of the current CO_2 emissions caused by burning natural gas will be reduced by 2020 by implementation of the new energy concept, Science City. Other measures include closely monitoring and, wherever possible, reducing emissions caused by business travel. By using more electricity in favour of less fossil fuel consumption, the university reduces carbon emissions. One example is a big heat pump in the river Limmat, where some additional electricity replaces larger amounts of CO_2 loaded district heating.

Minimizing air emissions

ETH Zurich closely monitors NO_x emissions from its heating plants as well as VOC emissions from its laboratory activities. In 2009, NO_x emissions were 64 mg/m^3 compared to 80 mg/m^3 in 2008. New, state-of-the-art gas boilers contribute to the lower concentrations. Overall, VOC emissions were 18t in 2009 compared to > 20t in 2008.

Lowering amount and impacts of paper use

"Papers" are still key products at any research organization. This does not preclude a strong focus on reducing paper consumption and on improving the environmental output of the remaining consumption. In 2009 and 2010, paper use was 60.8 million pages and 61.6 million pages respectively (compared to 63.9 million in 2008). Key to the paper-reduction strategy is increasing use of online documents in education and administration, and raising awareness among students and staff. Paper sourcing at ETH Zurich is increasingly being shifted to recycled fibres, corresponding to about 46.5% (2009) and 44.3% (2010) of paper consumption by weight. For the remaining virgin paper, ETH Zurich promotes the use of paper that meets the criteria of the Forest Steward-ship Council for responsible forest management (FSC label). The goal is to eliminate non-recycled, non-sustainably forested paper sources completely.

Staff and students boost recycling

A key environmental goal of ETH Zurich is increasing the recyclable portion of its waste stream. Reuse of chemical substances by introducing storage rooms, and recycling of solvents and other materials such as CDs/DVDs and electrical waste contribute to this. High awareness and consistent support of students and staff have been essential for reaching ETH Zurich's recycling goals, from large volume waste streams down to the small "Nespresso" coffee pods.

Safe handling of hazardous waste

As a top international research institution, hazardous materials have to be used for certain research activities. ETH Zurich promotes economical use of hazard-ous material. Staff and students are trained to ensure correct and safe disposal. In 2009/2010, ETH Zurich disposed of 108t/95t of hazardous material, of which 51t/47t were waste solvents sent to treatment facilities for safe incineration or reuse as fuel in the cement industry, depending on the concentration of chem-icals such as chloride. Only small amounts of waste, approximately 5 tons/year (e.g. heavy metals) are directed to underground landfill (old salt mine). This compares to 1210t (2009) and 1170t (2010) of non-hazardous waste disposed of via the municipal waste stream, and destined for incineration.

Energy: trend to lower use at ETH Zurich

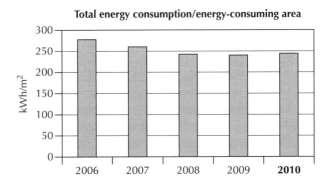

Total energy consumption/energy-consuming area

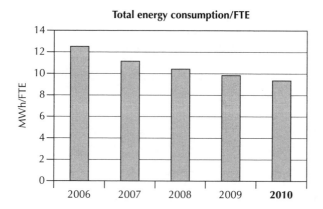

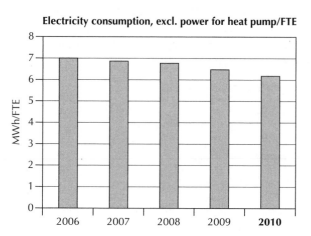

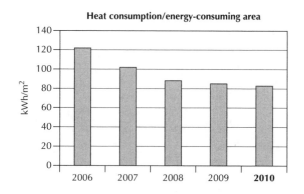

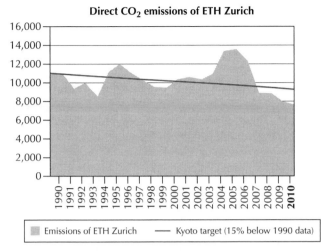

Direct CO$_2$ emissions of ETH Zurich

▦ Emissions of ETH Zurich	— Kyoto target (15% below 1990 data)

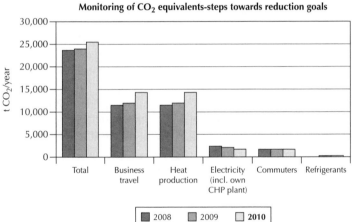

Monitoring of CO$_2$ equivalents-steps towards reduction goals

■ 2008	■ 2009	☐ **2010**

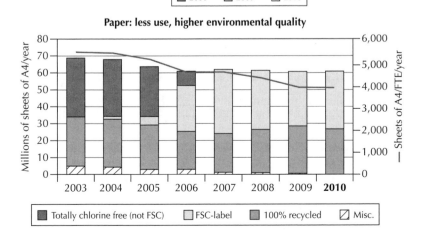

Paper: less use, higher environmental quality

■ Totally chlorine free (not FSC)	☐ FSC-label	■ 100% recycled	▨ Misc.

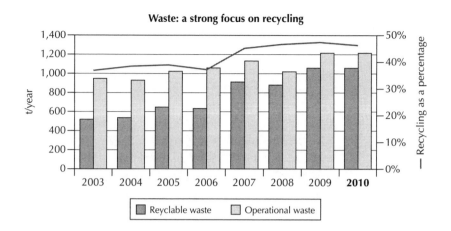

Waste: a strong focus on recycling

Lessons learned from ETH Zurich:
The process is as important as the result

First experiences with the new ETH Zurich sustainability report revealed positive results: The systematic process to compile GRI-relevant data led to increased internal awareness of the importance of sustainability. Particularly, the integration of social issues launched important and interesting discussions on what to consider as relevant for sustainability within an academic environment. The results show that the analysis of the environmental performance was as important as gender issues, legal aspects or the integration of sustainability in the overall strategic planning process. The report also underlines the importance of a strong intuitional commitment to sustainability on the highest level of decision-making. This is especially true when it comes to the implementation of goals and objectives.

The decision of the Executive Board of ETH Zurich to follow the GRI guidelines highlights the commitment to making the "Ivory Tower" more transparent to all partners in society and industry.

PRACTICAL EXPERIENCES FROM EPFL

This section illustrates the manner in which EPFL manages its environmental impact, monitoring for more than the past ten years essential parameters such as primary energy and CO_2, water and paper consumption, as well as the waste-recycling rate.

EPFL: 40 years of sustainability on its Ecublens site

During the 1970s, at the height of the oil and environmental crises, the people in charge of building the EPFL campus outside the city set very demanding environmental goals for the time regarding ecological building, which was not yet called sustainable building. Heating and cooling entirely ensured by lake water, with heat pumps and converters, thermal insulation far ahead of its time, natural ventilation and lighting, green roofs, extensive and indigenous landscaping, servicing by a metro line, etc. are many of the responsible and visionary choices that were implemented with great determination.

Certified in 2006, EPFL's environmental management program is modeled on the Swiss Confederation's and keeps the impact of the campus's activity under control year after year. For EPFL, it is now time to make known even more clearly its environmental targets, to set ambitious goals and to report annually on the results using a global tool within the GRI framework. A first report in 2010 carried out within the ISCN-GULF framework shows the way and indicates the necessary adaptations in order to meet GRI criteria.

Key results from the EPFL 2010 report

EPFL required 18GWh of energy to ensure its heating in 2009 and 21GWh in 2010, as well as 55GWh of electricity in 2009 and 67GWh in 2010. The increase in these two figures can be explained by the campus's growth (opening of the Rolex Learning Center, a Minergie-certified building), a particularly harsh winter and the launch of several demanding laboratories (white rooms, IT). With an exceptional level of 56% of heating from renewable sources in 2009, unchanged in 2010, EPFL is setting an example. For electricity, although the Swiss mix is particularly favourable with its share of hydraulic and nuclear, the 0.4% of electricity from renewable sources is low and justified the creation of the Solar Park on the EPFL's rooftops. This will enable a gradual increase of that rate: 1.2 MW will be in production by the end of 2011 and 2 MW by the end of 2012. Related to square metres or number of users, requirements in heating and electricity remain stable over time. As future buildings and renovations conform to high standards of insulation and high occupation rates, it will be possible to keep heating consumption well under control. However, it seems that electricity requirements, in particular for scientific processes, will increase regularly over the coming years.

An innovative Master Energy Management Program for EPFL

The first full environmental assessment of EPFL was carried out in 2001 and clearly showed the stakes. A first calculation indicated 19,830 tons of carbon emissions, of which 1,360 for electricity, 8,530 for buildings (over a duration of 80 years), 8,490 for professional (academic) and private (commuting) travel, 1,280 for heating, 1,070 for water and 685 for paper. Regarding primary energy, it is therefore clearly electricity and its production mode that should be the focus, whereas it is the private and professional mobility, as well as the buildings' lifecycle, that have the greatest impact on CO_2 emissions. Considering the very rapid evolution of the worldwide energy debate, EPFL's management has decided to put together by the end of 2011 a new Master Energy Management Program that sets ambitious goals for primary energy and CO_2, and to accelerate its implementation over the coming years, with strong measures from the point of view of efficiency, energetic autonomy, resorting to renewable energies and user behaviour.

UNIL-EPFL Mobility plan

With over 30 tons of CO_2 emitted every semester day by students and staff to get to the campus, 88% of which are caused by car drivers, private mobility is an important challenge for the reduction of impacts. Many measures in favour of soft mobility have curbed these effects, in particular by a 5% increase of the modal proportion allotted to bikes over the past five years. In this, the creation of 1,300 secure bicycle parking places, the restoration of changing rooms and showers, the creation of a repair workshop, the setting up of the first Swiss public bike-sharing system that is free for the staff and students, have opened the way. A Mobility plan shared with Lausanne University will enable further improvements until 2014, thanks to a very comprehensive package of measures connected with soft modes, incentive to use public transport, innovative management of parking lots and campus planning (lodgings for students and staff).

Drinking water, paper, waste

In addition to the efforts that take priority for reducing the consumption of heating, electricity and mobility, other aspects require sustained attention, among which the consumption of drinking water and paper, and the production of waste. Although in international comparison these elements have been well under control for many years, EPFL means to continue leading the way. Whereas water consumption is particularly efficient with 17,885 litres per year and per person (15,996 in 2009), as is paper consumption with 3,384 A4 sheets per year and per person (3,977 in 2009), it is now the proportion of recycled paper certified by the Forest Stewardship Council that is the object of the most attention. Indeed, with 23% of recycled paper in 2010 (27% in 2009), EPFL still has a broad potential for improvement and the paper purchasing and use policy is undergoing revision in order to increase the proportion of recycled paper massively over the next few years.

Regarding waste, EPFL produced 1,228 tons of all types of waste in 2010 (1,037 in 2009). The increase is essentially due to the opening of the Rolex Learning Center, which caused an influx of many visitors during the year 2010. However, with a recycling rate of 62%, EPFL has its various waste-treatment chains well under control. In 2010, the delivery of food leftovers from the restaurants to the City of Lausanne's methane production plant notice-ably improved the assessment. For special waste, the creation in 2011 of a reinforced safety, prevention and hygiene service will enable to respond ever more appropriately to the increase in requirements.

HEAT Specific consumption of buildings at EPFL (comparable climate)

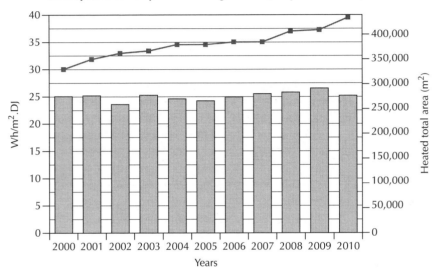

ELECTRICITY Specific consumption of buildings at EPFL

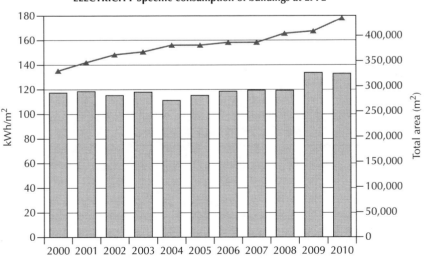

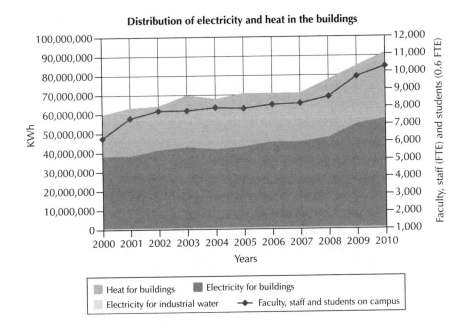

Distribution of electricity and heat in the buildings

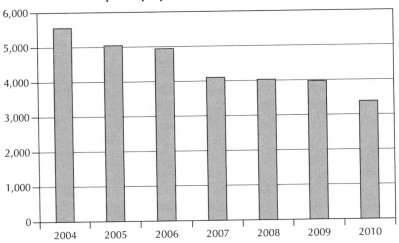

Paper use per person at EPFL (A4 sheet/person*year)

EPFL 2020

With global climate issues, it is essential for technological universities to continue leading the way in sustainable development and to ensure a responsible running of their campus. Of course, energy issues appear to take priority, but social dimensions also require constant attention: equal opportunities (male-female, disabled people), social and cultural integration, childhood, safety, physical and psychological health, sport, dietetics, etc. The economic aspect also deserves close attention, for example the cost of studies, grants, students' employability, the institution's efficiency, the ethical management of funds, etc.

The action initiated by ISCN and consolidated through GULF, with the determined support of ETH Zurich and EPFL, will enable the establishment of the standards necessary for the management of technological universities, both consumers of resources and purveyors of solutions for the future, and to lead the way for numerous other university or industrial campuses.

ISCN-GULF Charter Member Universities in Alphabetical Order

1.Brown University
2.Carnegie Mellon University
3.Chatham University
4.Columbia University
5.EPFL
6.ETH Zurich
7.Georgetown University
8.Harvard University
9.Indian Institute of Technology Madras
10.INSEAD
11.Johns Hopkins University
12.Keio University
13.KTH Stockholm
14.London School of Economics and Political Science
15.Massachusetts Institute of Technology
16.Monterrey Institute of Technology and Higher Education
17.National University of Singapore
18.Peking University
19.Pontifical Catholic University of Peru
20.Princeton University
21.Stanford University
22.The University of Hong Kong
23.Tsinghua University
24.University of Cambridge
25.University of Gothenburg
26.University of Luxembourg
27.University of Oxford
28.University of Pennsylvania
29.University of Tokyo
30.Yale University

PART III

••••••••••••

Implications for University Teaching and Learning

CHAPTER 10

A University Culture of Sustainability: Principle, Practice and Economic Driver

Linda P.B. Katehi

INTRODUCTION

Sustainability — as we use the term in our classrooms, capitals and marketplaces — has evolved and taken on an almost mythical quality. The word is ripe with meaning, yet not well defined, and actions in the name of sustainability are similarly wide-ranging and varied.

As early as the 1800s, economic philosophers such as Thomas Malthus and John Stuart Mill recognized resource limits and the need for maintaining resources for future generations. Interest in sustainable resource use faded from view, however, as the Industrial Revolution brought higher standards of living to more developed regions.

The Green Revolution of the mid-20th century, with its enormous technological advances, promised to eliminate hunger and to sustain humanity at previously unimaginable levels (Wharton, 1968; Evenson & Gollin, 2003). By the 1960s and 70s, however, environmental costs associated with growing human populations and intensification of resource use were entering the public consciousness. Rachel Carson (*Silent Spring*, 1962), Paul Ehrlich (*The Population Bomb*, 1968) the Club of Rome (*Limits to Growth*, 1972), E.F. Schumacher (*Small is Beautiful*, 1973) and others gave voice to these rising concerns.

For much of society, the energy crises of 1973 and 1979 were crystallizing events, directly connecting the emerging principles of sustainability to our energy consumption; our dependence on access to limited resources to support economies, governments, lifestyles and future generations was suddenly apparent. Responding to these challenges, the United Nations in the early 1980s established the Brundtland Commission to study global sustainability. The Commission's definition of sustainable development — that in which the needs of the present are met without compromising the ability of future generations to meet their own — is one of many in use today (Brundtland, 1987).

Academics, in their roles as innovators, scientists and philosophers, have been critical players in identifying these global problems and their potential solutions. University administrators were also quick to stake out leadership roles in global sustainability in a coordinated manner during the 1990s, as marked by the Talloires Declaration (University Leaders for a Sustainable Future, 1990), which recognized the unique abilities and responsibilities of universities to advance the study, teaching and application of environmentally sustainable practices.

In recent years, the notion of sustainability has expanded from a narrower focus on natural resources to include resilient and durable social, political and economic institutions, without which globally sustainable outcomes are unlikely. The Great Recession that began in 2007 and its long aftermath have further highlighted the need for sustainable financial models for institutions as diverse as governments, NGOs and research universities.

Today, there are dozens (if not hundreds) of definitions of sustainability circulating in academic and popular media, adding to the elusive and sometimes confusing nature of discussions on sustainability. Rather than selecting an existing definition or building a new one, I suggest in this paper a conceptual framework that can give structure to consideration of a range of sustainability topics. Then, I discuss unique aspects of academic culture that give research universities an unparalleled role in establishing the principles, modelling the practices and driving the new economics of sustainability.

A CONCEPTUAL FRAMEWORK FOR SUSTAINABILITY

Instead of continually reworking definitions and interpretations of sustainability, it is time to shift our thinking. Sustainability cannot be simply a definition. It must reflect the processes at work at local and global scales that will determine what resources we leave to subsequent generations.

Many of the proposed "solutions" to global sustainability have a fundamental weakness: they assume that some entity will be able to enforce a single set of policies across the planet. Our attempts to apply global governance to problems of similar scale, such as those associated with the Kyoto Protocol on greenhouse gas emissions, have met with much frustration and limited success. Sustainability is likely to prove even more intractable with this type of approach, since the concept, at the outset more nebulous, will also be defined differently across cultures.

Therefore, a reasonable analysis of global sustainability must take into account the inherent differences between countries and cultures. Once basic survival needs are assured, the drive to obtain status, as defined by local culture, is of central importance to human actors. Societies prioritize very different sets of needs; within societies, individuals' expectations and preferences are molded by cultural forces independent of their own will (Marx, 1904). These constraints shape a society's preferred vision for the future, as well as its capacities for modifying its constituents' behaviours.

In addition to these cultural constraints, each locality has its own set of environmental constraints. Sustainability requires acting purposefully in the context of these constraints, then analysing how choices made in the local system will contribute to the potential for sustainability at the global scale.

For any given locality, sustainability requires maintaining — over the long term — supplies of resources essential to the well-being of individuals in that society. Nations dependent on irrigated agriculture may prioritize access to fresh water, while island nations may see the conservation of thin soils as most important. In addition to key natural resources like energy and food, other factors such as clean air and water, natural habitats, access to education, human health and aspects of cultural heritage may be prioritized in a given society.

All localities are, of course, embedded in the larger framework of the planet, and with it all the other localities and their collective activities. At the global level as well, there is a set of resources that must be maintained above a critical threshold to allow all the localities to maintain their human well-being. These global resources represent an absolute constraint on the sum of human activities.

Economic modelling suggests that, at the global scale, economic stability and even growth are possible given the constraint that some set of sustainability indicators must, at a minimum, stay stable over time (Martinet, 2011). It is a daunting task to model how the effects of different societal values and choices interact at the global scale to influence the shared pool of resources. These interactions, however, are the relevant ones for the real-world bargaining processes by which sustainability must be attained.

Inherent differences lend themselves to different sets of solutions, which rarely directly scale up to the global level. Because of these local differences in constraints and visions, societies are often not willing to adopt common global policies, but they may be far more likely to share common tools from which they can develop locally adapted policies.

Inevitably, we are locked in a world of divergent opinions and values. Local and global definitions of sustainability will always be in tension, as will local and global desire and capacity for effecting behavioural change. Scientific research will not resolve these conflicting viewpoints. Universities must therefore take the lead in expanding the toolkit available for advancing sustainability in the face of all these challenges.

THE UNIVERSITY CULTURE OF SUSTAINABILITY

Higher education embraced the concept of sustainability early (Wright, 2002), though it took many years for passion and beliefs to translate into focus and action. The world's universities have a compelling responsibility to be at the forefront, breaking down barriers, taking risks and modelling sustainability. Universities are uniquely situated to take this leadership role, and, in fact, no other entity or system may have the ability, capacity and positioning to do so. A university culture of sustainability fuels the principles, practices and economies of sustainability, while being reinforced by them (Figure 1).

Figure 1: The relationship between a university culture of sustainability and the principles, practices and economic drivers of sustainability are self-reinforcing

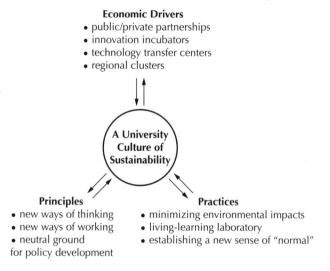

Economic Drivers
- public/private partnerships
- innovation incubators
- technology transfer centers
- regional clusters

A University Culture of Sustainability

Principles
- new ways of thinking
- new ways of working
- neutral ground
  for policy development

Practices
- minimizing environmental impacts
- living-learning laboratory
- establishing a new sense of "normal"

What factors make universities so well placed to respond to the challenges of sustainability? They are inherently multidisciplinary, enabling a diversity of research and opportunities for collaboration. Universities are grounded in their region, allowing them to adapt to a locality's unique needs, while simultaneously driving the region's economy. They are less tied to the short-term cycles (elections and quarterly reports) constraining our political and economic systems, freeing researchers to do the basic research necessary for innovation, while providing a neutral platform for open debate. The world's universities are the independent agents — the honest brokers — who create partnerships bringing science and policy together, then provide the necessary analysis, knowledge, tools, research and commitment to public service.

Public land-grant institutions, which have always enjoyed the support of their states in providing access to education, are now watching states quickly distance themselves from the land-grant commitment. At the same time, the public has found it difficult to reconcile its expectations of access to public education with its unwillingness to support that access, either indirectly through taxes, or directly through tuition. Universities have been widely criticized as irresponsible and unmanageable amid pressure to reduce size and cost, while simultaneously providing high quality. Efforts to reduce expenditures and size frequently conflict with state policies and with the public's expectation and appetite for a state-of-the art college experience.

It is against this backdrop, and perhaps because of it, that research universities must reorganize and change fundamentally. They are being driven to work more smartly and efficiently. They must become leaner enterprises while simultaneously innovating on the battle lines of the world's most challenging issues. Universities have long been seen as institutions whose mission is to tackle society's most pressing challenges.

Universities are busy creating these models of the future, testing strategies and forming partnerships. A culture of sustainability is being integrated into everything we do at the university, whether oriented towards the institution and its surrounding communities, or towards the larger society and our world. Instilling our actions with the core values of sustainability — a respect for people, the environment, and future generations — will allow those passing through our universities to integrate these concepts into their own principles, practices and economic decisions.

Sustainability as Principle

Driven by a changing organizational culture, universities are embracing, developing and disseminating the principles of sustainability in their curricula, research programs and outreach efforts. The world's universities have the potential to bring everyone together on an even playing field: industry, environmental advocates, government and academia. A multidisciplinary approach allows universities to foster new ways of thinking and working, which is necessary in tackling the complex issues of sustainability.

Universities develop new ways of thinking, by investing in both basic and early-stage research. Increasingly driven by short-term interests, the private sector has tended to devalue research and development compared to earlier parts of the 20th century. For example, the deregulation of the energy markets drastically reduced private investment in R&D during the 1990s (Margolis & Kammen, 1999). Because of their educational mission and commitment to public service, universities encourage greater risk-taking. For example, at our newly opened August A. Busch III Brewery and Food Science Laboratory, two rooms were built without any assigned uses, intentionally leaving them available for future innovations.

Universities also develop new ways of working. Many of our greatest challenges today, sometimes referred to as the "wicked problems", require collaborative and multidisciplinary approaches to develop solutions. With their diversity of academic departments, large universities have the infrastructure to create these multidisciplinary dialogues. They must, however, be willing to break down the academic silos and work across disciplines and with their surrounding communities. At UC Davis, the newly created Agricultural Sustainability Institute provides the institutional framework to allow faculty, staff and students from both social sciences and traditional sciences to collaborate on research projects investigating the impact of our food system on society. Accompanying its directors are a team of 24 full-time staff, 9 professorships in a range of disciplines, 150 other affiliated UC Davis faculty interested in sustainable agriculture and over 150 students; its association with the UC Cooperative Extension Program expands its reach to the business and public communities. Obviously, this effort represents a significant investment and a determination to make progress on an important societal issue.

Universities develop sound policies, by providing neutral ground for discussion and debate. For example, when the governor of California wanted to develop a Low Carbon Fuel Standard for transportation fuels, rather than turning to his agencies, he instead turned to UC Davis and UC Berkeley. A team of 20 researchers developed the policy by grounding it in science while simultaneously taking the politics out of the process. Industry, environmentalists and policymakers were involved from the start (Farrell & Sperling, 2007a). We know business cannot thrive unless our foundation is healthy and stable. We also know that cleaning the planet's air and water is not just good for our environment — it also creates jobs and improves the economy. So together, industry and academia created the first policy in the United States to steer the petroleum industry toward low carbon. It was eventually adopted in California almost as written — and it requires a 10% reduction by 2020 in greenhouse gases emitted by transportation fuels (Farrell & Sperling, 2007b). The northeast states in the U.S. are now considering a similar standard and there is also interest in it on the national level. UC Davis has also been consulting in Canada, Europe and China on models for low-carbon economies.

Sustainability as Practice

Universities have a responsibility to be leaders in implementation of sustainable practices. At the most basic level, sustainable practices, such as green buildings and energy efficiency projects, save money and minimize impact on the environment. However, as places of higher education, universities can turn their campuses into living laboratories, which serve as a testing ground for new research, while engaging students in experiential education.

Higher education is competing with the background "education" that comes from one's surroundings — such as that from superhighways, shopping malls, urban sprawl, entrenched industries, television and non-stop advertising — in establishing a sense of what is "normal" to our youth (Orr, 2002). The innovative research and operations policies that are outgrowths of universities' cultures of sustainability can directly engage students in sustainable practices, and challenge what students perceive as "normal". This engagement will pay dividends for society as these students, our future leaders, carry these innovative practices into their workplaces and personal lives. Universities act as drivers of social change by challenging our very ideas of "standard practices".

As an example of the tight integration of sustainable practice with student learning, UC Davis is building what will become the largest zero-net energy community in the United States, West Village (Finkelor *et al.*, 2010). The first phase will open in fall 2011, housing students who will bike and ride the bus to classes. The buildings incorporate cutting-edge energy and environmental design, and the community will generate renewable electric power. At face value, this project is simply an effort to reduce energy costs, while minimizing environmental impacts. Yet, it is much more than that. The project is a public-private partnership involving many of UC Davis' research centers, including The Energy Efficiency Center, The Energy Institute, The Center for Water-Energy Efficiency, The Western Cooling Efficiency Center, The California Lighting Technology Center and The Biogas Energy Project. West Village provides a platform for university researchers to work across disciplines and apply their research to real-world scenarios. The project will eventually include homes for our faculty, retail space and a dynamic village center. The project — because it is sustainable, coherent and comprehensive — will serve as an international model.

A more targeted example of the living laboratory at UC Davis is the California Lighting Technology Center — a university-sponsored collaboration with industry — charged with developing more sustainable lighting. Our campus is implementing a US$39-million initiative to apply efficient new technologies, not only to save money, but also to use the campus as a large-scale testing ground. The new lighting technology deployed in parking garages, for example, serves as a prototype to assess the quality of the technology and to see if better lighting reduces crime around the garages. Lessons learned from these experiences will improve the products, thus speeding the adoption of more sustainable infrastructure in the rest of the community and nation.

Practices should not be limited to large, multimillion-dollar initiatives. Smaller-scale initiatives often provide the greatest opportunities to engage students, providing valuable experiential education in core sustainability fields. For example, students at UC Davis can train and work in organic agriculture at our Student Farm, or conduct research at the Russell Ranch Long Term Research on Agricultural Systems (LTRAS). The students' work is not simply a classroom exercise: the produce from the Student Farm is sold through a CSA (community supported agriculture) to Davis community members, while the tomatoes from Russell Ranch are used by Sodexho in its campus dining operations. Connecting educational opportunities with operational practices is an essential part of building a sustainable framework.

By taking a leadership role in sustainable practices, universities minimize their environmental impact, provide a testing ground for applied research, engage students in experiential learning, and establish a new set of expectations for "how things should be" that students can take with them to future employment. Fine-tuning practices in the university setting allows researchers to make the necessary modifications to scale up these practices to best serve society. When combined with innovation hubs catalyzing technology transfers to the private sector, sustainable practices can catalyse regional economies.

Sustainability as Economic Driver

The coordinated push for sustainability has invigorated the generation of knowledge in science, technology and policy. This new knowledge is driving innovation and the creation of new products and services. The biggest challenge and opportunity for any organization — and for public universities particularly — is to channel our new culture of sustainability into ideas and behaviours representing a paradigm shift.

Universities have demonstrated their capacity to act as regional economic drivers, as evidenced by dynamic economic zones like Silicon Valley and Rochester, NY. Communities leverage research and people emanating from the university, along with private partnerships, to develop clusters of economic and technological innovation. Universities can create centers to bring disciplines together to move ideas out of the lab, establish incubators to develop projects separately from the university setting, and finally are capable of creating centers to transfer these technologies into the workplace. Today, sustainability is driving innovation and creation of new economies (Nidumolu et al., 1998); universities and their communities have a head start on being able to productively respond to these new opportunities.

Often, advances on campuses can be directly applied beyond the university. For example, student teams at UC Davis have developed a solar-powered light that is less expensive than candles or kerosene — it also emits far less carbon. Already tested in Zambia and Nigeria, the light could make a significant difference in quality of life and in carbon emissions for the 1.5 billion people still using petroleum-based fuel to light their homes (Creed *et al.*, 2010). As another example, Professor Pamela Ronald recently developed a flood-resistant rice strain through precision breeding with three to five-fold increased yields under flood conditions in Bangladesh, India and Indonesia. Universities provide a unique platform for these types of intellectual advances, which translate to increased productivity with a reduction in our use of resources. UC Davis is committed to enabling this kind of technology, while simultaneously training a new generation of educators and leaders to understand the complexities and interdisciplinary nature of sustainability.

Aiming to invigorate partnerships that spur creativity, UC Davis has designed an innovation incubator — the Engineering Translational Technology Center. This is an on-campus facility where faculty can develop their projects while ensuring separation of intellectual property and technology transfer between the campus and start-up companies. While universities are well known for their knowledge generation services, they are historically not as good at transferring these technologies to the private sector. Complex intellectual property policies typically hinder researchers from commercializing technologies developed on campuses. Privately funded, our Engineering Translational Technology Center provides a platform for researchers to turn their ideas into private businesses in a familiar and secure setting. Incubators are already demonstrating their potential to transfer ideas into the workplace: UC Berkeley's Business Incubator has helped secure $1.7 million in funding for zipReality.com.

Along similar lines, UC Davis has established the first university-based Energy Efficiency Center focused on transferring relevant technology into the marketplace. We have also invested in a Center for Entrepreneurship to bring science, engineering and business together to move ideas out of the lab and into the world. Thanks in part to these efforts, UC Davis has formed 34 start-up companies since 2004 — 9 of which formed last year alone. We would like to improve this number and create close to 15 annually. UC Davis is now in the process of creating an Innovation Hub to connect research with entrepreneurs, accelerate the transfer of campus discoveries into commercial products, and develop the local and regional economy.

In the 1950s, Stanford's Frederick Terman had a specific vision — to foster a cluster of high technology firms around the Stanford campus in order to keep the talented Stanford graduates in the region. That cluster became known as Silicon Valley, responsible for many of the innovations behind the computer revolution, and creating one of the strongest regional economies in the nation. This plan succeeded for three reasons — it linked students and faculty with surrounding firms for jobs, created an Industrial Park on the Stanford campus to incentive firms to relocate, and it used incubators to catalyze technology transfers from the classroom to the workplace (Huffman & Quigley, 2002). This is what we are doing at UC Davis, demonstrating the power of universities to drive economic change.

All of these initiatives feed into our plan for UC Davis: providing higher productivity by enhancing output while reducing our use of resources, a reflection of the extent to which an ethic of sustainability has permeated our university culture. Our plan will generate growth by creating new ideas, new relationships and new structures, by reducing bureaucracy and embracing risk taking, and by encouraging and supporting free thinking about the opportunities and responsible planning against the challenges. This is the new university: an intensive and intentional organization that can find meaning and order in unconstrained thinking, providing focus and a disciplined approach.

CONCLUSIONS

A century ago, visionary leaders established a regionally based network of agricultural experiment stations at land-grant universities and colleges to connect university research with farmers to solve real-world problems (Hatch Act 1887, Smith-Lever Act 1914). This network enabled universities to create tools to overcome local constraints, while simultaneously sharing their tools with other stations to help farmers to provide enough food for the nation.

Today, we are faced with a similar predicament in which localities, facing different environmental and social constraints, are both contributing to and being impacted by the global issue of sustainability. Universities have demonstrated their ability to drive economies and social change. An organizational culture of sustainability must be at the heart of the university's principles, practices and economic partnerships in order to ensure that the innovations and dynamism emanating from campuses advance the dual goals of local and global sustainability.

Universities must act, and as they do so, they must break from the past. The traditional university as isolated actor will not conquer the future, and may not even survive into the future. Behaviours and structures must fully embrace collaboration and multi-disciplinary solutions. Tools must be created and shared. These frameworks are beginning to be built: R20, an innovative international effort bringing together local governments, NGOs, corporations and educational institutions, enables collaborations leading to concrete action to combat climate change and build the green economy.

The world's universities must be bold and creative, yet disciplined and frugal. It is possible. If universities work together, as partners and collaborators, they will be the models, the living laboratories and the solution.

REFERENCES

Brundtland, G.H. (1987). The U.N. World Commission on Environment and Development: Our common future. Oxford: Oxford University Press.

Creed, B., Kreutzberg T. & Salomon, A. (2010). Lighting the Way Nigeria. *International Energy Technologies, University of California, Davis*, [online] Available at <http://piet1.ucdavis.edu/projects/zambia-bangladesh/ReplacingFuelBasedLighting2010 DLablFinalPresentation.pdf> (Accessed August 30, 2011).

Evenson, R. E. & Gollin, D. (2003). Assessing the impact of the Green Revolution, 1960 to 2000. *Science*, 300, pp. 758-62.

Farrell, A.E. & Sperling, D. (2007a). A Low-Carbon Fuel Standard for California, Part 1: Technical Analysis. Institute of Transportation Studies, University of California, Davis, Research Report UCD-ITS-RR-07-07.

Farrell, A.E. & Sperling, D. (2007b). A Low-Carbon Fuel Standard for California, Part 2: Policy Analysis. Institute of Transportation Studies, University of California, Davis, Research Report UCD-ITS-RR-07-08.

Finkelor, B. *et al.* (2010). West Village: A Process & Business Model for Achieving Zero-Net Energy at the Community-Scale. *UC Davis Energy Efficiency Center*, [online] <http://eec.ucdavis.edu/ACEEE/2010/data/papers/2271.pdf> (Accessed August 30, 2011).

Huffman, D. & Quigley, J.M. (2002). The role of the university in attracting high tech entrepreneurship: a Silicon Valley tale. *The Annals of Regional Science*, 36 (3), pp. 403-19.

Margolis, R.M. & Kammen, D.M. (1999). Evidence of under-investment in energy R&D in the United States and the impact of federal policy. *Energy Policy*, 27 (10), pp. 575-84.

Marshall, J.D. & Toffel, M.W. (2005). Framing the elusive concept of sustainability: a sustainability hierarchy. *Environmental Science and Technology*, 39 (3), pp. 673-82.

Martinet, V. (2011). A characterization of sustainability with indicators. *Journal of Environmental Economics and Management*, 61 (2), pp. 183-197.

Marx, K. (1904). *Preface to a Contribution to the Critique of Political Economy*. Chicago: C.H. Kerr.

Nidumolu, R., Prahalad, C.K. & Rangaswami, M.R. (2009). Why sustainability is now the key driver of innovation. *Harvard Business Review*, September Issue, pp. 56-65.

Orr, D.W. (2002). *The nature of design: ecology, culture, and human intention*. New York: Oxford UP.

University Leaders for a Sustainable Future (1990). The Talloires Declaration. Washington: ULSF.

Wharton, C. (1968). The Green Revolution: cornucopia or Pandora's box? *Foreign Affairs*, 47, pp. 464-476.

Wright, T.S.A. (2002). Definitions and frameworks for environmental sustainability in higher education. *International Journal of Sustainability in Higher Education*, 3 (3), pp. 203-220.

CHAPTER 11

Universities: serving as, and educating global Citizens

Heather Munroe-Blum and Carlos Rueda*

GLOBAL CHALLENGES AND GLOBAL CITIZENSHIP

Four years ago, in Sydney, Australia, 2.2 million citizens turned their lights off for one hour to take a stand against climate change. Last March, only four years later, 5,251 cities in 135 countries responded to the same call and turned their lights off for "The Earth Hour", including places such as the United Arab Emirates, Bolivia and Palestine (Earth Hour, 2011). The symbolic action of "The Earth Hour" has become the world's most engaging climate change initiative.

Today, almost every person who has been exposed to the concept of climate change is able to tell a story, show a video or state a fact relating to the impact of climate change. They are realizing that national or regional boundaries, the same ones that define an important part of social identities and loyalties, do not matter in the dynamics of climate change. They also see themselves as part of the problem, and of the solution. According to a poll conducted among 25,000 people in 23 countries, the most serious global problems are: extreme poverty, the environment or pollution, the rising cost of food and energy, the spread of human diseases, terrorism, climate change, human rights abuses, the state of the global economy, war or armed conflicts, and violation of worker's rights (BBC, 2010). The different local and global responses to these challenges, such as the "The Earth Hour" movement, reveal strong supranational feelings of unity and responsibility, the two drivers shaping our identity as global citizens.

The reactions towards those global challenges, together with the revolution in technology and communications, are distinctive characteristics of young citizens. Holden Thorp, President of University of North Carolina at

129

Chapel Hill, and Buck Goldstein refer to "the millennial generation" in their book *Engines of Innovation*:

They were born between 1981 and 1993... Approximately 40% of millennials in America are non-white, and 20% have a parent who is an immigrant. Eighty per cent have participated in some form of community service, and they are generally optimistic about the future... [Also] they generally think of themselves as entrepreneurial. Ninety seven per cent of them own a computer and 94% own a cell phone; 76% use instant messaging to stay connected 24/7 (Thorp et al., 2010, p. 15).

Referring to their problem solving capacity, the authors note:

The demographic diversity... as well as their standards of intellectual achievement, technological facility, social commitment and entrepreneurial outlook, make them ideal partners in attacking great problems in a practical and timely manner. Their strong idealism combines with an increasing interest in what has come to be known as social entrepreneurship to create an important and influential constituency ready to engage the world's most challenging and exciting issues (2010, p. 15).

The challenge for universities is clear. How should universities respond to global challenges? How should universities adapt to educate "the millennial generation" as global citizens? In sum, how are universities — institutions that were founded to resemble "the universe", "the whole", "the world" — behaving as global citizens?

In 2007, the Glion Colloquium gathered to discuss *The Globalization of Higher Education*, compelling examples and strategies to create "universities in the world and of the world" (Duderstadt, Taggart & Weber, 2008, ch. 24). Four years after, written in the context of the 2011 Glion Colloquium on *Global Sustainability and the Role of Universities*, the current article aims to concretize seven directions in which universities can fulfill their role as global citizens. These directions are presented without a specific order, and some of them illustrated with examples of programs and initiatives at McGill University, a highly global, research-intensive and internationally interconnected research university, and its Desautels Faculty of Management — one of the university's highly internationalized and innovative communities.

Active engagement in global considerations

Are universities effectively engaging with global considerations, such as climate change? As example, a quick Google search with the words "climate change research center", identified more than 50 university-based centers or institutes devoted to research on climate change, and there is only in the English-speaking world of Google. Yes. We can be confident — universities are engaging with global challenges.

As universities sharpen their focus on addressing world problems, they are naturally doing so via new research-oriented multidisciplinary programs that foster collaboration, drawing on their current institutional assets. But university leaders might question their activities and priorities more deeply in the context of their role in addressing global challenges. As Harold Shapiro (2009), former President of Princeton University, notes:

In order to meet their obligations as a public citizen in the educational arena, universities need to constantly and transparently reevaluate whose interests are being served by the current policies and programs that surround the provision of their educational programs. [And universities need] to raise questions that society does not want to ask and to generate new ideas and understandings that help us invent a better future, at times even pushing society toward it.

We suggest two ways in which universities might engage more deeply. One, by embracing research and knowledge translation on global challenges that might not be receiving attention by other institutions or sectors. As an example, to what extent are universities engaging with post-disaster reconstruction, nuclear risk, health systems research, international financial regulation or business ethics? Two, by adapting university educational activities in response to global challenges. To what extent are universities educating and training people to understand and take effective action in relation to problems, such as these above?

McGill University, with students and faculty from every continent of the world, has made global health a priority. For example, significant research, policy, outreach and training activities in this field are channeled through the Institute for Health and Social Policy. Researchers at the Institute actively approach health considerations from a global perspective: briefing the United States Congress on the benefits of maternity leave around the world, or raising awareness of the impact of HIV/AIDS on the ability of African families to provide for their children. On the educational side, the International Masters in Health Leadership (IMHL), a joint program of the Faculty of Medicine and the Desautels Faculty of Management, is uniquely designed to give practising physicians, nurses and other health professionals effective engagement with the manner in which health care is organized in jurisdictions around the globe, and to support them in the implementation of change projects with teams inside and outside their organizations or communities, while learning from their experiences. In the words of IMHL Faculty Director, management professor Henry Mintzberg (2011): "The IMHL is unique and highly ambitious. We are setting out to change, not only education for health leadership, but the health system itself, by bringing into an ongoing forum the best of practising leadership from all aspects of health and from all regions of the world." The latest class graduated health professionals from 13 countries, including Uganda, Saudi Arabia, Italy, Iceland, England, the Philippines and Belgium.

Universities are positioned to actively engage global issues through interdisciplinary research platforms and innovative educational programs.

Transnational and connected research

In the last few decades, the development of regional clusters, modelled world-wide after the success of Route 128 in Massachusetts and Silicon Valley in California, has been a cornerstone innovation in economic policy. According to Richard Florida (2008), 10 mega-regions, which together have only 6% of the world's population, "account for 43% of the planet's economic activity and more than half of its patented innovations and star scientists".

Highly effective clusters have seen government, industry and universities working on shared goals in a three-way partnership — what Stanford professor Henry Etzkowitz (2008) calls the "triple helix" model — and then applying this on the world stage. It is clear that, in order to have impact in a field today, the best strategy is still to assemble a critical mass of smart people in your own back-yard. However, serious players in the R&D game connect their clusters to others.

Since 2006, key partners in Canada and California have been working together to pioneer a new type of large-scale international framework, one that networks government, industry and universities in both locales — a "double tri-ple helix". This Canada-California Strategic Innovation Partnership (CCSIP) is an entrepreneurial collaboration among the three sectors in innovation-inten-sive research areas, such as sustainable energy and bio-imaging technology. This "double triple helix" strategy is a promising model for future research partner-ships, taking a proven regional strategy and globalizing it. It uses shared priorities and strengths to quickly identify, and act upon, critical research questions that align with industry and community needs (Munroe-Blum, 2008, pp. 157-8).

When identifying partners, geographic proximity is typically a feature of economic clusters. Nevertheless, with respect to research and innovation clusters, universities can act globally. The increasingly competitive research and innovation performance of the BRIC countries (Brazil, Russia, India and China) demonstrates globalization and virtual clusters of research, innovation and talent (Munroe-Blum, 2010).

- In 2006, the BRIC countries produced half as many doctorates as all 30 OECD countries combined (OECD, 2009, p. 17).
- All the BRIC countries tripled their production of scientific articles in just over a decade (OECD, 2010, p. 45). In 2007, China also took the #2 spot — surpassing Japan — for volume of research articles pub-lished (National Science Board, 2010, pp. 0-9).
- In a survey of global firms planning to build new research and devel-opment facilities, 77% plan to build or are building them in China or India (The National Academies, 2010, pp. 6-11).
- China and India, also, have developed new products that are dramat-ically cheaper than their western counterparts: $2,500 cars and $100 computers.

The time when non-Western scientists had to partner with prominent Western scientists before achieving international acclaim is over. In the coming years, we are likely to see the situation reverse.

In our globalized world, one of the most important roles of universities is, and will be, forging international connections. Contemporary research and scholarly collaborations often demand a scale so massive, so daring, and requiring such a wide range of expertise, that it will increasingly be impossible for any single institution, organization or industry to assemble the necessary talent and infrastructure to tackle these on their own. And, perhaps most importantly, these establish networks of key players — the organizations and people that, when brought together, are most likely to jumpstart innovation.

Universities will benefit from connecting their research activities to intersectoral, international clusters of innovation, with a special emphasis on including one or more partners from the BRIC economies, where there exists a natural complementarity or synergy.

Open knowledge that flows

Initiatives that promote open knowledge are clashing with current property rights frameworks. Google's Library Project (2011) is an example of such an initiative, which it defends as follows:

Copyright law is supposed to ensure that authors and publishers have an incentive to create new work, not stop people from finding out that the work exists. By helping people find books, we believe we can increase the incentive to publish them. After all, if a book isn't discovered, it won't be bought. That's why we firmly believe that this project is good news for everybody who reads, writes, publishes and sells books.

Out of the 21 library partners in this Google initiative, 15 are universities.

Universities contain knowledge in their libraries, but are also very active in the creation of knowledge for teaching and research purposes, thus, the same principle of information flow might well be applied to these latter activities and outputs.

MIT is at the frontier in their effort: OpenCourseWare (OCW) a free web-based publication of virtually all MIT course content given by almost 700 faculty members, with approximately half of the materials already translated into other languages (MIT OCW, 2011). This is achieving global impact. An estimated 100 million people use the source, with the majority of users outside the United States. As part of the initiative, more than 250 universities from around the world now share their educational content. OCW materials have helped educators in Indonesia improve their courses, entrepreneurs in Haiti launch their businesses, and students in Africa study with the confidence that they are accessing current, accurate information. The initiative aims to reach 1 billion minds in the next decade.

Initiatives such as Google's Library Project and MIT OCW use open flows of knowledge to have a positive global impact, and these demonstrate the leading role that universities play in this effort.

Achieving the right balance between closed and open IP is an acute problem for some key economic sectors. Currently, strong IP protection is framed as the only way to recoup major investment in a necessarily long and costly development process, yet that walling-off of knowledge may be, in part, the very reason that, for example, the number of new drugs created in recent years has fallen so dramatically. At universities, the traditional enclaves of closed IP — patents, licences, contracts and associated streamed income — have been viewed as effective means to monetize the impact of knowledge. But the new innovation era demands expanded notions of "technology transfer", models that support open innovation. To increase the impact of research and teaching on global considerations, all players in the innovation system must interact proactively to build trust and productive collaboration.

Universities can lead a reform of current IP constraints and act boldly in opening their knowledge to global use and applications.

Co-educate in global partnerships

The higher education sector is booming, especially in the developing world.

- In 1970, 28.6 million students were enrolled in tertiary education; in 2007, 152.5 million students were enrolled, a five-fold growth (UNESCO Institute for Statistics, 2009, pp. 9-10).
- In 1980, people from developing Asian economies accounted for 14% of the people who completed tertiary education worldwide. In 2000, those same countries were home to 25% of degree holders (National Science Board, 2010, pp. 0-6).
- In China, the number of people graduating from universities and specialized colleges has nearly quadrupled since 2000 (UNESCO Institute for Statistics, 2009, pp. 9-10).

These educational trends respond to demographic and economic changes, and aggressive educational policies taken by developing countries to supply the increasing demand for higher education. Universities from developing and developed countries may look more ambitiously to build co-educational partnerships with the goal of increasing the quantity and quality of higher education.

The need for a truly global education is another motivation to build international partnerships. Universities that move away from international educational experiences as "bubble programs", where students are sheltered from the character and people of the very places they are visiting, to find the means in which to co-educate students in partnership between schools form different countries will have greatest impact. Business schools, in particular, may be setting the benchmark for other disciplines. Among the top 25 business schools in the world (*Financial Times*, 2011), at least 10 of them offer an MBA degree in partnership with another international school. In seeking to co-educate in global partnership, one of the main challenges for universities' senior administration and faculty will be to overcome the vicious circle of defining themselves as "elite" institutions, that should only "educate elites" among other "elite universities", with "elite" narrowly defined.

The International Master in Practicing Management at McGill University is a partnership of 5 business schools (in Canada, U.K., Brazil, India and China). The five schools train a common cohort of managers with a common, innovative learning framework developed collectively. In each country, each school is in charge of one of the five modules and delivers it with their own faculty and resources. Such opportunities can provide students with a rich global experience.

Universities can offer students the opportunity to be equally co-educated by schools from other countries and cultures, as one means of implementing global education.

Social entrepreneurship with local and global impact

The history of many universities is linked to an entrepreneur. McGill University, for example, was founded on the vision and generosity of James McGill, a Scottish immigrant merchant who, in the 1700s, came to the land that would become Canada. We can find similar origins in Cornell University, Johns Hopkins University, the National University of Singapore and the Instituto Tecnológico de Monterrey.

Entrepreneurship is in the DNA of the university, making our institutions great places for the attraction of talent with a hunger to test new ideas. Nevertheless, it must after be stimulated and rewarded. As Thorp and Goldstein note (2010, p. 20):

Don't the smartest people in our society gravitate toward academic communities? Isn't academia known for discovering new ways of doing and seeing things? Didn't the World Wide Web get started to foster knowledge sharing among academics, and wasn't social networking (the newest form of knowledge transfer) invented by undergraduates on a college campus? And in terms of resources, what institutions on our society have more financial resources dedicated to attacking the world's big problems? There is obviously something missing in the mix, and we believe, as you might expect, the missing ingredient is entrepreneurship.

Entrepreneurship, in the university context, includes the transfer and application of the knowledge and technology that flow from university research. But it does not stop there. It means, for professors and students, bringing the energy and expertise of universities to bear on problems that have an impact on society: for example, creating and evaluating a more effective biomedical device, sharing advice with policymakers in societies transitioning to democracy, or helping communities devise sustainable solutions to nutrition problems, and doing so via creative new approaches to teaching and learning.

Teach for America (TFA) was founded by Wendy Kopp in 1989, a Princeton University student, and emanated from her senior thesis on how to help eliminate educational inequity in the United States. TFA now recruits new college graduates and professionals, "TFA corps", to teach for two years in urban and rural communities throughout the United States. The goal of TFA (2011) is to impact students' performance via the work of TFA corps members, and to develop the members into lifelong leaders who will work towards educational equality. Since the beginning of the program in 1990, more than 20,000 corps members have fulfilled a commitment to TFA, and the organization has become one of the most desired employers in the United States and in 18 other countries where the network Teach for All has expanded to include U.K., Germany, Brazil, China, India, Israel, Lebanon and Pakistan. And it all started with the thesis of a senior college student.

The Jeanne Sauvé Foundation and McGill University annually host a group of accomplished young leaders from all around the world: The Sauvé Scholars. Financially supported by the Foundation, they live together in The Sauvé House, have McGill mentors and almost unlimited access to McGill and Concordia University courses, and take advantage of those resources and time flexibility to work on their projects during one year. One of the Sauvé Scholars, Arcie Mallari, from the Philippines and the founder of Silid Aralan, an educational NGO working with underprivileged school low-performers, was inspired through the Sauvé program to address the challenge of waste management for future generations. Mallari is launching iWastology, a web-based tool to raise awareness on the issue of garbage production through the eyes of schoolchildren from varying communities around the world. To date, there have been 100 Sauvé Scholars on the McGill campus, launching outstanding ventures to tackle global problems in their own countries and communities.

We can help to grow the entrepreneurial spirit within our universities, encouraging students and professors to act on their ideas and connect with partners and resources to effect social change.

Leadership style rooted in communities

McGill's Henry Mintzberg described the last financial crisis (2009, p. 1):

Beneath the current economic crisis lies another crisis of far greater proportions: the depreciation in companies of community — people's sense of belonging to and caring for something larger than themselves. Decades of short-term management, in the United States especially, have inflated the importance of CEOs and reduced others in the corporation to fungible commodities — human resources to be "downsized" at the drop of a share price. The result: mindless, reckless behavior that has brought the global economy to its knees.

This phenomenon not only highlights a "leadership crisis", but also points to the emergence of a new way of understanding change and the management of organizations. Barack Obama's 2008 presidential campaign was a milestone in animating a new style of leadership. In the words of Marshall Ganz (2008, p. 16), Harvard Kennedy School Professor and key trainer of organizers during the campaign:

Social movements' nature, as broadly based harbingers of change, create unusual leadership challenges: they are voluntary, decentralized and self-governing; they are volatile, dynamic, and interactive; participants are motivated by moral claims, but results depend on strategic creativity; and their capacity to make things happen depends on their ability to mobilize broad levels of commitment. As a result, perhaps their most critical capacity is consistent — formal and informal — leadership development. [The campaign] combined large-scale training organizing skills and, at the same time, developed innovative new media techniques to support the organizers and their local leadership teams in putting those skills to work.

Or what Mintzberg calls *Communityship*:

Communityship requires a more modest form of leadership that might be called engaged and distributed management. A community leader is personally engaged in order to engage others, so that anyone and everyone can exercise initiative. If you doubt this can happen, take a look at how Wikipedia, Linux, and other open-source operations work (2009, p. 2).

Organizations work best when they too are communities, of committed people who work in cooperative relationships, under conditions of trust and respect. Destroy this, and the whole institution of business and other organizations collapses (2010, p. 1).

This same revolution in leadership and management is also challenging traditional approaches to education, which have been based on classroom learning, to a new engagement in learning *within* organizations and communities, and moving into a "mutual learning" framework.

At McGill, the International Master in Practicing Management and the International Master in Health Leadership programs were conceived with a community approach for learning and organizational change. Each participant designated a team of colleagues who will do the program with him/her virtually, both to anchor the learning and to assess its consequences. This team debriefs on the learning after each module; welcomes guests to the managerial exchange and field studies; and together with the participating manager, promotes change in the organization as a result of this learning. This approach leverages the activity: for each in-person participant in the program, five or more people are trained virtually, multiplying the impact on the organization (Mintzberg, 2011).

University education may increasingly be reciprocal and community-based, and less dependent on the professor as "leader-expert".

Intercultural intelligence, empathy and courage

Globalization, in its many economic and social expressions, has resulted in a smaller world. For some cultures, as mentioned previously, this creates a comfort with global identity. For others, it represents a threat to traditional beliefs and life styles, awakening feelings of protectionism, tribalism and aggression. As Samuel Huntington (1993) in his article, *The Clash of Civilizations*, noted, cultural and religious differences will increasingly be a main source of conflict, requiring humans to develop enhanced capacity to coexist together. Indeed, civil conflict and war, paradoxically, may be triggered more readily with the pressures of globalization, as 9/11 and subsequent events have shown.

Thus, as the world is increasingly interconnected, for some it becomes smaller and intimidating. Global citizenship will require three important individual qualities: intercultural intelligence, empathy and courage.

Intercultural intelligence refers to a person's capacity to adapt to and effectively interact with new cultural contexts. It requires from an individual: the capacity and interest to gain knowledge about a new culture, the will and commitment to persevere in comprehending and engaging with the new culture, and transcending stumbling blocks such as disappointment or fear into the ability to engage effective action in a given intercultural situation (Early, Ang & Tan, 2006).

Empathy towards those who are "different" can assist people to turn feelings of indifference towards or fear of the "other" into compassion and involvement, resulting in understanding and positive connections. In the context of an increasingly connected world, empathy is the core to feelings of unity and shared responsibility and, together with multicultural intelligence, the distinguishing elements separating "international" from "global" citizens.

For centuries, humanity has built institutions responding to national, local and individual interests, and an important part of our loyalties, identities and emotions have been attached to a domestic mission. However, problems of global scope will not be resolved by citizens and institutions borne of limited and local perspectives and mission. A sense of adventure and courage may be necessary to foster adaptive change. Courage here does not mean aggression.

In the exercise of global citizenship, one's courage can be viewed as the ability to challenge one's own personal institutional and cultural perspectives and norms to embrace broader global norms and perspectives and to persevere in that effort of developing global citizenship. Indeed, both local *and* global engagement need not be mutually exclusive but, rather, mutually constructive.

University education, as a key element of institutional mission, is generally structured within the context of disciplines that pursue facts and knowledge, potentially under-focusing on the equally important personal learning associated with intercultural intelligence, empathy and courage (and multilingualism), characteristics that will be key for graduates that are successfully prepared to perform global tasks. The Economist Intelligence Unit's CEO *Briefings* (2006, 2007), based on survey data from over 1,000 senior executives across 40 nations, identified a lack of high quality talent to operate in multiple cultures as the greatest challenge facing international organizations. How can universities foster these qualities? Apart from co-educating in global partnerships, another key direction is to create environments that embrace and interact on a base of diversity, including intellectual, linguistic and demographic diversity.

McGill's Desautels Faculty of Management is located in downtown Montreal's multilingual, multicultural environment. Two-thirds of the school's faculty members come from abroad; each year, 75% of PhDs, over 50% of MBAs, and 25% of Bachelor students also come from countries other than Canada. With such diversity of experience and culture, the school's curriculum and environment naturally reinforce an understanding of global issues, with several new programs created specifically in support of that aim. The result is a panoptic, versus myopic, approach to living, working and learning together.

Universities can enhance the intercultural fluency of professors and students by creating environments that encourage multilingualism, and that respect and engage varied socio-economic backgrounds and disciplines, acknowledging the varied religions and cultures that serve as a backdrop to intercultural and global transactions.

In order to equip professors and students to act as civilized and responsible citizens, moving freely across borders and cultures, universities can play a role in enhancing attributes that explore and develop the values and skills associated with intercultural experience, empathy and courage.

FINAL REMARKS

Rapid global transformations, spurred on by a massive revolution in the nature and use of communication technologies, is spawning a sense of connectedness **and** dependency in "the millennial generation". Higher education may both require and facilitate global citizenship. A prime role for universities today is to foster actively the development of global citizenship in students and staff. Indeed, the case can be made that this will increasingly be a hallmark of success for the university, and its teaching and research programs.

The seven directions described here aim to support universities in embracing an institutional responsibility to promote in its faculty and students global citizenship. These can be viewed as an institutional menu, to be adapted to the needs of an institution and the individuals and committees it serves. In this sense, each strategy might be applied in consideration of the particularities of each institution: their respective organizational histories and cultures, funding sources and budgets, long-term missions and current priorities. The progress that may be achieved has the potential to be powerful.

Embracing global citizenship can be challenging; integrating this goal into an institutional mission and context may be dizzying but essential. Increasingly, globalization will require universities, their communities and members to adapt, and to foster the widespread desire, and means, to achieve global citizenship.

* The authors would like to acknowledge, with gratitude, Professor Henry Mintzberg's work in modernizing management education as an important inspirational source for this paper; and, the supportive contributions of Ms Caroline Baril in discussing and reviewing key elements of this paper.

REFERENCES

British Broadcasting Corporation (2010). *Poverty most serious world problem, says global poll.* [press release], 17 January 2010, Available at: http://www.globescan.com/news_archives/bbcWorldSpeaks- 2010/ (Accessed 1 September 2011).

Duderstadt, J., Taggart, J. & Weber, L. (2008). The Globalization of Higher Education In L. Weber and J. Duderstadt ed. *The Globalization of Higher Education.* Glion Colloquium.

Earth Hour (2011). *About the Earth Hour* (online) Available at: http://www.earth-hour.org/About.aspx (Accessed 1 September 2011).

Early, C., Ang, S. & Tan, J. (2006). *Developing Cultural Intelligence at Work.* California: Stanford University Press.

Economist Intelligence Unit (2006). *CEO Briefing: Corporate Priorities for 2006 and Beyond.* [online] Available at: http://graphics.eiu.com/files/ad_pdfs/ceo_Briefing_UKTI_wp.pdf (Accessed 1 September 2011).

Economist Intelligence Unit (2007). *CEO Briefing: Corporate Priorities for 2007 and Beyond.* [online] Available at: http://graphics.eiu.com/files/ad_pdfs/eiu_CEO_Briefing_2007.pdf (Accessed 1 September 2011).

Etzkowitz, Henry (2008). *The Triple Helix: University-Industry-Government Innovation in Action:* New York: Routledge.

Financial Times (2011). *2011 Global MBA's Rankings* [online] Available at: http://rankings.ft.com/businessschoolrankings/global-mba-rankings-2011   (Accessed 1 September 2011).

Florida, R. (2008). The Buffalo Mega-Region: Bigger than We Know. *Buffalo News*, 15 June.

Ganz, M. (2008). *Leading Change: Leadership, Organization, and Social Movements*. Harvard University Kennedy School of Government, (online), Available at: http://mitsloan.mit.edu/iwer/pdf/0809- ganz.pdf.

Google Books Library Project (2011) *What's the Issue?* (online) Available at: http://www.google.com/googlebooks/issue.html (Accessed 1 September 2011).

Huntington, S. (1993). The Clash of Civilizations?: The Debate. *Foreign Affairs Magazine*, 42 (3).

Massachusetts Institute of Technology Open Courseware (2011) *Site Statistics* [online] Available at: http://ocw.mit.edu/about/site-statistics/ (Accessed 1 September 2011).

Massachusetts Institute of Technology Open Courseware (2011). *Why Donate?* (online) Available at: http://ocw.mit.edu/donate/why-donate/ (Accessed 1 September 2011).

Mintzberg, H. (2011). *International Masters for Health Leadership* [online] Available at: <http://www.mcgill.ca/desautels/imhl/> [Accessed 1 September 2011].

Mintzberg, H. (2010) Developing Naturally: from Management to Organization to Society to Selves. In Snook, S., Nohira, N., & Khurana, R. ed. *The Handbook for Teaching Leadership*. California: Sage Publications. Section 2.

Mintzberg, H. (2009). Rebuilding Companies as Communities, *Harvard Business Review*[online] Available at: http://hbr.org/2009/07/rebuilding-companies-as-communities/ar/1. (Accessed 1 September 2011).

Munroe-Blum, H. (2008). The Innovation Society: Canada's Next Chapter. In Weber, L. & Duderstadt, J., eds. *The Globalization of Higher Education*. Glion Colloquium. Ch. 9.

Munroe-Blum, H. (2010). *Higher Education and Innovation: The Canada-U.S. Story*. Speech given in Boston, Massachusetts, 15 September 2010, (online) Available at: http://www.mcgill.ca/principal/speeches/lectures/fulbright2010/

National Academies (2010). *Rising Above the Gathering Storm, Revisited: Rapidly Approaching Category 5* (Executive Summary), Washington: The National Academies.

National Science Board (2010). *Science and Engineering Indicators 2010*, Virginia: National Science Board.

Organisation for Economic Co-operation and Development (2009). *OECD Science, Technology and Industry Scoreboard 2009*, Paris: OECD.

Organisation for Economic Co-operation and Development (2010). *The OECD Innovation Strategy*, Paris: OECD.

Shapiro, Harold (2009). *The University as Public Citizen*, Speech given at McGill University, 14 October 2009.

Teach for America (2011). *Mission*. (online) Available at: http://www.teachforamerica.org/our-mission (Accessed 1 September 2011).

Thorp, Holden & Goldstein, Buck (2010). *Engines of Innovation*. North Carolina: The University of North Carolina Press.

United Nations Educational, Scientific and Cultural Organization Institute for Statistics (2009). *Global Education Digest 2009: Comparing Education Statistics Across the World*, Montreal: UNESCO.

CHAPTER 12

Preparing the University and its Graduates for the Unpredictable and Unknowable

Alain Beretz

Les prévisions *sont* difficiles, surtout *lorsqu'elles* concernent *l'*avenir.
(Predictions are difficult, especially when they deal with the future.)

Pierre Dac

U niversities are a key player in the "knowledge society". But this increased influx of knowledge and the exponential rate of technical progress also generate anxiety and fear that could undermine the fundamental role of universities to elaborate and disseminate knowledge. Universities should not be locked into the sterile debate of the "knowledge society" *vs* "risk society" (Hansson, 2002), because this can only undermine their fundamental role and missions. But, if universities are here to take risks, to open new paths and to innovate in every sense, they have also to defend this role in society and implement policies and procedures that can secure this responsibility in a sustainable manner.

INTRODUCTION: SUSTAINABILITY AND THE UNPREDICTABLE/UNKNOWABLE

What is the exact nature of the "unpredictable" that we should be prepared for? Prevention of dangers, whatever their origin, is nowadays a central preoccupation. The word "preparedness" is used, for example, for describing the different measures against emergencies and disasters, i.e. do we have "in store"

143

the materials, structures or procedures to react to some major events, many of which are now environmental issues? Clearly universities can be key actors of this preparedness, and should provide some key components of this "preparedness toolbox", which should contain tools used both in research and education. In this volume, Chuck Vest discusses in detail the complex relationship between uncertainty and risk (Chapter 6). However, Andy Stirling (2010) reminds us that concentrating exclusively on risks can bring dangerous bias: "Overly narrow focus on risk is an inadequate response to incomplete knowledge. It leaves science advice vulnerable to the social dynamics of groups — and to manipulation by political pressures". Indeed, this debate cannot be reduced to a mere technical issue: Tannert *et al.* (2007) also state that "when it comes to decisions that affect people's lives and health [...] carrying out research to diminish uncertainty and, consequentially, risks can become an ethical duty".

Therefore, evaluating risks and being ready to respond to threats is not enough. We must not only be prepared for these unknown challenges of the future; a core role of universities is to *generate directly* the unexpected. Discoveries and major breakthroughs are not always planned nor expected; being prepared for the unknown and the unknowable is an absolute condition for scientific progress. It is also a key asset for the personal accomplishment of our graduates, although this latter aspect is usually underestimated. Major discoveries can indeed be considered as "black swans" (Taleb, 2010), as introduced by James Duderstadt in this symposium (Chapter 7). Universities should be a privileged provider of what we should here call "positive black swans", i.e. unexpected events that have a major impact, and can be the support for major breakthroughs and discoveries.

As it is usually seen in science, one basic question generates a series of others; some of them will be asked in this paper: What is sustainability in this context, how and why to prepare for the unexpected, and finally how do these questions impact on our basic academic missions, both as scholars and as teachers?

Although we all know that sustainability is one of the key issues of our times, the clear meaning of this concept for the evolution of the duties and objectives of modern universities is far from being straightforward, and many speakers during in this meeting have stressed this point. In French, sustainability is often translated as "*développement durable*". French is probably a beautiful language, but this translation is indeed tricky!

Firstly, there are two ways of understanding this "development": the first one is about growth and expansion, and the second one is more about maturation or evolution, but without necessarily a quantitative aspect. Speaking about growth in universities has of course a completely different meaning in the Western hemisphere and in developing countries. In the former, our sustainability is now clearly oriented on the qualitative side, aiming for a new role of universities, while, for the latter, universities will have to grow, sometimes almost from scratch, in order to become major assets of their country and secure for them a healthy and prosperous future.

Secondly, the "durability". Sustainability involves something more that durability, although we deal in universities with "durable" time frames; it also implies that we can *afford* whatever endeavour we are involved into, thus it also involves *accountability*. This is precisely why should budgetary issues are a core subject of university sustainability.

But maybe the main question of this paper is not only *how* universities can prepare for the unpredictable and the unexpected, but to ask *if* this should be considered a core mission of universities. Any scholar, when asked this question, will probably immediately answer "Yes!" because this issue actually sends us back to some of our basic academic duties and challenges, and we can easily assume that all these principles are rather straightforward for a university scholar of the 21st century.

Still, we should not just live on principles, but should examine candidly if we are really taking all the necessary measures to fulfil this duty, and to live up to these challenges. Then the question is not so much to discuss these basic principles, but to examine how they are implemented in the academic community, and what measures can be taken to apply them, as well as to make them well known in our society.

PREPARING THE UNIVERSITY FOR THE UNPREDICTABLE

In order to prepare for the unpredictable, the university needs to be itself a sustainable structure. It cannot afford to change its policies or priorities to answer short-term requirements of governments or economic stakeholders. Long-term sustainability is an absolute requirement if we want to be able to respond quickly to the unpredictable; it implies that universities are granted enough autonomy, both on academic and financial aspects.

The university as sustainable economic entity

This subject is analysed in more detail in other presentations at this symposium, thus it will not be covered in detail here (Newby, Chapter 20).

One main issue resides in the balance between the various mechanisms of financing of universities (for both research *and* education), i.e. between programmed, finalized financing on one hand, and basic, non-directed budgets on the other. At a time where financial accountability is a legitimate societal requirement, the plea for non-directed financing is not always popular with politicians; they will almost systematically prefer to invest massively in "applied research" or "technological degrees", where they see clear and immediate economic outputs. Our duty is therefore to provide stakeholders and decision-makers with sufficient data and proof that investing in basic, non-finalized subjects is indeed yielding significant economic returns, if one is patient enough. It is precisely these long-term investments that can produce these unexpected, unplanned results that carry the highest potential of innovation and subsequent economic value.

The university as an academic institution

Directed research: both a need and a danger

Universities were built on academic freedom as a central value. Researchers must be given the freedom and space to develop their ideas innovatively. But universities need to be well rooted in their societal environment, and thus any funding programme should ensure a well-balanced share between directed and non-directed research. This requires funding schemes to contain a significant part of bottom-up, investigator-led or non-directed research.

Use a long time frame for evaluating results

Many of the regulations and incentives (especially financial) to obtain forms of behaviour in universities are based on outcomes defined as desirable by authorities within a very short-term frame of reference, which is very often tuned with the duration of political mandates (Bolton & Lucas, 2008). Adhering only to these short-term calendars will dangerously shift our priorities and reduce the output of unexpected, Black Swan type of scientific breakthroughs. As Bernd Huber stated during one of our discussions: "Conservative universities can produce innovative solutions!"

Avoid restrictive research programming

In my own field of research, pharmacology, the standard drug discovery paradigm has shifted over the years more and more from serendipity toward a target-based approach, although it is difficult to say which of these two pathways has finally yielded the most significant results (Schlueter & Peterson, 2009). The advancements of science have now enabled us to identify precise molecular targets for many drugs. When such a target is validated (and this is in itself a complicated question), it can indeed lead to the discovery of original and successful new therapeutic agents; however, in many cases, it remains difficult to predict which targets will offer a real therapeutic benefit. In spite of the fantastic precision (and scientific interest) of the newly identified molecular targets, new drug development is presently stagnating. Such a shift to "targeted research" is also a general tendency of our research granting agencies. This is not in itself a disputable strategy; but concentrating all our research efforts on single target drug development carries the risk of restricting therapeutic innovation to well known pathways and strategies, and producing what is referred very often as a "me-too" discovery, rather than a major innovative therapeutic breakthrough. The unexpected or unknown will not be easily detected by such a research scheme.

Another strategy is sometimes referred to as "phenotypic". In this strategy, one goes back to studying the effects of drug candidates not on simplified targets, but on complex models, for example transgenic mice affected by a model disease. This global strategy is more prone to yield breakthrough advances, but it is costly and time-consuming. Ironically, it is sometimes difficult to find the pharmacologists and physiologists who can perform such global experiments because training and research programs have for many years extensively invested in molecular aspects of pharmacology, neglecting global physiology which was regarded as an old-fashioned domain. We now pay the price for this short-term planning.

Basic research as a central paradigm

When looking at the future, anticipation is one thing, vision quite another (Campbell, 2001). Basic science can yield unlimited and original thoughts about the future; and when scientists are (too rarely) given freedom to speculate, the result is fascinating: they are capable of shedding new light on the unforeseeable by focusing on what might take us there: cutting-edge basic science that might lead to unexpected technologies, and adventurous technologies that should lead to unpredictable, fundamental discoveries (Campbell, 2001). Of course governments, which provide directly or indirectly the vast majority of funds for universities, should have a word to say on research planning and research strategies. But universities have to convince them that the most useful knowledge is that grounded in deep understanding, and that it should not be relinquished for shallower perceptions of utility (Boulton & Lucas, 2008).

Leave some place for serendipity

According to the Merriam-Webster Online Dictionary, serendipity is "the faculty or phenomenon of finding valuable or agreeable things *not sought for*". Serendipity is a term coined by Horace Walpole, suggested by "The Three Princes of Serendip", the title of a fairy tale in which the heroes "were always making discoveries, by accidents and sagacity, of things *they were not in quest of*". This surely rings a bell and would suggest that, if we want to be ready for the unknown and the unthinkable, we should devise research and education systems in which serendipity remains possible. However serendipity cannot, and should not, be considered as the magic wand, or the only efficient source of scientific breakthroughs.

Defend academic freedom

"Academic freedom is not only seen as a goal in itself. It is important especially since it makes it possible for universities to serve the common good of society through searching for and disseminating knowledge and understanding, and through fostering independent thinking and expression in academic staff and students." (Vrielink *et al.*, 2010).

In this respect, academic freedom can be considered, not only as a "classical" value of universities, which is of paramount political and ethical importance, but also as a important tool to guarantee that we are given the means and leeway to stay prepared for the unpredictable. This is also an example that ethical values, not just technical schemes, are one of the major safeguards that are needed to guarantee that universities can remain prepared for the unpredictable and unthinkable.

PREPARING OUR GRADUATES FOR THE UNPREDICTABLE

Preparing our graduates for the unpredictable as scientists, scholars or skilled professionals

Knowledge is global, and knowledge is multidisciplinary

Universities are of course here to transmit knowledge, and especially knowledge with a true and immediate professional value. The "knowledge society" requires skilled individuals. This transmission of professional skills, often based on state-of-the-art scientific knowledge, is a clear mission of universities, and the transmission of pure, abstract knowledge cannot remain our single objective.

However, we need a broader and revised definition of the notion of "transferable skill", i.e., what type of professional abilities do we want our students to master, and what do we want them to gain from their years of academic training?

Geoffrey Boulton and Colin Lucas have summarized, in a position paper written on behalf of the League of European research Universities, this fundamental issue (Boulton & Lucas, 2008):

"The key to retaining the flexibility to exploit the unexpected lies in a fundamental understanding of the nature of phenomena. Such understanding continuously resynthesis specific knowledge in the form of general understanding that is broadly applicable [...] Basic research that compresses and generalises understanding in this way invigorates teaching that probes the limits of understanding. Together, they are the fuel for the university engine. Such generic understanding also represents a fundamental 'transferable skill' which can be applied to a much wider range of circumstances and phenomena than any catalogue of specific knowledge. It is a vital investment in the future [...] Universities serve to make students think: to resolve problems by argument supported by evidence; not to be dismayed by complexity, but bold in unravelling it."

Our curricula, but also our pedagogical methods, are thus key assets to prepare our students for uncertainty, for deep underlying issues and for the general context in which their knowledge will be applied. We thus have to face this double challenge: on the one hand, promote education that can transfer skills which correspond to an immediate demand of our society, while, on the other, providing our students with generic tools that will help them, throughout their life, to face the unexpected and remain original and creative.

The importance of research-based education in the construction of student skills

Research promotes in students a practice of positive criticism, adaptability, capacity to challenge and a constructive experience of failure. Research-based curricula provide a pedagogy based on students' autonomy. It makes it possible for them to challenge magisterial attitudes that, for some of us (students or professors), should remain indisputable.

Relying on research also means making the choice not to teach everything, but to base curricula on local expertise, and thus to get away from the notion of homogenous, administratively-decided programs and curricula that would be based on an objective, reproductive and stereotyped ideal of knowledge.

Preparing our graduates for the unpredictable as citizens

Research-based education does not only provide students with a learning method and technical know-how. It also provides an *ethical* framework, which is unique to the type of pedagogy developed in universities. These ethical principles are essential in the development of a sustainable society. Because it familiarizes students with collaborative, socially constructed knowledge, research-based education also promotes these collective values, which they can also apply to other fields of their professional or personal life.

By rooting deeply our mission in society, we should also make our graduates conscious that "when it comes to the main values in life, or to what should be done with our newly acquired knowledge [...] the answers are not scientific but political in nature" (Dubochet, 2003). Universities should not only train scientists, they must also educate them as citizens.

CONCLUSION

In summary, some key factors for universities to prepare for the unexpected and unthinkable could be:

- practise research-based education;
- put strong emphasis on basic, non-oriented, research;
- defend long-term, sustainable goals and values;

- consider all societal consequences of scientific, technological and scholarly issues;
- invest in **trust** towards universities.

Taken from the Glion declaration of 2009, sustainability in our academic field can be seen as requiring "collective scientific and technical expertise in the environmental sphere, but also economic, social and political policies that nurture sustainable communities". This sentence stresses two of the important issues facing universities in the 21st century: we have to provide *collective* expertise, and this expertise has to reach *far beyond* the traditional academic sphere. It thus links more closely the general question of our symposium, sustainability and the narrower subject of this paper.

This suggests that, in order to prepare for the unknown and unthinkable, a university has *itself* to be sustainable. We do need the universities to be fully sustainable institutions in order to guarantee sustainability in the present society, which Hansson has called "the uncertainty society" (Hansson, 2002).

We now live in a global environment of knowledge. If we want to capitalize on our academic assets, then why not use the tools, fundamental values and even the vocabulary of general environmental sustainability? Indeed we should consider universities as a global ecosystem. For Andy Stirling (2008), technological change, at a variety of scales is best understood, not as a race along a single preordained track, but — like biological evolution — as an open branching process more akin to organic growth, where random contingencies can play a crucial role, and he coins the term of "Evolutionary Dynamics of Technology".

In this sense, a university should not base its strategy on the determinist understanding of an oversimplified linear relationship between science and technology. Universities, just like our whole planet, require "biodiversity", supported by sustainable methods and procedures. It is well known that the global decline in biodiversity leads to associated declines in the services provided by ecosystems that support human societies (Corvalan *et al.*, 2005). This generic principle is fully relevant to the university ecosystem. Only a true "academic biodiversity" will guarantee that universities fulfil their missions and are able to respond to actual and future challenges.

Universities must be considered as a complex and fragile environment, not just as a knowledge factory. All stakeholders should ensure that universities remain the best environment for innovation to flourish. In this way we can set the stage for our society to be prepared for the unpredictable and unknowable. But whether we are on the right path remains totally unforeseeable.

REFERENCES

Boulton., G. & Lucas, C. (2008). What are universities for? LERU position paper. Available: http://www.leru.org/files/general/•What%20are%20universities%20 for%20(September%202008).pdf

Campbell, P. (2001). Vision things, Nature 409, 385 (*an introduction to*: Paths to unforeseeable science and technology, *Nature* 409, No. 6818).

Corvalan, C., Hales, S. & McMichael A.J. (2005). Ecosystems and human well-being: health synthesis: a report of the Millennium Ecosystem Assessment, Geneva: World Health Organization.

Dubochet, J. (2003). Teaching scientists to be citizens, EMBO reports 4, 4, pp. 330-332.

Duderstadt, J. J. (this book). "Global Sustainability: Timescales, Magnitudes, Paradigms, and Black Swans", in Weber, L. E. & Duderstadt, J. J. (eds), *Global sustainability and the Responsibilites of Universities*, Economica, Paris.

Hansson, S. O. (2002). Uncertainties in the knowledge society. *Social Science Journal*, 171: pp. 39-46.

Huber, B. (this book). "Research Intensive Universities in a Globalized World" in Weber, L. E. & Duderstadt, J. J. (eds), *Global sustainability and the Responsibilites of Universities*, Economica, Paris,

Newby H. (this book). "Sustaining World Class Universities — Who Pays and How?" in Weber, L. E. & Duderstadt, J. J. (eds), *Global sustainability and the Responsibilites of Universities*, Economica, Paris.

Schlueter, P.J. & Peterson, R.T. (2009). "Chemical Biology and Cardiovascular Drug Discovery", *Circulation* 12, pp. 255-26

Stirling, A. (2008). "Science, Precaution, and the Politics of Technological Risk". Ann. N.Y. Acad. Sci. 1128: pp. 95-110.

Stirling, A. (2010). Keep it complex. *Nature* 468, pp. 1029-1031

Taleb, N. N. (2010). *The Black Swan*, second edition, Penguin, London.

Tannert, C., Elvers, H.-D. & Jandrig, B. (2007). "The ethics of uncertainty". EMBO reports 8, 10, pp. 892-896.

Vrielink, J., Lemmens, P. & Parmentier, S. & The Leru Working Group On Human Rights (2010). Academic Freedom as a Fundamental Right. LERU advice paper Available: http://www.leru.org/files/publications/Academic_Freedom_final.pdf

CHAPTER 13

International STEM Education for Global Sustainability

Roberta Johnson

INTRODUCTION

O n a daily basis, people around the world face challenges that result from us all, together on our small planet, approaching the carrying capacity of our environment. The sustainability of humanity is determined by our ability to keep in balance the three pillars of society — our environment, and our economic and social systems. The social and economic costs of environmental degradation are very real to individuals, communities and economic endeavours. Similarly, economic systems based solely on exploitation, without consideration of resource depletion and community impacts, can have drastic impact on environmental quality and the quality of life in communities. As Jared Diamond has aptly demonstrated in his book, *Collapse: How Societies Choose to Fail or Survive* (2005), societies that ignore the intimate feedback between environmental problems and economic and social structures risk driving themselves to collapse. As noted by historian Arnold Toynbee in *A Study of History* (1961), "civilizations die from suicide, not by murder" when they fail to meet the challenges of their times. Or, as noted by historian Barbara Tuchman in *The March of Folly: From Troy to Vietnam* (1984), "A phenomenon noticeable throughout history regardless of place or period is the pursuit by government of policies contrary to their own interests."

- Were any of us prepared for understanding the interconnectedness of societal systems through our education, prior to our university experience?
- Is the small fraction of the global population that enters research universities the only segment of society that needs to understand this?

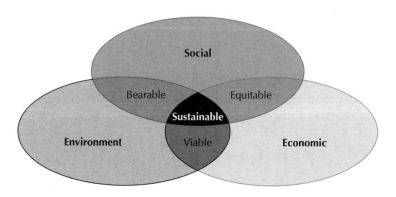

- Do we recognize the need to have a global population that understands the principles of sustainability, so they have a chance to put them into practice in their lives?

This paper argues that education and global sustainability are a coupled set — you can't achieve global sustainability without widespread sustainability education. Furthermore, education for sustainability must include STEM disciplines as well as humanities and social sciences, be made available internationally, and must be available where the bulk of the population is — namely at the primary and secondary levels — if we are to have any chance of making meaningful progress towards global sustainability.

The paper examines the sad state of education today globally, as well as economic, political and geopolitical complicating factors, and highlights the difficulty in educating for global sustainability when education itself appears increasingly to be unsustainable. Finally, the paper notes that leadership is desperately needed in advancing widespread sustainability education. Research universities have a key role to play in this arena — not only through education at the undergraduate and graduate levels, but also by building, testing and implementing successful programs that advance sustainability and sustainability education at the primary and secondary educational levels and through community engagement.

GLOBAL SUSTAINABILITY AND EDUCATION

Thoughts on Sustainability

Sustainability has been defined as *"Meeting the needs of the present without compromising the ability of future generations to meet their own needs,"* (Our Common Future, 1987). Because of the wide range of human needs, as well as the economic, social and environmental systems associated with satisfying and managing them, sustainability is inherently interdisciplinary at the largest scale.

Achieving sustainability solutions for humanity requires innovations involving not only science and engineering, but also economics, history, government, cultural studies, psychology and ethics, among other fields.

As John Muir once said (1911): "When we try to pick out anything by itself, we find it hitched to everything else in the universe." Pollutants travel the globe, emitted from factories on one continent only to pollute another. Excessive consumption of scarce resources by one country can have drastic consequences for other countries — whether per capita fossil fuel consumption in the U.S. and our resultant climate change debt, the conversion of ethanol for fuel in the U.S., reducing the availability of essential food stocks in Latin America, or the use of rare Earth minerals in industry and construction in China, and the resultant impact on availability of these resources in other countries. A massive, but not unimaginably large earthquake (USGS, 2011) and resultant tsunami inundate thousands of square kilometres of Japan including aging nuclear reactors unwisely placed on coastal, low-lying ground, producing a nuclear incident which threatens to put a widespread global halt on use and expansion of one of the most effective methods we have of producing energy without greenhouse gas emissions — a solution we desperately needed to address our climate change problem. We now know that we can't have a truly sustainable society at a local or national level — sustainability can only really be achieved on a global level, because the systems that are required for sustainability are interconnected and global.

Furthermore, unless sustainability, which inherently has the implication of maintaining the *status quo*, is approached from a perspective that addresses equity concerns and the aspirations of people, invariably some individuals and communities may not see the value of achieving global sustainability. Why would someone want sustainability, when they are on the bottom of society? The relative attractiveness of individual actions, when you have the choice of improving your quality of life through increased resource consumption or deferring your own consumption in the interests of unknown others on a global scale, is hard for people who have already been blessed with access to resources for generations to deal with. How much more difficult is it for those that have never had access to even a marginal quality of life to forgo the opportunity to improve their lot, relative to others? Attaining sustainability inherently requires an approach that facilitates the advancement of populations locked in poverty, suffering widespread governmental mismanagement, and with minimal access to education and opportunity.

The concept of sustainability is to some extent inherently at odds with the cultural mantra of freedom, accepted widely in Western society. If freedom or "liberty" is your core value (Jefferson, 1776), and it means being able to do anything you want to maximize your happiness and success independent of the impact of your actions on anyone else, then the concept of sustainability may threaten your core values. Because these values are deeply embedded in culture and family, and because values are formed when we are young by teaching and example, developing the values that are needed to move individuals to accept and act on approaches to global sustainability needs to begin when people are young, and leverage the tools that we have to impact young people. These include (but are not limited to) primary and secondary schools and educators, parents and grandparents, social and community organizations, religious communities and social media.

Education for Advancing Global Sustainability — Youth, Multi-disciplinary and International

Traditionally, education at all levels has been stove-piped into independent disciplines, with relatively little opportunity for interdisciplinary approaches except at the highest level. Not only are the Humanities, Social Sciences and Physical Sciences taught essentially in different worlds, but even within these worlds, there is little enrichment or cross fertilization between closely related disciplines. As a result, it's not surprising that students finishing secondary education have little knowledge of systems, let alone complex and interrelated ones. The large majority of students at the secondary level typically have little to no formal educational exposure to thinking about the interconnected systems that bind together the environment, economic and social systems, nor the opportunity to consider their complex interactions and scenario-based outcomes.

But why should this emphasis on sustainability begin in the primary and secondary levels, instead of waiting until students reach the university? As we know, while a significant fraction of young people in the developed world have the opportunity to have a university education, a significant fraction of young people drop out of high school. In the U.S., high school dropout rates ranged from 4% to 11% across the country in 2009 (Datacenter, 2009), with the dropout rate for black and Hispanic students (9.6 and 17.6, respectively) significantly higher than for Asian and non-Hispanic white students (Child Trends Data Bank, 2011). In 2006, the national on-time high school graduation rate — the percentage of entering ninth graders who graduated 4 years later — was 73% (Stillwell & Hoffman, 2008). Internationally, the Organization for Economic Co-operation and Development (OECD) provides reports on education systems, approaches and student attainment across OECD countries, many of which have reached a high level of economic development. *Education at a Glance OCED 2010 Indicators* (2010) reports that across OECD countries, an average of 80% of students complete upper secondary education, ranging from 26% in Turkey to 97% in Germany. Of these students, an average of 56% of secondary graduates entered the equivalent of a four-year college or university in OECD countries, ranging from 25% in Luxembourg to

83% in Poland (in the U.S. in 2008, 69% of high school graduates had enrolled in an undergraduate education program the fall following graduation). (National Science Board, 2010). This means that in OECD countries, on average, only 45% of young people enter college — and even fewer complete their undergraduate education. For those who drop out of the educational system before university, the education they receive in primary and secondary school is likely to be the intellectual toolset they carry with them the rest of their lives. These numbers reflect the graduation and tertiary enrolment rates mainly in developed countries. We can expect that the number of students completing secondary education and continuing to college in less-developed countries to be much lower.

Finally, because leading individuals towards sustainability involves consideration of values, and the formation of values takes place mainly when we are young, weaving consideration of values into education across disciplines in the primary and secondary level is an essential and too-long neglected component of education at these levels (Fulghum, 1990). This is particularly important in the area of sustainability education, in which we need to encourage individuals to temper their urge to act solely in their immediate self-interest and, instead, to modify their behaviour in the interest of others, the environment and society in general.

If we are to have any hope to bring the difficult concepts of sustainability to the largest possible audience of learners globally, it must begin in the primary and secondary levels.

EDUCATION FOR SUSTAINABILITY WHEN EDUCATION ITSELF IS NOT SUSTAINABLE?

Are We at a Breaking Point for U.S. Education?

The previous section argues that, in order to have any realistic prospect of achieving global sustainability, education for sustainability must begin with youth, leveraging the tools we have to impact young people. Prominent among these are K-12 educators, with whom a significant fraction of students' time is spent before reaching majority. In order to advance sustainability education for this critical cohort, an effective strategy would be to work with teachers, providing professional development and support networks to assist them with integrating concepts of sustainability across the curriculum. Today's teachers, not unlike many of their students, have also had minimal exposure to the concepts of coupled systems and unanticipated outcomes that underlie sustainability issues — they similarly need help mastering these concepts, so they can bring them confidently to their students to facilitate their learning.

Unfortunately, these days in the U.S., K-12 teachers feel like they are under attack. A significant fraction of the U.S. population appears to not be willing to increase school funding to the level needed to adequately support K-12 education through increased tax rates, even if it is their kids who suffer the consequences. (According to the *New York Times* [2008], in the 2008 Vice Presidential debate with Joe Biden, Sarah Palin suggested that it was not patriotic to pay taxes). Facing the loss of collective bargaining rights, tenure, health and retirement benefits, coupled with stagnant or falling wages while teaching positions are cut and class sizes balloon, it's not hard to understand why teachers are demoralized. States and school districts across the country can't afford to support the teachers needed for the curriculum as it exists today, let alone to revise and extend the curriculum to integrate sustainability.

At the university level, the cost of a university education is rapidly moving out of reach of a large fraction of graduating high school seniors. In the U.S., the norm for private or out-of-state tuition at "public" universities is ~$50K per year. While a few families may have these resources stashed away for their children, and some families can qualify for financial aid based on severely limited financial resources, a large portion of the remaining class of graduating seniors finds the option of a first class education at a liberal arts college or research university out of the question. As a result, students and families are incurring significant debt to finance their education. With the current prolonged economic recession, there is no longer the assurance that quality, high paying jobs will be available after graduation from college, which will allow the students to repay this debt. Nevertheless, because the possibility of increased tax revenue appears to be out of the question, state governments find themselves needing to continually slash funding for state colleges and universities, shifting more and more of the burden of increased costs onto students and their parents.

Given the apparent unwillingness of a significant fraction of the U.S. public to provide support for improved education at the K-12 or university level, and the limits on financial resources of individual families, we appear to be approaching a point where a major paradigm shift is needed in our approach to education. Indeed, many would argue that this shift is already underway to some extent at the university, and even K-12 level, with the growth of alternative internet-facilitated learning systems which bypass the traditional institutions of learning, for better or worse, and replace them with distance-learning and remote mentoring.

Reflections on the Status of Education Globally

Of course, educators in the U.S. are comparatively lucky. In many schools in less-developed countries, teachers may not even have running water or floors in their schools, let alone books, paper and pencils, or computers to use with their students. (ICSU, 2011). There are enormous variations in the quality of schools globally, from very well equipped establishments to those that may not even have a proper classroom for its students. A large proportion of parents in developing countries are unable to have their children admitted to the better-equipped schools because of a lack of financial resources or cultural constraints.

International studies of student achievement provide some insight into the relative success of educational efforts in a wide range of countries globally, lending support to the assertion that investment in education, and respect for education and educators, result in positive learning outcomes. OECD's Program for International Student Assessment (PISA) and the International Association for Evaluation of Educational Achievement's Trends in Mathematics and Science (TIMSS) studies demonstrate that average students in more developed economies have higher achievement scores than those in the emerging and less developed countries. While most OECD members are the economically developed countries, the PISA 2009 test had participation not only from 34 OECD countries, but also 41 countries or economies outside the OECD. PISA tests a representative sample of 15-year-olds in each country every third year, and assesses students' levels of scientific, mathematical and reading literacy and not with respect to the school curricula in the participating countries (OECD, 2010a, b). TIMSS aims to test mathematics and science achievement that is broadly aligned to the school curriculum, given that all test items are used in each of the participating countries. Fifty-nine countries (37 for grade 4 and 50 for grade 8) from all continents took part in TIMSS 2007 (TIMSS, 2007).

Finland, which ranked at or near the top in successive PISA testing from 2000-2009, attributes (FNBE, 2011) their success to multiple factors — structural and cultural:

- equal educational opportunity for all students irrespective of domicile, gender, financial situation or linguistic and cultural background
- a five-year program of Master study for all teachers, including at the primary level
- very high social status for teachers (although not necessarily very high salaries)
- becoming a teacher is the highest priority among young people, and only the top performers at school become enrolled in teacher education
- high expectations and hope, but also high unemployment rates among young people after the political shifts around 1990 provided an atmosphere where young people (and their parents) understood the significance of getting a good education.

In PISA 2009 (OECD, 2010a, 2010b), the top scores in science were achieved by Shanghai-China, followed (in order) by Finland, Hong Kong-China, Singapore, Japan, Rep. of Korea, New Zealand, Canada, Estonia, Australia, the Netherlands, Chinese Taipei, Germany, Liechtenstein, Switzerland, the United Kingdom, Slovenia and Macao-China. All these were well above the OECD average. The top scores in mathematics were achieved by Asian countries and Finland. The countries with the highest overall reading performance — Finland and the Republic of Korea, as well as Hong Kong and Shanghai — also have among the lowest variation in student scores. Asian countries that appear to share positive attitudes towards the value of education consistently perform better in PISA test results.

These results show that in at least some countries around the world where education and educators are respected, where they are provided the tools and the training needed to provide quality education, and are reasonably well-paid, students demonstrate higher achievement levels in multiple disciplines than where this is not the case.

Education for Sustainability is Essential — But We Must Also Save Education Itself

Education is essential to move humanity to global sustainability, and this education must start when the bulk of the population is still in school and forming their values. Yet we seem to face insurmountable challenges to merely adequately fund education as it is today — let alone to improve it to the point where we can integrate a strong thread of sustainability, so that students graduate equipped to handle the challenges of our complex and interconnected world.

In the absence of the societal will to fund education adequately, we are well past the time when we need to be developing and implementing, at a large scale, radically different educational strategies that will provide the opportunity for quality and affordable education for the vast majority of students globally. Rather than wasting time continuing the apparently futile attempt to support our existing expensive educational infrastructure, it is time to begin planning for a time not long from now when educational resources are delivered almost entirely online, with students working individually or in small groups in a range of venues, when educators are largely remote facilitators of learning, where learning at the secondary and university levels have extensive project and service-based learning components, and where schools and universities become research, collaboration, and testing facilities available to local learners and educators, equipped with quality resources and capabilities, but not teaching staff.

WHAT ROLES SHOULD THE RESEARCH UNIVERSITY PLAY IN ADVANCING GLOBAL SUSTAINABILITY?

Some of the papers in this volume focus on the role of research universities in advancing global sustainability in areas that are central to research universities today — namely undergraduate and graduate education, research and innovation. The recommendations presented here take the research university's role a step further — reaching out meaningfully to K-12 educators and community.

It is unfortunate that the pressing need to develop and implement globally sustainability systems arises at a time when resources are so severely limited, and education systems are under such stress. At the present time, leadership is desperately needed in advancing widespread sustainability education. With the paralysis that comes with difficult economic times and political gridlock, governmental decision-makers and program directors can find it impossible to move forward novel and well thought out programs due to a lack of financial resources and political pressures. Yet the clock is still ticking on our need to educate our youth on sustainability, and to develop the next generation of sustainability-enabled professionals. Some one — or some ones — must step up to help provide leadership in this vacuum. Research universities, as the home of the few who have had the opportunity for advanced education, are natural sources of the expertise we need to do research within and across disciplines with a focus on sustainability issues — helping to develop solutions to vexing interconnected problems. But precisely because of their specialized expertise, research universities should take their role several steps further.

Researchers developing promising approaches on sustainability issues should be encouraged to bridge the chasm between research and implementation, so that university-based innovation is more effectively moved out from the university research sector to the real world. While many research universities have excellent schools of education, in addition to their STEM departments, dysfunctional collaboration between science discipline departments and the schools of education is legendary at research universities. The reason for this is perhaps not surprising — education researchers are rewarded for research on innovations in pedagogy, typically tested at the small scale in individual classrooms, and reported in their research literature, similar to the motivations of scientists in their own disciplines. Neither has an explicit motivation to scale up innovative approaches that work on a large scale. For this reason, many exciting new approaches to learning are tested and documented, but never succeed at making it into widespread implementation. In the area of sustainability, we can't afford to lose lessons learned, as promising approaches to sustainability education are developed, and not implement the best of them at larger scales. As university faculty work on developing approaches to sustainability education, they should be encouraged to take these efforts a step further to ensure that their innovations are actually implemented in educational systems.

A major area of concern, considering the sad state of education today, is how to develop effective educational strategies that use technology for education and reconfigure our approach to education. Research university faculty can make significant contributions here, working with educators, to develop and test new approaches, and then, once proven, work to implement these solutions at the large scale. Note that distance learning, as implemented today in K-12 and universities, leaves much to be desired. In order for the new paradigm shift mentioned above to be effective, online learning materials must become much more engaging, enable more meaningful faculty interactions, and be designed so that it is not possible to beat the system and defeat the learning objective.

There is another role for faculty at research universities that should be actively encouraged. Many university faculty have been accused of living in "Ivory Towers", engaging little with their communities and, many times, not taking the time to describe their research within their communities. This lack of engagement can lead to a lack of trust between university faculty and the public, leading to negative consequences, such as we have recently seen in the area of climate change science. As researchers work on sustainability, it's also important to engage actively in community, and develop trust there, so that when we share difficult messages, the larger community will have a basis upon which to trust — or at least not immediately discount — what we say.

Of course, all of this takes time from university faculty — some of it in areas of effort that are not traditionally valued in the university reward structure. If universities are serious that they want their faculty and students to become engaged in advancing sustainability, they must develop reward structures that meaningfully account for these efforts in ways equivalent with the traditional focus on publications, grants and teaching. Without a reward structure that places a reasonably equivalent value on these efforts, only a very small fraction of university faculty will chose to work in these areas.

The scope of effort needed for global sustainability education is vast and daunting — and it needs to ramp up in earnest soon. Some leadership is needed to facilitate, connect, and where possible, coordinate the activities of the many different organizations, researchers, and programs that are working to advance the sustainability agenda. A quick search on Google shows that there are many groups trying to make a difference in this area, working on different scales, and many dependent on transient grant funding. An internationally-based leadership organization could provide the essential glue that is needed to help the sustainability community advance with a semblance of organization and facilitate the leveraging of resources among groups so that all have the opportunity to advance more rapidly together, building on each other's successes and programs.

Finally, we should all remember that the most essential element of a global sustainability solution is our youth. Whether in primary or secondary school, or in the university, our youth are the individuals who will need to create the sustainable world of the future, and they have the greatest stake in that endeavour. Furthermore, they have enormous energy and motivation, and are comparatively inexpensive. In all of our sustainability activities, we should remember to engage youth as broadly as possible, taking advantage of their energy, their enthusiasm, their insights, and their facility at networking and communication to help rapidly advance the sustainability agenda.

REFERENCES

Child Trends Data Bank (2011). http://www.childtrendsdatabank.org/?q=node/162

Datacenter (2009). The Annie E. Casey Foundation. http://datacenter.kidscount.org/data/acrossstates/Rankings.aspx?ind=73

Diamond, J. (2005). *Collapse: How Societies Choose to Fail or Survive*. Penguin books, New York.

FNBE (2011). Finnish National Board of Education. http://www.oph.fi/english/sources_of_information/pisa

Fulghum, R. (1990) *All I Really Need To Know I Learned In Kindergarten*, Villard Books: New York.

ICSU (2011). Report of the ICSU Ad-hoc Review Panel on Science Education. International Council for Science, Paris. ICSU. The author had the pleasure of chairing the Ad-Hoc Review Panel, and part of this paper draws on the report.

Jefferson, T. (1776) "We hold these truths to be self-evident, that all men are created equal, that they are endowed by their Creator with certain unalienable Rights, that among these are Life, Liberty and the pursuit of Happiness." *United States Declaration of Independence*.

Muir, J. (1911) *My First Summer in the Sierra*, Houghton Mifflin Company, Boston and New York.

National Science Board (2010).
http://www.nsf.gov/statistics/seind10/c1/c1s4.htm

New York Times (2008). "Palin's kind of patriotism". 7 Oct. http://www.nytimes.com/2008/10/08/opinion/08friedman.html

OECD (Organisation for Economic Co-operation and Development) (2010a), PISA 2009 at a Glance, OECD Publishing. http://dx.doi.org/10.1787/9789264095298-en

OECD (Organisation for Economic Co-operation and Development) (2010b), PISA 2009 Results: What Students Know and Can Do — Student Performance in Reading, Mathematics and Science (Volume I) http://dx.doi.org/10.1787/9789264091450-en.

OECD Indicators. (2010). http://www.oecd.org/document/52/0,3746,en_2649_39263294_45897844_1_1_1_1,00.html#ms

Stillwell R. & Hoffman L. (2008). Public School Graduates and Dropouts From the Common Core of Data: School Year 2005-06, First Look. NCES 2008-353rev. Washington, DC: National Center for Education Statistics.

TIMSS (Trends in International Mathematics and Science Study) (2007). International Science Report: *Findings from IEA's Trends in International Mathematics and Science Study at the Fourth and Eighth Grades*. IEA, 2008, pp. 73-4.

Toynbee, A., (1961) A *Study of History*. Oxford University Press.

Tuchman, B. (1984). *The March of Folly: From Troy to Vietnam*. Ballantine Books, New York.

USGS (2011). U.S. Geological survey. http://earthquake.usgs.gov/earthquakes/world/ events/1952_11_04.php, http://earthquake.usgs.gov/earthquakes/states/events/1964_ 03_28.php, http://earthquake.usgs.gov/earthquakes/world/events/1960_05_22.php

World Commission on Environment and Development (1987) *Our Common Future, Report of the World Commission on Environment and Development*. Published as Annex to General Assembly document A/42/427, Development and International Co-operation: Environment August 2

PART IV

•••••••••••••

Implications for Research

CHAPTER 14

Global Environmental Sustainability: An "All-Hands on Deck" Research Imperative

Tim Killeen

INTRODUCTION

T he two-way interaction of societal activity with environmental processes now defines clear and present challenges to our well-being. Human activity is changing the climate system and the ecosystem services that support human life and livelihoods. The changes are occurring at an unprecedented and often bewildering pace. The Earth's hydrological cycle is intensifying and weather records (e.g., floods, wildfires, droughts, heat waves, etc.) are being regularly revised upwards. The vulnerability of societies to disruptive change is increasing as the world's population itself grows, as resource limitations of all kinds become more evident, and as people are drawn to live in unsafe settings, often in conditions of poverty.

Reliable and affordable energy is essential to meet basic human needs and to provide for economic stability, but many environmental problems arise from unsustainable approaches in harvesting, generation, transport, processing, conversion and storage of energy. Climate change is a pressing anthropogenic stressor, but it is not the only one. Growing challenges are associated with poverty alleviation, development pathways for the world's most vulnerable societies, biodiversity degradation, ocean acidification, freshwater availability, hazardous extreme events, coastal vulnerabilities, infectious diseases and food security, to name a few. The three "E's": environment, energy and economics, in particular, form a strongly coupled but presently unstable tripod on which everything depends. In fact, any family of solutions worthy of the simplest definition of sustainability (*meeting the needs of the present without compromising the ability of future generations to meet their own need*) (World Commission, 1987) will require detailed consideration of the interplay of these factors in new and creative ways. Furthermore, in the time domain, solutions will need to address both the long-term *mitigation* of deleterious effects (through, for example, building a low carbon global economy) as well as near-term *adaptation* to changes already underway (through, for example, more effective conservation of freshwater stocks globally and creating greater levels of societal resiliency).

To compound these challenges, detailed solutions are not always self-evident and the problem of global environmental sustainability is one that is sometimes referred to as "Wicked" (Rittel & Melvin, 1984) or even "Super-Wicked" (Levin *et al.*, 2008) — terms used in social planning to describe problems that are difficult or impossible to solve because of incomplete, contradictory and changing requirements that are hard to recognize until after solutions have been tried. Moreover, because of complex interdependencies, the effort to solve one aspect of a wicked problem may reveal or create other problems. More ominously perhaps, super-wicked problems are characterized as ones for which 1) time is running out; 2) there is no central authority; 3) those seeking to solve the problem are also causing it; and 4) time-inconsistent discounting occurs (meaning that individuals may make choices today that they their future self would prefer not to make, despite using similar reasoning).

So, in short, we have a global sustainability "perfect storm" on our hands — and on "our watch" — one for which the scientific and technological tools are not, as yet, sufficient, and where responsive societal decision-making processes are arguably too slow and too erratic.

Despite the difficulties, the urgency to identify viable pathways for a healthful future for humanity is well documented and much diagnostic work has been accomplished (Intergovernmental Panel on Climate change, 2007; National Research Council, 2008 and 2011). And, of course, we have magnificent research universities distributed around the world that are, at first glance, almost perfectly designed to create the needed trans-disciplinary knowledge *and* build the human capital base to define and implement such pathways. But I believe that there is a mismatch in cadence between the evolution of the complex emerging sustainability challenges and our evolving state of readiness to respond — a mismatch that demands a new "call-to-arms" for the modern research university.

Part of this mismatch comes from a dangerous misreading of the times scales at play. Even though many recognize the issues at stake, they feel that there is time to work it out — perhaps over decades, perhaps over one or more generations. It is actually very hard for humans — with our inherent optimism, our yearning for stability, and our awe of nature — to fully internalize the stressors, to recognize the imperatives for collective action and then react in responsive ways. Intuitively for many, the world feels too big and too complex to be under any kind of disruptive human control. Our aspirations, our desire for a high standard of living, our financial and community-based investments for the future and for economic growth, and our religious and ethical beliefs often lead us to assume that continued progress, growth and a promising future are at least a possibility if not an absolute birthright. These human factors — and the central and even dominant role of human decision-making in creating a level of sustainability — bring to the fore the social sciences and the arts and humanities in a fundamental new way and in a very challenging intimate partnership with science, engineering and technology.

We have an historically unique and pivotally important race on our hands: a race between the development, dissemination and application of the knowledge needed to create a sustainable future and a fast moving opponent: the deleterious and disruptive changes, now well underway, that might/will sap our ability to respond in the future. If often strikes me as ironic that this race is such a tight one, with the two horses running neck and neck together at this moment in history (in fact — an even more humbling thought — during our professional careers!) In an ideal world, after all, the required knowledge base could have been available and well-accepted a century or two ago. And, in a non-ideal world, we would never have had even an inkling of what hit us.

I argue here that, because of the need to win this race and because of their unique ability to educate and mobilize the world's brain trust across the full range of disciplines, research universities have the following urgent and specific responsibilities:

- To *transform* education — and not just postsecondary, but the full spectrum of formal and informal education — to educate, engage, empower and energize the next generation of problem solvers;
- To *drive* a robust international and collaborative research agenda designed to identify, invent, test and deploy solutions designed to address the formidable challenges of global sustainability;
- To *insist* on building both disciplinary depth and trans-disciplinary breadth of research and education, connecting the science, engineering, technology, mathematics, social sciences, arts and humanities disciplines in service to society;
- To *assess* the need for societal action, to transmit authoritative information to stakeholders and then *take ownership* of the process of transition of knowledge to application, working in new partnerships.

In this contribution, I describe activities underway to address the second imperative above: defining and carrying forward a vigorous and urgent interdisciplinary research agenda. I describe new plans at the agency (NSF), national (U.S.), and International (ICSU) levels designed to create a much more fully coordinated sustainability research agenda. Unfortunately, these plans have not yet been adequately driven — or even fully embraced — by academia. However, they all point to the *urgent need for strong research university leadership* to be manifested in building the knowledge base to shape humanity's common future and ensuring that it is a sustainable one for generations to come.

NO TIME TO WASTE

The changes underway in the global climate system are occurring at a rate that exceeds the projections made at the time of the most recent Intergovernmental Panel on Climate Change (IPCC) report in 2007. This is due to increases in greenhouse gas emissions from many parts of the world, coupled with the relatively modest international efforts to limit those emissions and the rapid economic development of China, India, Brazil and other countries (to be celebrated, of course, from the perspective of poverty alleviation). Although decadal predictions are notoriously difficult to make in detail, sophisticated numerical climate system models, running on supercomputers, are able to show plausible responses with a degree of regional fidelity.

These changes will have profound consequences for fresh water availability, food production rates and for the occurrence frequency of extreme events, such as heat waves and droughts. In one study, conducted by the International Food Policy Research Institute (IFPRI, 2011), by the year 2050, continued warming and the accompanying changes in regional precipitation would reduce the production of rice globally by 27% (Mark Rosegrant, private communication). Such changes would, in turn, affect childhood malnutrition significantly, with an estimated increase of 22% of malnourished children by the year 2050 due to the effects of climate change on food production. Clearly, such studies are subject to much uncertainty, since they have to include imperfections in our understanding of climate change, particularly chained modeling projections of both precipitation and temperature regionally, as well as land use patterns, economic development and crop productivity, and assumptions of biome shifts and market variability. The point here is not that these numbers are strictly correct, but that societal management in the near future will increasingly demand such multi-disciplinary collaborations and projections, with results that have major public policy implications.

Freshwater scarcity is also a very near-term problem. In 2006, the International Water Management Institute reported that water scarcity affected fully one third of the world's population. IPCC projections indicate that this proportion will grow over the next years. It is estimated that more than 2 million children die of diarrhea each year due to badly managed and polluted waters.

Figure 1: Modeled Temperature anomalies with respect to 1870-1899 baseline; IPCC A1B scenario[1]

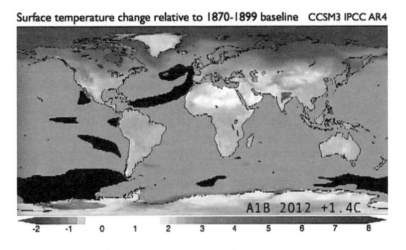

More than 500 million subsistence farmers lack irrigation water and are mired in poverty (Rijsberman, 2008). Water rationing in the rapidly growing cities in Africa and Asia is already the norm. The U.N. Millennium goals include a commitment to halve the number of people without access to safe potable water and, although significant progress has been made in Asia, Africa still lags. It is estimated that a diet of 3,000 calories per day requires at least 3000 litres of water to produce, so population pressures will further stress the freshwater security equation. All these water-related issues are likely to become more severe and much more complex to manage with climate change.

So, although it is possible to ponder global environmental sustainability questions from an academic standpoint at leisure and with a sense of distance and perspective, these changes are in fact occurring at rates that can and will simply overwhelm some of the traditional academic processes, where a typical graduate student maturation interval is about five years. Connect the two processes and you find the ratio is 0.1 C global-mean temperature increase per graduate student cycle!

So, Research Universities must respond and respond quickly to these onrushing, complex and multifaceted sustainability questions that demand science and technology analyses, coupled with deep understanding of human decision-making processes under conditions of large — and sometimes poorly defined — uncertainty. These challenges will undoubtedly stress Research Universities in ways that are quite unusual and it is likely that many institutions will simply fail to be relevant to the times. Those that do step up, however, will play an historical role for the future of human well-being.

SCIENCE, ENGINEERING AND EDUCATION FOR SUSTAINABILITY, SEES: A US NATIONAL SCIENCE FOUNDATION INITIATIVE

Funding agencies are beginning to appreciate the need for vigorous new approaches to support the scope and interdisciplinary function of what might be called global environmental sustainability science. One such agency is the National Science Foundation of the United States (NSF). NSF established the Science, Engineering, and Education for Sustainability (SEES) investment area (NSF, 2011) in FY2010 in order to promote the research and education needed to address the challenges of creating a sustainable human future. The SEES portfolio emphasizes a systems-based approach to understanding, predicting and reacting to change in the linked natural, social and built environment. Initial efforts were focused on coordination of a suite of research and education programs addressing future changes in climate and environment, with specific attention to incorporating social and cultural components of sustainability solutions. Eight solicitations were released in 2010 and 2011. These included the following:

- Water: Sustainability and climate
- Ocean Acidification
- Biodiversity (jointly with China)
- Regional and Decadal Earth System modeling (jointly with the U.S. Department of Agriculture and the U.S. Department of Energy)
- Climate Change Science Education (federated with similar efforts by NOAA and NASA)

- Sustainability Research networks
- Sustainable Energy Pathways
- Sustainability Research Fellowships

In all cases, natural, engineering and social sciences were required elements for successful proposals, connecting the environmental, economic, and energy-use elements of the problem, as well as the human capacity-building aspects. SEES is expected to be a five-year effort, extending through FY2015. Continuing efforts will focus on supporting research that facilitates global community sustainability, specifically by building connections between current projects, creating new nodes of activity, and developing the interdisciplinary personnel needed to address sustainability issues.

Efforts such as SEES are designed, not just to conduct frontier research, but to build the community of researchers able and capable of conducting the kinds of interdisciplinary studies relevant to sustainability. New partnerships of natural and social sciences are quickly emerging and the SEES program will be carefully evaluated for effectiveness in the context of important outcomes related to sustainability.

THE UNITED STATES GLOBAL CHANGE RESEARCH PROGRAM, USGCRP

In addition to individual agency activities, such as NSF/SEES, there is a growing emphasis on multi-agency coordination in support of the sustainability research enterprise. The United States Global Change Research Program (USGCRP) is a 13-agency cross cutting program of the federal government designed to further research in global change, including mandated support for the furtherance of international collaborations.

The USGCR is finalizing a new ten-year strategic plan and vision that will be made available for public comment in the summer of 2011. The new vision for USGCRP has already been released and is of: A nation, globally engaged and guided by science, meeting the challenges of climate and global change. The mission of the new USGCRP is "to build a knowledge base that informs human responses to climate and global change through coordinated and integrated federal programs of research, education, communication and decision support". The emphasis for the next ten years of the U.S. federal effort in global change research will be to develop what is being called an "end-to-end" approach, that is, developing the science and technology, but also applying the emerging knowledge base to key applications in society. The USGCRP recognizes that "meeting society's expanding demands for planetary resources, while preserving our global environment is one of the greatest challenges the world faces". Draft USGCRP materials state that:

"Sustainability requires finding ways to accommodate a growing population and its economy while assuring environmental goods and services needed to maintain our modern way of life will be available for present and future generations. Never in history has there been a greater need for well-founded science to help inform government, business, and public sectors in their efforts to meet this challenge, whether in their roles as voters, investors, homeowners, business owners, or stewards of the planet."

"The rapidity of the global change occurring today — in temperature, sea level, ice sheet thickness, ocean chemistry, and land surface change — far exceeds anything in recent geological history. The potential implications of this rapid change are profound, including dramatic increases in the severity of heat waves, floods, fires, storms, crop yields, habitat destruction, and water shortages, all occurring too quickly for ecosystems and human communities to adapt gradually. Business as usual could lead to irreversible changes, such as loss of summer sea ice and glaciers, accelerating extinction of species, and changes in critical ocean circulation patterns."

The USGCRP (2011) recognizes that the "challenge is urgent" and will emphasize several key components including:

- Integrated Observational Systems
- Integrated Modeling
- Regular Sustained National Climate Assessments
- An Interagency Climate Portal
- Climate Adaptation Science
- Climate Services
- Enhancing International Partnerships

The USGCRP also recognizes the importance of social sciences to the new end-to-end approach and is reaching our to academic social sciences community to build capacity. As the U.S. federal inter-agency effort moves towards a more end-to-end approach to the science of global change, the U.S. Research Universities will see opportunities for new levels of integrated sustainability research.

A PATHBREAKING "ALLIANCE" TO ESTABLISH A TEN-YEAR INTERNATIONAL INITIATIVE ON GLOBAL ENVIRONMENTAL SUSTAINABILITY

The NSF agency program and the USGCRP inter-agency programs have been influential in also seeding a new international coordinated research effort of relevance to the world's research universities. The Belmont Forum (2011) was established in the Fall of 2009 and is a high level group of the world's major and emerging funders of global environmental change research and international science councils. It is co-chaired by leaders of the National Environmental Research Council of the U.K. and the NSF Geosciences Directorate in the U.S. Two key members of the Belmont Forum from outside the funding agency community are the Executive Directors of the International Council of Scientific Unions (ICSU) and the International Social Sciences Council (ISSC), representing international academia from the natural and social sciences.

The Belmont Forum founding was inspired by recognition that the understanding of the environment and human society as an interconnected system, provided by Earth System research in recent decades, now needs to be built on, to provide knowledge for action and adaptation to environmental change. It aims to accelerate the international environmental research most urgently needed to remove critical barriers to sustainability, by aligning international resources.

At its fourth meeting, in Cape Town, October 2010, the Belmont Forum spearheaded a proposal for a new Alliance between funders, researchers, operational agencies and users, to deliver a 10-year environmental science research mission for sustainability. This new partnership for user-driven research was described recently in *Science Magazine* (Reid *et al.*, 2010). The Alliance partnership will launch its research mission at the Planet Under Pressure Conference, London, March 2012. The ten-year Initiative will be designed to address what has come to be called the "Belmont Challenge": *To deliver knowledge needed for action to mitigate and adapt to detrimental environmental change and extreme hazardous events*.

It is understood that addressing this challenge will require:

- Information on the state of the environment, through advanced observing systems;
- Assessments of risks, impacts and vulnerabilities, through regional and decadal analysis and prediction;
- Enhanced environmental information service providers to users;
- Inter- and transdisciplinary research which takes account of coupled natural, social and economic systems;
- Effective integration and coordination mechanisms, to address interdependencies and marshal the necessary resources.

With initial priority foci for the Belmont Forum group of funding agencies being:

- Coastal Vulnerability;
- Freshwater Security;
- Ecosystem Services;
- Carbon Budgets;

• Most vulnerable societies.

Meeting the Belmont Challenge will require much more effective coordination and integration across these elements than has been achieved to date. An integrating conceptual framework with a focus on aligning resources towards an holistic environmental change decision-support system is essential to drive effective coordination and integration of the diverse disciplinary, institutional and financial resources to meet the current global environmental challenges.

The proposed framework for the ten-year initiative is comprised of ideas for:

• Systematic targeting and integration of observations and research to overcome critical limits to predictions;
• Overarching strategic governance to establish key priorities among competing demands and promote cooperation;
• A greater voice for users in informing the research priorities;
• A step-change increase in collaboration across scientific disciplines, especially those between the natural and the social sciences and geographical areas;
• A profound increase in collaboration across geographical regions with a special emphasis on enhancing scientific capacity in developing countries; and
• Improved mechanisms for major transnational funding that overcome current constraints to cross-border support while respecting national requirements and statutes.

The Belmont Forum and this new "Alliance" of Funding Agencies, Researchers (through the participation of ICSU and ISSC), Operational Agencies and Users is pathbreaking in that it offers the possibility for creating a research agenda that is feasible, intellectually rich, fundable and of tailored service to society. Such connective elements have previously occurred on a much more ad hoc basis without explicit a-priori planning. Although Research University leadership has not yet played a role in the development of this international sustainability research initiative, it is anticipated that key opportunities for these institutions will flow from the improved international coordination and alignment of resources to support an aggressive research agenda.

In addition to the Belmont Forum, the International Group of Funding Agencies for Global Change Research (IGFA, 2011) is re-evaluating its role in coordination with the Belmont Forum (which serves as the Council of Principals for IGFA). IGFA will focus on energizing regional research networks, such as the Inter Americas Institute (IAI, 2011), the Asian Pacific

Network (APN, 2011) and AfricaNESS (IGBP, 2011). It will also work to establish strong linkages between scientific funding agencies and development aid agencies worldwide.

CONCLUSIONS

This paper has attempted to illustrate the societal urgency of developing an effective, end-to-end interdisciplinary research agenda for global environmental sustainability. Many new efforts and programs are underway on the agency-specific, national and international levels that will augment present efforts in systematic ways. It is critically important that the Research Universities play their ordained role fully: aggressively educating and empowering the needed human capital to address these historic challenges, while also identifying and driving a vigorous research agenda that address the super-wicked problems of our century in a timely and effective manner.

However, it must be said finally that neither the Research University Community, its leadership, nor the other players in global environmental sustainability stakes (funders, operational organizations, non-profits, stakeholders of various kinds, etc.) should work in isolation. The challenge of sustainability will clearly need everyone, or as President Obama said one day in Ohio in July 2008:

"The fact is, the challenges we face today — from saving our planet to ending poverty — are simply too big for government to solve alone. We need all hands on deck."

REFERENCES

APN (2011). Asia-Pacific Network for Global Change Research. www.apn-gcr.org

Belmont Forum (2011). www.igfagcr.org/index.php/belmont-forum

IAI (2011). Inter-Americas Institute, which seeks to support interdisciplinary global change studies in the Americas. www.iai.int

IFPRI (2011). *Food Security, Farming, and Climate Change to 2050*, IFPRI, Scenarios, Results, and Policy Options. http://www.ifpri.org/publication/food-security-farming-and-climate-change-2050, http://dx.doi.org/10.2499/9780896291867

IGFA (2011). International Group of Funding Agencies for Global Change Research. http://www.igfagcr.org/index.php

IGBP (2011). International Geosphere-Biosphere Programme. http://www.igbp.net/page.php?pid=412

Intergovernmental Panel on Climate Change (2007). *"Climate Change 2007"*, Cambridge University Press.

Levin, K, Bernstein, S., Cashore, B. & Auld, G. (2008). "Playing it Forward: Path Dependency, Progressive Incrementalism, and the 'Super Wicked' Problem of Global Climate Change." DOI: 10.1088/1755-1307/6/50/502002

National Research Council (2008). *America's Energy Future*. Washington DC.

National Research Council (2011). *America's Climate Choices*. Washington DC.

NSF (2011). National Science Foundation. http://www.nsf.gov/sees

Reid, W. *et al.* (2010). "Earth System Science for Global Sustainability: Grand Challenges", *Science* (30) pp. 916-917.

Rijsberman, F. R. (2008) *Every Last Drop*. http://bostonreview.net/BR33.5/rijsberman.php, September/October.

Rittel, H. & Melvin, W. (1984). "Dilemmas in a General Theory of Planning", pp. 155-169, *Policy Sciences*, Vol. 4, Elsevier Scientific Publishing Company, Inc., Amsterdam, 1973. [Reprinted in N. Cross (ed.), *Developments in Design Methodology*, J. Wiley & Sons, Chichester, pp. 135-144.]

USGRP (2011). United States Global Change Research Program. www.globalchange.gov

World Commission on Environment and Development (1987). *Our Common Future*, Published as Annex to the General Assembly document A/42/427, Development and International Co-operation: Environment, August 2.

CHAPTER 15

Research Intensive Universities in a Globalized World

Bernd Huber

INTRODUCTION

As president of a German university and chairman of the League of European Research Universities (LERU), it is my special interest to discuss the role of research intensive universities and their impact on global sustainability from a European point of view. One may wonder why the perspectives of European universities should be particularly interesting in terms of globalization. Another question would be what impact Europe's research intensive universities have on promoting and progressing sustainability as a goal that must be pursued? Looking at the numbers, Europe represents one of the largest economies in the world; it is one of the richest areas in terms of per capita income. And, it is also one of the largest higher education and research areas in the world. In 2009, almost 20 million students were pursuing a degree in higher education in one of the 27 member states of the European Union. For 2008, the EU member states had 1.3 million researchers (Eurostat, 2011). At this point, one may note that the differences from the United States and China are only minor — in 2006, Europe ranked third in total numbers, counting 1.33 million researchers compared to 1.4 million in the U.S. (as of 2007) and 1.6 million in China (as of 2008) (European Commission, 2011). To understand the current situation and the perspectives of European universities in an increasingly globalized world and their influence on global sustainability, it is helpful to have a brief look into the recent past.

DEFINING GLOBALIZATION
AND RESEARCH INTENSIVE UNIVERSITIES

Since the end of the last century, globalization has become one of the key-words on the international agenda. The term was first introduced to describe the rapid increase in world trade and the higher mobility of production factors across the world. Similarly, the process of globalization was accompanied by a decline in transportation cost and rapid improvement of international communications. Today, products that indicate "Made in Germany" might also contain parts that were manufactured in China, Brazil or Turkey. The same applies, for example, to the food industry — globalization allows customers to buy typical groceries from Italy or Japan all across the world.

The term "globalization" is often used more broadly these days, to describe the enhanced interdependence of national states in the fields of economy, politics and culture, especially induced and boosted through the internet and other technical achievements regarding communication and information. One effect is that the world is seemingly moving together, and even getting "smaller", as long distances between people and countries no longer matter. Events in one part of the world affect other parts more than in the past, simply because all information spreads almost in real time. A good example for the triumph of the World Wide Web and fast communication are the recent revolutionary movements in the Arabic countries. Without smartphones, twitter or facebook, the protesters would have had more difficulties organizing rallies and protests, and these would not have spread to other countries so quickly or at all.

The ongoing globalization process through enhanced communication and easily available information (e.g. through television or World Wide Web) is a great chance to learn about and acknowledge the diverse cultures, habits and everyday lives of the world's population. But at the same time there is also the danger that by the dominance of some leading economies and cultures, this diversity is lost, and the economic and political forces at work lead to a homogenization of cultures and lifestyles across the world.

However, globalization influences the way the topic of sustainability — which can be defined as one of the grand challenges of our time — can and must be discussed. The positive outcomes of globalization as mentioned above create a framework within which sustainability can be tackled the best possible way. An ideal and at the same time responsible use of all available resources — be it food and water, energy or the creativity and innovative potential of the world's brightest minds — can be communicated to the world's population more efficiently with the tools that globalization is offering. Then, finally, people's well-being worldwide can be tackled, achieved and maintained. To sum it up, one can say that globalization can be used to educate people, therefore a well functioning system of higher education is the key to a sustainable management of the available resources: A higher education system that enables the best brains to do research and come up with innovative solutions brings the world forward and needs to be used to ameliorate the lives of the world population.

THE RESPONSE OF EUROPEAN UNIVERSITIES TO GLOBALIZATION

Although the term globalization has only become popular in the last century, globalizing tendencies have always existed. Universities, research and researchers have always had a "global" impact. One could say that the universities of the Middle Ages were already truly international institutions with scholars from many parts of the world attending them or at least corresponding with each other. By doing this, they were working beyond countries' frontiers and across language barriers, with Latin being the lingua franca of the age. The truly international approach driven only by the desire to exchange and enhance knowledge has always been a trait of universities until the present day.

For various historical and other reasons, the term "European universities" used in my contribution refers only to the institutions in continental Europe, as the situation in the United Kingdom differs in many respects from the rest of Europe.

European universities are among the oldest in the world; there are proud, old institutions like the Sorbonne or the universities in Bologna, Prague, Heidelberg and Geneva, to name just a few. Nevertheless, one must say that ten years ago, at the beginning of this century, European universities were in deep crisis. For reasons that will not be discussed in detail in this contribution, the higher education system had become highly sclerotic, underperforming and non-competitive on a global scale — thus not sustainable any longer. The situation of European universities at that time could be described as performing badly with not much funding. This picture has, in my view, dramatically changed over the last years. In many countries, we have seen sweeping reforms at universities, a process of modernization has been set in motion and far-reaching initiatives have been undertaken. In the next paragraph, some of the key steps will be highlighted.

On the one hand, there is more autonomy and less bureaucracy at European universities. For example, Germany and recently France have introduced reforms which drastically reduce the dependence on the state. To give you one example for such a reform at Ludwig-Maximilians-Universität München: A key step for higher education in Europe to become more open and more international was the introduction of a system of common degrees across Europe.

This is the so-called Bologna process that facilitates and thereby increases the mobility of students and graduates. Consequently, a student with a Bachelor degree from the Netherlands can now do his master's in Germany.

In addition to this massive change for European higher education, in 2009, the right to appoint professors was delegated to the universities, so now the presidents/rectors directly appoint professors, whereas, before, the government had this right and could also reject appointments submitted by the universities.

One of the most important steps has been to introduce competition into the university system. For example, Germany has introduced the so-called excellence initiative. Similar programs are now also run in Spain and in France. At the European level, the ERC (European Research Council), which funds world-class research on a competitive basis across Europe, has been established. And we have experienced a significant expansion of the system of higher education and research. For example, in Germany, it used to be the case that 25% of a cohort attended higher education institutions. This proportion is now nearly at 45%. We have more than 2.2 million students in Germany, and this number will increase to almost 3 million over the next years. Similarly, the number of researchers has increased to more than 300,000 today from 240,000 a couple of years ago (Hochschulrektorenkonferenz, 2011).

Summing this up, one can say that the university landscape has undergone some wide-ranging changes: universities gained more autonomy, the degrees have been harmonized, competition between the institutions has been strengthened, and an overall expansion can be observed. All this is, of course, part of an effort to make Europe globally competitive and a place that is attractive to both people and businesses. In return, this also serves sustainability.

WHERE DO WE STAND NOW?

It is then natural to ask — where do we stand now? From a global perspective, we observe what you may call a catch-up process. Consider for example international rankings of universities. As an academic I should add that this kind of league tables raises various difficult methodological issues. Keeping this in mind, rankings nevertheless reveal some interesting tendencies. One well-known league table has been developed by the *Times*. Their current ranking for 2010 shows that only 14 universities from continental Europe are among the top 100 (Times Higher Education, 2011).

This reflects the deficiencies of European universities in the past that I have mentioned above, and it also shows that catching up to the top positions takes time. But I am confident that when the full benefits of the recent reforms kick in, one will make out a significant improvement of the position of European universities in these ranking tables. For example, the potential for improvement can already be deducted from the fact that more than 40% of the universities in the positions 100 to 200 in the ranking are from continental Europe (Times Higher Education, 2011).

If you consider the current situation from a European perspective, my view is that higher education and research in Europe are "moving together". A common European Research Area is being formed which brings together the triangle of research, innovation and higher education. But in this regard, one also has to mention that not all of Europe's universities perform in the same way. It is mostly the western European states that contribute powerfully to this triangle.

From a national perspective, one can say that the increased competition has induced a process of differentiation across universities in many member countries. Some universities are on the way to become truly internationally oriented, research-based universities while other ones are developing their strengths in a national or regional context; others are focussing on their role as teaching institutions. One must be clear about this process of differentiation: the procedure is not easy, as it raises various difficult and sometimes painful issues. But it opens the perspective for a highly competitive and successful system of higher education and research that can support the efforts to achieve and maintain global sustainability.

WHERE DO WE GO NEXT?

What lies ahead for the future of research intensive universities? How will their performance contribute to global sustainability? In my view, the answer is clear. Europe has to further strengthen and improve the performance of its system of higher education and research. It needs to be emphasized that the benefits of higher education, research and innovation are not only key drivers for innovation, economic growth and prosperity. Investment in universities and research goes beyond economic considerations. We need more research and thus more innovation to tackle the great challenges of our time — like food, energy, climate change and health. In short, all of these challenges come down to one major challenge that mankind has to face together: sustainability. In my view, European universities can make a significant contribution to these issues and therefore serve global sustainability.

Higher education in Europe has become more open, more international, by, for example, introducing a system of common degrees across continental Europe. As already mentioned, this is the so-called Bologna process: In order to homogenize degrees to make them more comparable and to allow students to fulfil part of their studies at institutions Europe-wide without losing precious ECTS points or seminars at their home institutions, the "new" Bachelor and Master system facilitates and thereby increases international mobility of students and graduates. Even if the current results of this reform leave room for discussions and critique, there is one trend that has gained impetus over the past decade and more so over the past few years. According to the OECD, more than 2.7 million students of the higher education system were attending universities abroad (OECD, 2007). Recent evidence indicates that this figure has further increased over the last few years: Many students consider a stay at a university abroad not only as an intellectual challenge and an asset to their academic transcript, but also as a rewarding personal experience, or, as a clear step into an economically better future; this applies especially to students from developing countries who take the knowledge gained at foreign universities back home to ameliorate the situation there. A truly globalized profile of a student today includes at least a stay abroad and an internship in a country other than his or her country of origin. International and transnational companies are looking for staff who are not only well trained, but who have already gained intercultural experience, speak several languages and are prepared to easily work in a multicultural environment.

For all non Anglo-Saxon states, this leads to major strategic considerations regarding their teaching and also their research output in form of publications: In what language will classes be taught? Are the staff willing and able to teach in a language other than their native tongue? Can they write their research papers in English with the same quality as in their mother tongue? Today, English has become the lingua franca in science. But in the humanities, the situation is often still quite different, reflecting the specific cultural background of the various subjects. Globalizing the student body and the faculty and serving an international market will then require countries like Germany to offer a larger part of their curriculum in English.

But globalization does not only affect teaching, it has a deep impact on research as well. Internationalization through attracting the best researchers and students from all over the world is the outspoken goal of many universities and even states. With declining birth rates and an economy that needs well educated employees, most developed countries have a keen interest in preserving their standard of living by being at the forefront of economic and social innovation.

But what are the potential risks for the future of research-intensive universities? One point that is worrying is the future role of basic or so-called blue sky research. There is always a certain tendency among politicians to support research which promises directly applicable results and immediate benefits. Blue sky or basic research often looks less attractive from a short-term perspective. But, let us be clear, in the long run, the innovation process is driven by the results of basic research. One brief example: CERN in Geneva is one of the leading research institutes pursuing basic research in the field of physics. The prototype of the World Wide Web which has changed the daily lives of all of us was developed at CERN in the early 1990s as a project to facilitate the sharing of information among researchers. Only a few years later, the World Wide Web has revolutionized the way we work, the way we consume media, the way we discuss openly and communicate with each other beyond borders — nearly every aspect of our lives. This example underlines that we need to make sure that research policy and funding policies leave ample room for basic and blue sky research which is so crucial to develop the unthinkable.

Finally, there is one more aspect that needs to be stressed when discussing the future of research intensive universities in a globalized world. Our understanding of the role of universities has changed over time. Today, we emphasize the contribution of universities to qualify young people, to research and innovation, and to sustainable economic growth and prosperity. This is legitimate. But let us not forget the cultural and societal dimensions of the role of universities. This concerns in particular the role of arts and humanities at universities. The departments of arts and humanities are not a by-product or a luxury, no — arts and humanities are crucial to understand ourselves, our history, our culture, our society. Therefore, we have to take care that arts and humanities remain an integral part of our universities. I think that this is one of the elements that make sure that our universities and, as a result of the universities' contributions, our societies face a bright future and the prospect of global sustainability.

REFERENCES

European Commission, Directorate-General for Research and Innovation (2011). *EUR 24211 — Innovation Union Competitiveness report*. Luxembourg: Publications Office of the European Union, p. 88.

Eurostat (2011). *Tertiary students (ISCED 5-6) by field of education and sex [educ_enrl5]*. Available at: http://appsso.eurostat.ec.europa.eu/nui/show.do?dataset=educ_enrl5&lang=en (Accessed 15 June 2011).

Hochschulrektorenkonferenz (2011). *Hochschulen in Zahlen 2011* (pdf). Available at: http://www.hrk.de/de/download/dateien/Hochschulen_in_Zahlen_2011.pdf (Accessed 15 June 2011).

OECD (2007). *Number of foreign students in tertiary education, by country of origin and destination (2005) and market shares in international education (2000, 2005)*. Available at: http://www.oecd.org/dataoecd/17/10/39308963.xls (Accessed 15 June 2011).

Times Higher Education (2011). *The World University Rankings 2010*. Available at: http://www.timeshighereducation.co.uk/world-university-rankings/2010-2011/top-200.html (Accessed 15 June 2011).

CHAPTER 16

The contribution of Research Universities in solving "Grand Challenges"

Georg Winckler and Martin Fieder

A CHANGING WORLD

Obviously, the world is changing rapidly, and not only for the better: Grand challenges for society are arising and demand solutions. Some challenges can be foreseen, some may occur without warning. When societal problems can be predicted, responsible governments have to address their solutions. Early research has to contribute to meeting upcoming challenges.

The European Union's foresight and forward-looking activities have a long tradition: societal trends are analysed, and knowledge gathered by these analyses becomes part of planning for the future ("The world in 2025, Rising Asia and socio-ecological transition").

As the public authorities increasingly aim at analysing and addressing future challenges, public expectation about the relevance of science and research of universities will change: the abstract aim of increasing the GDP will not be an end of research, but research should rather focus on tackling "themes" and achieving solutions to societal problems. Such a strategy might also enhance the interest and enthusiasm of researchers and the public alike (Winckler & Fieder, 2005). As the arising challenges are multidisciplinary, they cannot be the subject of a "single" scientific approach, but will need different contributions from various fields in order to be addressed fully. Of course, the traditional Humboldtian goal of "education through science" (*Bildung durch Wissenschaft*) will not change.

Broad and transdisciplinary themes are identified by the European Commission (2009) in the report "The world in 2025". In this document the European Commission also addressed the rise of a "multipolar world", with new players such as China. In the report *Preparing Europe for a New Renaissance. A strategic view of the European Research Area*, (European Commission, 2009a) the European Research Area Board (ERAB), a high-level advisory board to the European Commission addressed, for instance, the following grand challenges (European Commission, 2010):

- climate change
- health care
- ageing societies
- reduced availability of resources (energy, water).

In the report "Realizing the New Renaissance", (European Commission, 2010), ERAB recommends immediate, mid-term and longer-term actions which were developed and divided into four broad fields: unite the European Research Area in a global context; strengthen the interplay between science, society and politics; enhance open innovation; guarantee that the European Research Area delivers excellence and cohesion.

The solution of the Grand Challenges calls for a "paradigm shift in what the role and place of science should be" (ERAB 2009a, p. 9). The interaction between science and society and the collaboration of the public with the private sectors in the form of open innovation, play a major role in the strategic view to be developed. As research and innovation are particularly important to solve grand challenges, society should be ready to raise expenditures in the E.U. for R&D to 4% to 5% of GDP.

Tackling the new themes will also require new ideas, discoveries and the creation of talents. To realize the potential of research, the way research is done should be changed too. Strengthening the European Research Area should help to establish this new renaissance and should be marked by free movement of people (mobility of staff and students) and ideas ("open science"), and also by promoting "high-risk/high-gain" research.

Yet, unfortunately, the question remains, whether European universities will be willing to foster the idea of a "New Renaissance" as universities seem to be too much prisoners of their past.

UNIVERSITIES AS PRISONERS OF THEIR PAST

Today, universities play a central role for higher education and frontier research in Europe. Obviously, universities and their contributions are needed for creating a new renaissance.

However, European universities are still very occupied with their own affairs. This inward orientation may hinder a more goal- or theme-oriented approach to research:

- European universities are mostly organized along national and regional borders, although the Bologna and Lisbon process have helped to reduce the fragmentation *of the university landscape* within Europe. Yet, there is still too much provincialism within (Continental) European universities. There is still no real Europe-wide labour market for scientists and educational staff, as language, legal and practical barriers still exist. About 97% of graduates working today as faculty members at European universities had all their employment in the country in which they received their Ph.D. (Winckler, 2010).

- Universities are usually too *hierarchically organized*, a fact that strongly hinders creativity (Sawyer, 2006). It diminishes research opportunities for young scholars.

- The proportion of *blue sky research* may be too high. This does not mean that basic research should be reduced, but that research activities should be bundled along themes. The volume of blue sky research should be retained in the future, but research in line with tackling grand challenges has to grow over-proportionately. Research on grand challenges will be more and more the prime target of European research funding.

- Total fertility rates in Europe dropped after the "baby boom" in the 1960s to 1.6 children per woman in the year 2010 (source: population reference bureau; http://www.prb.org/DataFinder/Geography/Data.aspx?loc=413). Low birth rates will not only affect the health care and the pension system, but will confront universities with a *decrease in the number of domestic students*. Attracting the best brains from abroad, however, requires a degree of openness and internationalization of universities in (Continental) Europe which they do not yet possess.

- Universities indulge in an *idealistic* and often *self-referential* way of doing research. A pragmatic approach towards research should be adopted: universities should accept the interest of society in new research themes, especially when meeting grand challenges.

- Last, not least: *resources and money* are *not used efficiently*. In the sciences, for instance, cooperation between scientists across institutional borders may lead to better use of resources. There is a need for more cooperation between universities for better use of resources and for an increase in the quality of higher education (Taylor, 2011).

Will universities perform better when rankings and quantitative measurements of the quality of research such as impact factors gain importance? In general, of course, competition may lead to a more efficient allocation of resources. Yet there are reasons to doubt that ranking competition improves the efficiency of the university sector: the performance measurements of universities with respect to rankings often suffer from poor data quality. There is too much noise in the data (Bookstein *et al.*, 2010). In addition, rankings may have a language bias as illustrated by the *Times* Higher Education Ranking: *In the ranking of 2010, universities in English-speaking countries perform on the overall score better than universities in non-English-speaking countries (non-English-speaking countries: N = 78; mean avg score = 55.6; English-speaking countries: N = 122, mean avg score = 63.6; ANOVA = 22.56 P < 0.01).*

Furthermore, ranking competition may decrease the much needed openness of science, as cooperation across universities gets impeded. A comparable problem may arise by "over-emphasizing" impact factors and citations as a quality indicator for publications, as the impact of a journal predicts the number of citations that an article receives (Perneger, 2010). In addition, in cultural markets anything of average quality may emerge as top ranked if it is driven by social influences (Lorenz *et al.*, 2011)

Universities should not become like professional football clubs, chasing after the big names only and forgetting how to form new research teams between universities working on upcoming research themes.

TOWARDS A NEW WORLD OF RESEARCH AND INNOVATION

The structure of scientific research is on the way of a radical change. Very likely, this change may allow researchers to address themes of arising global challenges more effectively. What is needed is that universities move from the *ivory tower* to a more universal approach to research. Such moves might increase research output, but will also bring new challenges to traditional research institutions and funding bodies.

This trend is already indicated by the increasing share of researchers in business and enterprises: In the economically leading countries (measured by the overall size of GDP) Canada, China, France, Germany, Italy, Japan, Russia and the U.K. (Figure 1) (no data available in this form for the U.S., only amounts of budgets are known, Figure 2), with the exception of the Russian Federation and the U.K., the full-time equivalents of researchers in business and enterprises have conspicuously risen during the last 10 years. Concerning research staff in higher education institutions (universities), there is also a rising trend in Canada, France, Italy and for the U.K. In Germany, China and the Russian Federation, the number of full-time staff in higher education institutions seems to remain stable. However with the exception of Italy and the U.K., the rise of the number of researchers in business and enterprise is much steeper than for the higher education sector. Particularly in China and Canada, the number of researchers in business and enterprise increased strongly compared to the other sectors. Governmental research and research in private nonprofit organizations remain in all countries on a very low and increasingly marginalized level. For the U.S., R&D investment in business enterprises rose steeply from 1981 onwards (Figure 2).

Figure 1

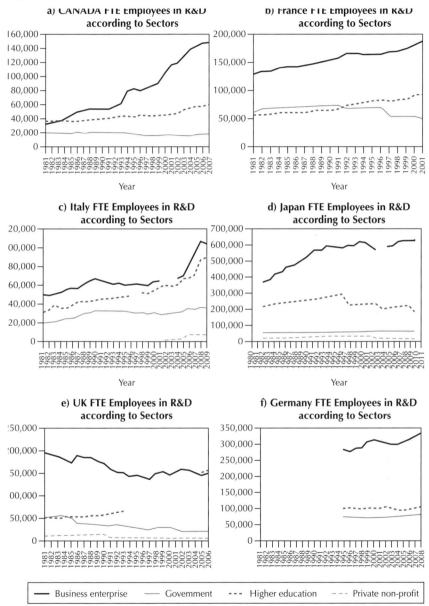

Figure 1

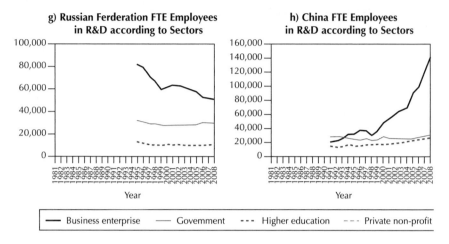

g) **Russian Ferderation FTE Employees in R&D according to Sectors**

h) **China FTE Employees in R&D according to Sectors**

—— Business enterprise   —— Govemment   - - - Higher education   - - - Private non-profit

Figure 2 : US R&D Investements in Mio. $

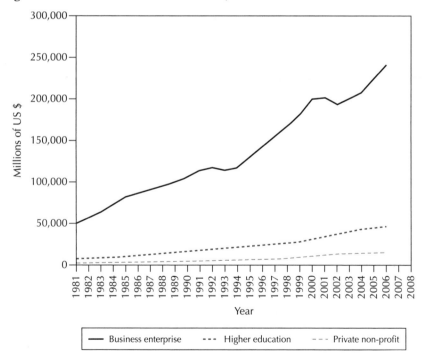

—— Business enterprise   - - - Higher education   - - - Private non-profit

Yet not only the number of researchers and financial resources in the business sector rises overproportionately, but also open innovation seems to gain importance as a new form of cooperation. The paradigm of open innovation assumes that firms can and will use external ideas as well as internal ideas. The research boundaries between a firm and its environment have thus become more permeable; innovations can easily be transferred (Chesbrough, 2003). Over the past few years, open innovation has become a concept on which more and more enterprises rely (examples: http://en.wikipedia.org/wiki/Open_innovation).

In addition the more radical concept of "crowd sourcing" has gained importance: Tasks are being distributed to a number of individuals often working and solving problems in their free time. *The best known example for crowd sourcing might be Wikipedia itself,* although the founder of Wikipedia, Jimmy Wales, refuses the term "crowd sourcing" for Wikipedia.

Both open innovation and crowd sourcing may represent examples of how research universities may behave in an open system where information flows freely. Universities will increasingly act like "open clubs" attracting part or fulltime co-workers who research and publish for a limited time for a university. Especially the science parks around universities will constitute a potential, mobile recruiting field for short-term jobs at a university.

As a consequence, the borders of universities may become very permeable. Non-professional scientists may engage themselves in research and may publish with a university (a kind of academic crowd sourcing). It is up to the universities to use this potential in the future. An excellent starting point could be keeping and intensifying the contact with alumni. Universities should think about what they are able to offer to potential non-professional "outside researchers" (for instance a sophisticated further education). This may boost the reputation and visibility of universities.

All these new developments such as "open innovation", "crowd sourcing" and "open science" may foster the tackling of the "grand challenges", for which societies have an interest and, thus, will provide financial means. Research funds should be prepared to finance these newly emerging structures of research, e.g. a certain proportion of the finances should be used to support "open science startups".

Additionally also higher education and teaching are on the way to a dramatic change: Via Apple's iTunes numerous podcasts of courses are offered completely for free. Stanford, particularly, is highly active on iTunes. Furthermore Stanford also uses iTunes to keep in touch with the community interested in the affairs of the university.

Another impressive example for open education and open teaching is MIT, due to the MIT OpenCourseWare. Per definition, "MIT OpenCourseWare" (http://ocw.mit.edu/index.htm) is "a free publication of MIT course materials that reflects almost all the undergraduate and graduate subjects taught at MIT". Via OpenCourseWare MIT offers materials and information, but not any degree or certificate.

As a consequence, access to knowledge becomes free and everyone who wants to gain knowledge and who wants to prepare him/herself for a study can do so, without paying (high) fees. To gain a degree or certificate, however, students have to enrol at a university.

It can be assumed that many more examples of open teaching content will be soon on the net and will enable people around the world to get in touch with the newest scientific development, again potentially enabling people outside the traditional academic borders to engage in science and research. Additionally, by increasing the proportion of "open education" the general participation rate will also increase. Furthermore, new technologies will flood the educational sector. Rupert Murdoch already signalled that News Corp is to make a significant new push into the education technology market (*Financial Times*, 25 May 2011, p. 19).

A CHANGING ROLE FOR UNIVERSITIES

As borders of universities may become more permeable and as more and more research opportunities and data are no longer restricted to specific research groups, innovation activities can be conducted worldwide by many researchers and even by the general public. For many scientific fields, data can be downloaded from the internet completely free of charge; the main restrictions are the existing bandwidth of the internet and the organizations and documentations of scientific data repositories (*Science* special issue on data, *Science* 331, 639-806). But, despite these technical obstacles, everyone who is capable of analysing data can do so, as also the tools of analyses are available for free and in open source (the free statistical program R (The R Project, 2011) that started to develop into a general tool for analyses of data in all fields, is a perfect example of the new trend). The problems that arise in this context are: who pays for gathering and storing of the data and who pays for fast internet connections, who owns the data and who guarantees the compliance with ethical principles when using the data?

However, despite these problems, the positive effects might outweigh the negative ones by far: Data are not lost on "private" servers or computers, but could be re-used for many different research issues. Many more scientists, especially from developing countries, could use data for scientific publications without paying for their use. This trend will foster research and innovation as many more "brains" can work on scientific questions and problems and overall, data and knowledge becomes more sustainable.

Ultimately, the concept of "open science" will prevail: New knowledge will be generated and disseminated rapidly by giving up the rights over using this knowledge. "Open science" facilitates the generation of further knowledge, helps students in moving towards frontier knowledge and boosts the innovation system. The benefits of "open science" stem from the significant positive external effects it creates.

The increasing share of business and enterprise research may point to a trend that might be even stronger in the future. Research has become so open and feasible that it will increasingly be done outside universities; external organization will play a more important role in knowledge production, challenging the traditional role of universities. As mentioned above "crowd sourcing" might become common in academic knowledge production.

Due to this reason, the education and particular graduate education at universities will become more important. Increasingly universities may become certifying agents for those who participate actively in research elsewhere and marketing institutions to bring research more directly to society and to the economy.

There are two trends corroborating this line of argument in the U.S.: (1) the rise in the proportion of FTE researchers working for business and enterprise, (2) the growing rate of proposal submissions from "non-research-intensive organizations" which points to the importance of research outside traditional structures: E.g. *during the 5 years between 2000 and 2004, the proposals from research intensive organizations increased by only 42% whereas proposals from all other organizations increased by 58% (National Science Foundation, 2007).*

Furthermore, the budget allocation since 2002 of national science funds in the U.S. reflects the growing importance of research outside of "traditional research organizations".

All these trends challenge the traditional roles of universities, as more and more frontier research and more and more research concerning the grand challenges will be conducted elsewhere.

At the moment, universities seem to fail to satisfy the demand of knowledge societies, particularly in the case of Ph.D. education (*Nature*, 472, 261). A Ph.D. is traditionally produced along narrow academic criteria and often narrow scientific fields. Hardly any interdisciplinary research takes place. Research labs are in a herd competition with each other only. As a consequence, in virtually all countries, there is a relatively slow increase in job offers on the job market for Ph.D.s. In Germany, for instance, only 6% of the Ph.D. graduates end up in full-time academic positions for an unlimited period. In Japan, the situation is even harder for Ph.D.s. Highly qualified young scientists represent a "treasure of human capital" that lies fallow, but the conclusion of Mark Taylor (2011) in *Nature* might be too pessimistic: "Reform the Ph.D. system or close it down." Particularly those young scientists dropping out of the academic world could foster scientific thinking and a commitment to research elsewhere in society or in business: Highly skilful and educated young scientists, who "spread" into societies, could be compared to the social descent of well educated persons from the higher social strata in the 18th and 19th centuries, a fact that, among other reasons, may have fostered the industrial revolution (Clark, 2007).

What might be the consequence for universities? Instead of evaluating future trends in research more effectively, Continental European universities pursue similar, traditional aims, adopt quite the same measures to achieve these aims and fail to occupy new and "ecological" niches. Making a university unique and fit for the future requires differentiation and a balance between local interest and a global view, especially concerning quality management of education and research. It is not clear how universities learn that cooperation between them will be an urgent need in the future (Winckler & Fieder, 2010).

HOW TO SECURE THE FUNDING OF UNIVERSITIES?

The increasing permeability that will characterize the borders of a university, the enhancement of "open science" and of "open innovation" will make the research university more dependent on attracting public funds. Of course, private donations may complement public money, but private money will more and more respond to the commitment of research universities to tackle "real issues" and to focus on the grand challenges for society.

Universities have to acknowledge that other competitors on the "research market" will come into play, eroding the monopoly rent of doing frontier research. Universities should be open for themes of importance for society, e.g., participating in cooperation with academic, but also with non-academic, organizations in solving the grand challenges. Schumpeterian innovation rents might be earned there. Yet, by moving into this direction, universities need to be less self-referential, more pragmatic and more open-minded.

Securing the funding of a university in the future will also press the university to organize itself more flexibly and less hierarchically.

CONCLUSION

Open Science, open innovation and open education will gain importance. The human potential that will be engaged in research will grow particularly outside the established research organizations, as publications, data and programs are more and more available for free via the internet. It is wise to invest in this growing overall research capacity from a European respectively governmental perspective, particularly to better address the "grand challenges". It is important for research universities to learn to be active in this growing sector. However, that requires a more outward-looking attitude than is common today.

REFERENCES

Bookstein, F., Seidler, H., Fieder, M. & Winckler, G. (2010). Too much noise in the Times Higher Education rankings. *Scientometrics*, 85, pp. 295-299.

Chesbrough, H. (2003). Open Innovation: The New Imperative For Creating And Profiting From Technology. Harvard Business School Press, ISBN: 1-57851-837-7.

Clark, G. (2007). *A Farewell to Alms: A Brief Economic History of the World*. Princeton University Press, ISBN-10: 9780691141282.

Cyranoski, D., Gilbert, N., Ledford, H., Nayar, A. & Yahia, M. (2011). "Education: The Ph.D. factory. The world is producing more Ph.D.s than ever before. Is it time to stop?" *Nature* 472, pp. 276-279.

European Commission. (2009). Directorate-General for Research. Socio-economic Sciences and Humanities The World in 2025. *Rising Asia and socio-ecological transition*.

European Commission (2009a). First report of the European Research Area Board "Preparing Europe for a New Renaissance: A strategic view of the European Research Area."

European Commission (2010). Second report of the European Research Area Board (2010) "Realising the New Renaissance: Policy proposals for developing a world-class research and innovation space in Europe 2030."

Lorenz, J., Rauhut, H., Schweitzer, F. & Helbing, D. (2011). How social influence can undermine the wisdom oft he crowd effect. Proceedings of the National Academy of Science of the United States of America 108, pp. 9020-9025.

McCook, A. (2011). "Education: Rethinking Ph.D.s". *Nature* 472, pp. 280-282.

National Science Foundation (2007). *Impact of Proposal and Award Management Mechanisms*. Final Report.

Perneger, T. V. (2010). "Citation analysis of identical consensus statements revealed journal-related bias". *Journal of Clinical Epidemiology* 63, pp. 660-664.

Sawyer, B. K. (2006). *Explaining Creativity: The Science of Human Innovation*. Oxford University Press, ISBN-13: 978-0195304459.

Science special issue on data (2011). *Science* 331, pp. 639-806.

Taylor, M. (2011). Reform the Ph.D. system or close it down. *Nature* 472, p. 261.

The R Project for Statistical Computing (2011). www.r-project.org

Winckler, G. (2010). "Innovation Strategies of European Universities in the Triangle of Education Research and Innovation". In: Weber, L.E. & Duderstadt, J. D. (eds.) (2010) *University Research for Innovation*, Economica, London, ISBN 978-7178-5797-9.

Winckler G. & Fieder M. (2005). Declining Demand among Students for Science and Engineering? In: Weber, L.E. & Duderstadt, J. D. (eds.) (2005) *Universities and Business Partnering for the Knowledge Society*. Economica, London, ISBN 2-7178-5190-9.

Winckler, G. & Fieder, M. (2010). Kooperation zwischen Universitäten und wissenschaftlichen Fächern. In: W. Mantl, ed. *Phänomenologie des europäischen Wissenschaftssystems*. Nomos Verlag EURAC Research, pp. 303-313.

PART V

•••••••••••••

Engagement with the Wider Community

CHAPTER 17

University 2.0: the University as an economic and social Driver

Rafael Rangel

INTRODUCTION

This paper intends to renew certain paradigms that tend to limit the vision and functions of universities and advance towards the University 2.0, a scheme focused on society and that brings about concrete changes. The University 2.0 works in two great aspects: economic development models and social development models, in collaboration with state government, federal government, private businesses and foundations. By way of example, a description is provided of the case of the Tecnológico de Monterrey System, which has performed a long series of adjustments to become, besides a world-quality educational institution, a decisive agent for social change in Mexico.

In the construction of a commitment with the communities in which our universities are inserted, several challenges must be faced. Certain paradigms must be left behind because they tend to limit the vision and functions of universities and we must advance towards University 2.0, a scheme focused on society and that brings about concrete changes.

With this objective, the set of modifications applied to the organizational structure of a university, the activities and vocation of an educational institution must focus on a radical and visible transformation that brings it to become a new type of institution.

On this path towards strengthening its commitment with society, the Tecnológico de Monterrey System has carried out a long series of adjustments that, over the years, have brought it to be, besides a world-quality educational institution, a decisive social change agent in Mexico.

The Tecnológico de Monterrey System is comprised of four educational institutions:

- The Monterrey Tech Institute, which has 31 campus with 102,832 students in classes taught by 8,500 faculty,
- The TecMilenio University, comprised by 33 campus currently serving 29,012 students,
- The Virtual University, which with a scope that includes 63 countries, serves 13,312 postgraduate students and 129,870 students in social and entrepreneurial programs, and
- The Tec Health, which congregates a school of medicine for close to 2,000 students, research centers, collaborative medical services institutes, a hospital and a health care center.

Among its most relevant activities, it performs an important task through its Research Centers, which employ 2,300 researchers, of whom 272 are members of the National Researchers System, and that are assembled into 126 work groups. The work of these groups generates on average, annually, 42 applications for patents in the areas of biotechnology and life sciences, sustainable development, information and communication technologies, manufacturing and design, mechatronics automotive and aerospace, entrepreneurship and family businesses, management, public policies, education, social sciences and humanities.

Throughout its history, the Tecnológico de Monterrey System has adapted its strategies not only for offering quality education, but also for aiding Mexico in facing its day-to-day challenges.

CHARACTERISTICS OF THE TRADITIONAL UNIVERSITY

In this section, rather than the common approach consisting in disapproving of traditional education by means of the simplification of its characteristics under reductionist points of view, an attempt is made to distinguish certain behaviours that the university has maintained over time and whose existence is not justified. Thus, far from the intention of describing the traditional university as a set of mistakes, it is pertinent that some of the traits that characterize it be recognized.

Among the habitual activities performed by a university, three are highlighted: education, research and extension. Generally, the quantity and quality of the graduates are used as results indicators for the first of these activities; for the second, the quantity and quality of publications, participation in forums and patents obtained; for the third, the number of participants enrolled and, therefore, revenues obtained.

In this sense, it is necessary to note that the visible results of these activities, that is, the aforementioned indicators, reveal a strong tendency to focus primarily on the immediate context where the traditional university exists. The preceding means that the impact that students have on society is restricted almost exclusively to the effect that they can have once they have graduated from the institution, and not before. By this same token, knowledge generated from the work performed by their researchers is, at the most, published in prestigious journals in the corresponding disciplines, participation in international forums is performed in front of academic colleagues, and patents, in the best of cases, seek to highlight the achievements of the applicants, with a limited interest for positively impacting society. Finally, it is convenient to state that traditional universities see extension work as an additional source of revenue, and not as an opportunity for collaborating with social change.

The previous characteristics, in such a manner combined, offer a panoramic view of the nature of the traditional university that is based on an essential trait: its isolation with respect to the society in which it exists and to which it owes itself.

In the face of this scenario, Rosovsky (2002) comments: "External influences on the university have multiplied and they are penetrating its activities with increasing frequency. Government and business are the major sources of influence."

The traditional university fulfils those functions in accordance with how it was conceived, but requires deep critical questionings: are the graduates the only path through which a university must aspire to transform the world? how fruitful for humanity are the investments in research that universities carry out? what are the obligations that all universities must fulfil with respect to the community that have created them? in what sense must the mission, vision and purposes of a university be adjusted with a view to its resolving the issues of the period in which it operates? Before this situation, and in a more optimistic tone, Rosovsky clarifies the following:

"To summarize: the ivory tower does not describe the modern research university: learning and service are always present. External influences are becoming more powerful for many different reasons: the power of government, the search by commercial interests for knowledge within the academy, the perpetual need for more resources within the university, and not least — the opportunity for individual faculty members to make economic gains."

Even, and with respect to the case of Harvard which, also according to Rosovsky, can be applied to other universities, this author states:

"As defined pejoratively, the ivory tower is a myth, because in modern institutions of higher education there has always existed tension between service to the public and

more contemplative scholarship. What the historian Bernard Bailyn (1991) wrote about Harvard a decade ago remains true for many universities in different parts of the world". "Harvard has never been an ivory tower, a closed universe of scholars talking to scholars and students. It has always been, has had to be, open to the world, responsible to its founding and governing community — hence in the service of society — and yet at the same time devoted to the demands of learning for its own sake. That balance between learning and service is the heart of the institution and it has shifted in emphasis from time to time."

From the previous questions, with the crucial nuance provided by Rosovsky, who establishes a fertile platform for a new paradigm, this reflection offers a series of proposals integrated under a single concept: the University 2.0.

THE UNIVERSITY 2.0

Weber (2002) retakes his concepts of *responsiveness* and *responsibilities*, to speak to the duality faced by the university's missions. *Responsiveness* refers to that immediacy which has been spoken to before; this is, it is expected that the university educates professionals prepared for the challenges of the moment, both in the economic aspect as well as in the public sector, and that it offers programs that ensure access to university for the greatest possible number of students, among other conditions. As is palpable, answering society's demands implies more than teaching or research; nevertheless, it is necessary to address the other pole of the duality posed by Weber, and that implies assuming a crucial responsibility with the society where the university is located:

"Universities are one of the oldest surviving institutions, clearly older than modern States. Moreover, they remain practically the only institution able to secure and transmit the cultural heritage of a society, to create new knowledge and to have the professional competences and the right status to analyse social problems independently, scientifically and critically."

The difference then, between *responding* and *being responsible* lies in that, in the first case, universities must be receptive to what society demands of them, while in the second, they must have the ambition to guide insights and proposals for the benefit of society.

Differently from the traditional university, and in concordance with Weber's ideas, the concept of University 2.0 that is proposed in this document, although supported on the same bases, brings each of them to transcend the limits set by the previous model between the activities of an educational institution and the social flow within which it operates. In this manner, the University 2.0 prolongs the effects of education, extension and research towards environments that are beyond the traditional context and have impact on different components of the environment where it functions. This relationship of the University with society, based on the urgency for the integration of priorities and the need for designing educational programs based on what is posed by society, the market, the importance of the research, is described by Williams (2002) in the following terms:

"If the university leaves its graduates generally unprepared for the responsibilities of citizenship, what will be the consequences? College graduates should be prepared to lead lives of civic engagement in addition to individual success. If we are ignorant of our history, government and the fundamental ideals and values that distinguish our society, we cannot be good citizens. Education has been the best predictor of civic involvement, and higher education now serves as the nation's most important common ground and is essential to the future of a democratic society."

Along this same route, the activities of the University 2.0, on the basis of education, research and extension, educate students as citizens with significant knowledge, which is ready for being applied in the appropriate contexts and with ethically focused intentions and purposes, program their extension offerings with a social focus, direct their research work, as well as their publications, participation in forums and patents generation, towards the formulation of pertinent developmental models.

But, beyond that production, and due to said efforts towards transcendence of its work, the University 2.0 generates developmental models appropriate to the context in which it finds itself. These models are, primordially, the core of the institution's work, and, due to that, are replicable by other instances, easily maintained for their permanence and, in general, simple, as well as being generated and owing their permanence to a scheme that, by means of alliances, ensures constant evolution and therefore, its usefulness for each community.

CREATION OF DEVELOPMENT MODELS

The University 2.0 carries out these alliances, the basis of its functioning, with private enterprise, governmental instances and international foundations with which it interacts in long-term relations, clearly established and organically articulated in such a manner that they produce palpable and measurable results.

Among other attributes, this scheme ensures that the developmental models generated are sustainable and transferable so that their use can be extended, with the necessary adaptations, to a great variety of contexts. Among them, the Tecnológico de Monterrey System has concentrated its efforts in fostering two developmental models: economic and social.

Economic development models

With the participation of the state government, the federal government and private businesses, the Tecnológico de Monterrey System is carrying out two main efforts for bringing about Mexico's economic development: the Technological Parks and the Strategic Business Opportunities Observatory:

The Tecnológico de Monterrey System currently has 16 technological parks, to which five, under construction, are about to be added. These parks are structured based on a series of different participating groups that are working in a physical space that includes certain components.

The participating groups are comprised of students, graduates, entrepreneurs, businesses and faculty; these groups carry out their developmental activities in physical spaces that include three components: a section destined to incubating companies, an accelerator for the same and an area destined to facilitating the *landing* process, thanks to which companies are able to establish operations in Mexico.

On the other hand, the Strategic Business Opportunities Observatory is an information system that has the objective of identifying, in each region of the country, those products and sectors with high market potential. This instance, thanks to a vast information platform, drives the creation of businesses and regional economic development by means of products and services such as the *Anatomy of the economic clusters with the greatest impact on Mexico's development*, *The competitiveness of the Mexican States* and the *Identification of strategic opportunities for the development of each Mexican state*, whose contents are published and made available to users by means of different schemes.

Social development models

The social development models, equally transferable and sustainable, have a set of participants appropriate to their purpose: state government, federal government, private institutions and foundations. In this sense, the Monterrey Technological Institute System has concentrated its attention on two fundamental strategies: the Community Learning Centers and the Training Programs for Basic Education Teachers and Administrators.

The Community Learning Centers maintain a strong orientation towards extending quality education throughout the country with support from a technological base (*e-learning*) which contributes sufficient capacity for carrying the Tecnológico de Monterrey System's programs even to places with very difficult access by any other means. As an added value, these centers have facilitated the creation of businesses in different states of Mexico.

From the year 2001 to date, the Tecnológico de Monterrey System has opened 2,329 centers of this type in Mexico, the United States, Central and South America. As result of this work, quality education has been provided to 254,423 persons in these countries, with highly relevant impacts.

It is convenient to highlight that the tutors in these centers, who, in a responsible and solidary manner carry out the most important processes in this effort, are Tecnológico de Monterrey undergraduate students.

On the other hand, the Tecnológico de Monterrey System has devoted itself, using on-line programs and with the support of the Tecnológico de Monterrey's campuses throughout Mexico, to offering training programs for Basic Education Teachers and Administrators of the Mexican governmental educational system, with the objective of supporting their development and increasing the quality of their performance. Among these programs' main achievements are three diploma level courses:

- The Diploma level course in Educational Quality and Teaching Skills
- The Diploma level course in Significant Learning of Mathematics using the PISA and ENLACE approaches for secondary education, and
- The International Diploma level course in Teaching Competencies Monterrey Tec-Cambridge.

Under this heading, between 2006 and 2010, training was provided for 52,129 participants from the different official schooling levels.

CONCLUSION

When facing the high demand of current challenges, governments focus their efforts on what is urgent and on corrective solutions; given this situation, universities must direct their own efforts towards what is important and to preventive solutions.

With the firm conviction that education is the basis for development, the Tecnológico de Monterrey System has implemented different strategies that bring it to comply with the principles that sustain the concept of University 2.0.

Citizens' training of students requires the experience of joining this scheme. This is not merely a social service program: the university has the obligation and the opportunity for reducing the social gap and preventing the disintegration of the structures that sustain humanity by means of deep-rooted, replicable solutions and with a medium- and long-term vision for reducing the malaise of the most vulnerable sectors born from a growing inequity in reference to the distance between their own situation and that of the sectors that have the most. This phenomenon can be called *social warming*, and the only way to reduce this social warming is to bring education and entrepreneurship to each and every human being on the planet.

The tendencies to isolation and limitation corresponding to the traditional university are left behind. Universities must reduce the gap between the sectors that have progressed and those that have fallen behind and must become pillars for the progress of civilization, essence and raison d'être of the notion of University 2.0.

REFERENCES

Bailyn, B. (1991). "Fixing the Turnips". *Harvard Magazine*, March-April Issue.

Rosovsky. H. (2002). "No Ivory Tower: University and Society in the Twenty-First Century". In Hirsch, W. & Weber, L.E. (Eds.), *As the Walls of Academia are Tumbling Down* (13-30) Paris: Economica.

Weber, L.E. (2002). "Universities' Responsiveness and Responsibilities in an Age of Heightened Competition". In Hirsch, W. & Weber, L.E. (Eds.), *As the Walls of Academia are Tumbling Down* (61-72) Paris: Economica.

Williams, H.M. (2002). "The ever Increasing Demands Made on Universities in the United States by Society and Politicians". In Hirsch, W. & Weber, L.E. (Eds.), *As the Walls of Academia are Tumbling Down* (53-60) Paris: Economica.

CHAPTER 18

Research Universities
and sustainable Development
with special Reference to India
and IIT Madras

M. S. Ananth

INTRODUCTION

Rapid advances in technology have had dramatic consequences. The environment that moulded life on earth over many millennia is being altered and even replaced dynamically, endangering the very life whose quality science and technology seek to improve. The overwhelming concern of all societies today is that of sustainability of human civilization on this planet. India is particularly at the crossroads having to meet the challenge of addressing two kinds of basic needs of her population: food, shelter and clothing for one part, and energy, materials and communication for the other. In this context educational institutions have a socially important role to play and an economically important opportunity. Of the three components of education, namely knowledge, know-how and character, they have the responsibility, more than ever before, of building character in their students. They have to cope with the problem of dealing with sustainability as a research and education issue, while preserving their core values and maintaining dynamic equilibrium with their local environment. This paper uses IIT Madras (Indian Institute of Technology) as an example to illustrate the role of premier research institutions in this context. The author recalls Mahatma Gandhi cautioning mankind nearly a hundred years ago about the unsustainable nature of human greed and concludes that it is time for us to revisit traditional wisdom, while looking ahead for a sustainable future.

The present has been described as the "best of times" and the "worst of times" (May, 2005). The "best of times" because science and technology have made living more comfortable than ever before. The "worst of times" because our environment is being altered and even replaced dynamically, endangering the very life whose quality science and technology seek to improve. The focus of all nations today is on sustainable development (SD) that alone can save our planet.

The Stockholm Resolution of 1972 And The Rio Declaration of 1992 (Agenda 21) identified rights and responsibilities for sustainable development. The right is simply that of every human being to live a healthy and productive life in harmony with nature by exploiting the State's resources for sustainable development. Among the many responsibilities are: equitable development and environmental protection globally through cooperation among all nations: in conservation, protection and restoration of the health and integrity of the Earth's ecosystem, in transfer of knowledge as well as technologies for SD, in judicial and administrative facilitation and in countering the effects of any environmental disaster. One of the important components in these declarations is the effective participation of indigenous people, especially women and youth in SD.

THE INDIAN CONTEXT

India is no longer a poor country: she is a rich country in which many poor people live. She is the second largest consumer market. She has the second largest pool of scientists and engineers. She offers the most challenging problems in development. For about 40% of our population, the basic needs are food, shelter and clothing; for about 30% of the urban population, the needs are energy, materials and communication (as in developed countries). The challenge is to address both kinds of needs even though addressing the former set is obviously her priority. In a world in which knowledge is power, India cannot ignore the latter set. In so doing our attitudes will need a significant change. Indians will have to learn to be proud of their nation and for good reasons:

- The clean and healthy nationalism of our independence movement;
- The difficult yet wise choices in at least five important post-independence debates: Democracy vs Totalitarianism, Secularism vs Fundamentalism, Globalization vs Self-reliance, Defence vs Development and Centralization vs Federalization;
- The "green", "white" and "brown" revolutions leading to self-sufficiency in food, milk and oil seeds;
- Achievements in defence, atomic energy, space, manufacturing and software.

However a lot remains to be done. The empowerment of women is critically important for sustainable development. India too has taken some steps in this regard: there are nearly a 1000 colleges exclusively for women, there is a National Commission for women to look into legal issues and so on. We celebrate Women's day on 8 March every year. Yet the very existence of such provisions, important as they are, reflects the lack of gender-equality in our society. In the final analysis it is educated women who can make a difference to the status of all women in our society.

THE CHANGING ENVIRONMENT

The all-pervasive nature of technology has resulted not only in a large variety of jobs that require new skills, but also in a rapid obsolescence of traditional skills. Society demands higher education to cater to a much wider spectrum of technical skills and to provide continuing education to upgrade the skills of the older graduates. The competitive nature of Indian society, the increase in consumerism and the information explosion have increased the accountability of educational institutions. The highly competitive and increasingly global economy has forced Indian industry to look for emerging technologies and R&D to provide the global competitive edge. Professional institutions have a socially important role to play and an economically important opportunity in this context.

The changed environment calls for greater flexibility and responsiveness in the university. Coping with these changes while preserving its core values (Strategic Directions Report, Indiana University, 1996) poses a variety of challenges. IIT Madras, for example, has articulated its core values in its Strategic Plan (The Strategic Plan of IIT Madras — Vision 2010): developing human resources to serve the nation, recognizing teaching as a unifying activity, nurturing integrity, creativity and academic freedom and retaining a willingness to experiment with new paradigms. Institutions of higher learning will have to cope with contemporary social realities and influence government policy, especially with regard to sustainable development, while remaining apolitical, autonomous, socially relevant and yet sufficiently detached to serve the need for objective evaluation and constructive criticism. They should also actively protect themselves from all outside efforts to abridge their autonomy and academic freedom. Universities in India must devise ways of providing education for at least four to five times the present student population within the next decade, while maintaining their dedication to excellence and high standards of performance.

Universities have to work out a healthy balance between specialization that caters to a current technological demand and wholeness of knowledge. They should educate students to cope with the confusion of values that follow from technology's threats to sweep humanity off its cultural feet. Rapidity of change creates a historical attitude. Universities have the problem of identifying and preserving that which is good in its past, while dealing with contemporaneity and relevance. They should create a vibrant community of learning that is willing to articulate, profess and defend its core values, while being open to healthy winds of change.

ENGINEERING EDUCATION

To discuss the challenges in the context of engineering education we briefly describe the three well-defined aspects of engineering education: *knowledge, know-how and character*.

Knowledge enables one to understand what one learns in relation to what one already knows. Each knowledge-area has an invariant core consisting of fundamentals based on universal laws that provide a phenomenological description and an outer layer of constantly improving empirical knowledge of particular systems and of constantly changing applications of increasing sophistication and complexity (Ananth, 1997). The invariant core provides the continuity in education while the applications provide the excitement and the education relevant to the current demands of the industry. Although the fundamental theory is itself invariant, it should be emphasized that applications constantly provide new insights into the working of the theory. The rapidly changing tools (the most obvious one being the computer and associated software) have had a very significant role on our entire approach to education.

Know-how is the ability to put knowledge to work. It requires the purposeful organization of knowledge from many different areas of learning. Know-how is taught through design courses, project work, industrial training and other opportunities for individual initiative and creativity. Elective courses on technology often provide descriptions of successfully implemented know-how, while those on emerging technologies describe attempts at doing so.

Character is the most important component of education. It is easy to recognize, but character-building processes are difficult to define and implement. Character traits such as honesty, truthfulness, integrity, initiative, competitiveness, self-esteem, leadership and the ability to work both alone and as part of a team have an invariant value. In the pre-scientific and pre-technological era preceding the wars, religion played a significant role in character-building even among the intelligentsia. This is no longer true and what compounds the problem is the fact that the intelligentsia have an increasingly disproportionate role in social development. The educational institutions now, more than ever before, have the responsibility of character-building.

EDUCATION AS A SURVIVAL TOOL

Education has become an essential tool for survival (Ananth, 1997). Rapid advances in technology have had dramatic consequences. The environment that moulded life on earth over many millennia was until the last century hardly influenced by the life that it so generously supports. Technology has changed this situation drastically. The environment is being altered and even replaced dynamically. The survival of life in the old environment was governed by a process of natural selection — species that adapted better to the environment survived better than those that did not. The new environment — especially the modern, urban environment in which most of mankind lives — is almost entirely artificial and survival in such an environment is governed by what one might describe as "artificial selection".

The human species in the new environment has two levels of survival. There is, on the one hand, the level of economic survival of the individual and, on the other, that of the civilization as a whole. There is often a conflict of interest between the two levels of survival. During the last decade, capitalism has emerged as the only sustainable form of government and advances in technology have magnified manifold the profit-making capacity of commercial organizations, these conflicts have become diverse and at the same time more subtle.

Thus the tools for the survival of the individual or institution (TSI) are *information, resourcefulness, an elastic conscience and some professional skills.* Information is picked up from many places — television, radio, newspapers, magazines and even conversations with others. This component has increased explosively in this age of information and communication technology. Resourcefulness is picked up "on the street". The urban environment today throws together people with widely different world views and occupational compulsions: the social worker and the marketing manager, the environmentalist and the industrialist, the conservative and the liberal, and so on. It is increasingly necessary for each to be able to appreciate the other's point of view and to develop an elasticity of conscience for peaceful coexistence and meaningful debate. Except for professional skills, formal engineering education has little to do with the imparting of these tools.

On the other hand, the tools for the survival of a civilization as a whole (TSC) are *knowledge, an abiding faith in the power of professional knowledge to improve the quality of life of all people and a sense of ethics, objectivity, aesthetics and history.* Educational institutions have an important role to play in this regard.

The objective of the university is basically to educate and prepare students for a variety of challenging careers. Such an education places powerful tools for the survival of the individual in the hands of the student at an impressionable age. It should therefore simultaneously attempt to equip the student with tools for the survival of civilization as a whole; it should, for example, inculcate in the student a sense of responsibility, an awareness of the ability of these tools to help society, as well as to cause damage.

The larger aim of institutions of higher learning is to serve the nation by producing value-added human resources through *education*, by creating a wealth of knowledge through *research* and by developing and transferring technology as a *service* in the sustainable development of the country and the improvement of the quality of life of our people.

THE TSC AND TSI COMPONENTS OF PROGRAMME

Courses in the humanities, social sciences and management should attempt to inculcate in the student a sense of history, ethics and social responsibility. The purpose of the humanities component is to persuade the professional to entertain questions regarding ends and values so that he does not lose the human direction in the pursuit of technological development and to caution him that a purely rational view of the world based on the inevitability of scientific progress cannot cope with a fragmented, culturally diverse society full of complex emotional problems. These are predominantly tools for the survival of the civilisation. A keen sense of aesthetics in the approach to and in the solution of technological problems is also largely a matter dealing with TSC. Aesthetics is a concept that varies with time, and today it is important to inculcate in the student the notion that the more eco-friendly and the more sustainable a technology, the more aesthetically pleasing and in the long run more economical it is likely to be.

The "know-how" imparting component should include exposure to real-life problems and teamwork and opportunities for individual initiatives such as participation in research, in seminars or in design competitions. The importance of teamwork, as well as that of individual initiative as tools for the survival of the civilisation cannot be over-emphasised, especially in the Indian context.

UNIVERSITY EDUCATION

The university is recognized as the most traditional of all our institutions and yet it is the major instrument of the change in our social, economic and political systems in the last few decades. Higher education therefore has an important role to play in sustainable development. The most important factors in the new paradigm are:

• Multidisciplinary education with environment as part of all learning;
• Values and ethics as part of all learning;

- Equity, justice, cultural and environmental sustainability should be the prime goals of economy and qualitative change should be a measure of success in development;
- The learning process has to be a lifelong one.

The educational programmes should include courses on sustainability, extramural talks by experts from the government, as well as non-governmental organizations. The most important task of the University is perhaps that of developing the right attitude of the students towards nature.

RESEARCH

Faculty at IITM, as in other research universities all over, are working on emerging challenges such as climate change, loss of biodiversity, resource depletion and deteriorating environmental quality at the local, regional and global levels. The global and interdisciplinary nature of these problems, their complexity and the urgency of the situation make it necessary for premier research and teaching institutions across the world to join hands with each other and with other stakeholders in order to develop solutions to problems of sustainability. The Indo German Centre for Sustainability (IGCS) at IIT Madras (Rajan, Murty & Philip, 2011) has been set up to take up long-term research and developmental studies which would eventually lead to sustainable water, waste, energy and land management practices. The objective of IGCS is to synergize the efforts of Indian and German faculty and students in research, training and policy advocacy in the context of sustainability. As a first step towards achieving this goal, the centre plans to take up research studies in two major areas: water and waste management for the sustainable development of urban river basins. The sub-themes of interest are: water resources management, wastewater management, solid waste management, flood protection and river/stream water quality, management of wetlands and of air quality.

The water resources management sub-theme focuses on evolving macro-level management strategies and practices for efficient (from an economic perspective) and equitable (from a societal perspective) utilization of water resources in the urban and the semi-urban areas of the basin addressing different competing needs, such as agricultural, drinking water supply, industrial and flood mitigation, while preserving the ecological integrity. Other sub-themes will focus on a sub-basin level, but in a holistic fashion. The sub-basin level studies will involve management of (i) wastewater (ii) flood water disposal and water quality in rivers and streams, (iii) air quality, (iv) solid waste and (v) wetlands. Emphasis will be laid on analysing the technical, social, economic and political context of the basin alongside changes in its hydrological and environmental dimensions over the past two decades, in an attempt to arrive at meaningful policies for basin management in the future.

LOCAL SUSTAINABILITY

At a local level the idea of sustainability is built into the vision of IIT Madras (The Strategic Plan of IIT Madras — Vision 2010): *To be an academic institution in dynamic equilibrium with its social, ecological and economic environment, striving continuously for excellence in education, research and technological service to the nation.*

The implementation of this vision is clearly in three parts — activities that strive to achieve dynamic equilibrium with social, ecological and economic environments. The idea of the first part is to try and solve problems for society using appropriate, not necessarily high, technology. For example, IIT Madras has developed affordable import substitutes in medicine, devices for children with cerebral palsy and devices to reduce drudgery in coir spinning. There are about 30 on-going projects in which many faculty and students are involved. Their work is their source of satisfaction not monetary rewards.

IIT Madras is located in a 230 acres (93 hectares) of sylvan forest land with over 400 species of plants, 100 species of non-native plants and over 10 species of invasive plants and 200 species of animals. The second aspect of the vision is about managing this incredibly beautiful, yet sensitive ecological environment. A bio-diversity study by a group of experts, posted on the website of IIT Madras, has helped formulate suitable maintenance measures needed to preserve our biodiversity. Two pocket books, one on animals and one on plants, provide information to the stakeholders in a manner that helps them get involved meaningfully in this activity.

The IIT Madras Research Park, the first university-based research park in India, attempts to help IIT Madras achieve dynamic equilibrium with its economic environment. Innovation and competetiveness are recognized today as being central to any nation's survival in today's globalized world. Louis Pasteur observed that "discovery is the result of chance meeting a prepared mind". The role of university-based research parks in the Silicon Valley during the last decade of the 20th century presents a lesson for others in this regard. Names of Indian students, especially those from the IITs, appear in a significant fraction of the IPR generated during this period. It appears as if the IITs were preparing minds that met "chance" in Silicon Valley! Innovation resulted from bringing together unlike minds: R&D personnel from the industry who understand the value of the ideas in the marketplace, professors who are subject matter experts with a width of vision and students with new ideas and a spirit to conquer the world. The IIT Madras Research Park hopes to play a significant role in making India the design house of the world!

CONCLUDING OBSERVATIONS

Nearly a hundred years ago, Mahatma Gandhi said "nature gives us enough for our need, but not for our greed". With the currently accepted ideas of development (which are beginning to be questioned seriously), what we are asking today is: "Can we be greedy and sustainable?" The answer is most probably a resounding "no". However, it is heartening to note that we are increasingly willing to reframe the question and gearing up to face the answers squarely. I think it is important to try and answer this question with humility which appears to be a highly under-rated virtue today and faith in God. Traditional Indian wisdom holds that the latter two qualities are pre-requisites for human beings to follow the path of "dharma" (righteousness). While looking outward to understand the world around us, it is necessary to simultaneously look inwards to understand one's Self. I believe that it is time for us to revisit traditional wisdom while looking ahead for a sustainable future.

REFERENCES

Ananth, M. S. (1997) *The Invariant Core of Engineering Education*, Proceedings of the INAE Conference on Engineering Education, 75-78, Addison-Wessley, New Delhi.

May, Robert. (2005). Presidential Address, The Royal Society, London, 30 November.

Rajan, S. C., Murty, B. S. & Philip, L. (2011) IGCS proposal from IIT Madras to the Department of Science and Technology, India, March 2011.

Strategic Directions Report (1996). Indiana University. Currently stored in the Indiana University's Online Library Catalogue.

The Strategic Plan of IIT Madras — Vision 2010. Available on the website of IIT Madras, www.iitm.ac.in as a pdf document under About Us.

CHAPTER

Regional Engagement and Sustainability: University of Aveiro in Portugal

Maria Héléna Nazaré

INTRODUCTION

I n the framework of the demographic evolution foreseen up to 2050, major issues related to sustainability include: food, natural resources (water in particular) and energy. These "grand societal challenges" affect all aspects of our lives and are not contained within geographical borders or specific scientific disciplines.

Starting from the imbalance in population and riches across the world, this paper concentrates on the European situation where the demographic decline **constitutes the most serious problem** and focuses on the role of universities and possible action in three inter-related areas:

- Research: Carrying out cutting-edge work and making it valuable for the global world and at the same time relevant for local/regional communities.
- Teaching and learning: Paying particular attention to the education mission, including lifelong learning and retraining, within the framework of both ageing population and shifting labour needs.
- Cooperation with society: Universities as promoters of good practices in regional networking for post-secondary education (municipalities, industry, professional and secondary schools) leading to better qualification of the workforce, improving employment and promoting the integration of immigrants.

To illustrate the above, I will present some initiatives, some of which have been taken by the University of Aveiro in Portugal, as an example of a responsible and inclusive institution, a research-oriented university which has managed to became an asset to its region. These examples will show very clearly that institutional autonomy and leadership are fundamental requisites to muster the creativity that is needed to deal with such complex issues.

SETTING THE SCENE

Population imbalance

The 2008 Revision of United Nations' *World Population Prospects* estimates that the world population will reach 7 billion this year (2011) and rise to 9 billion by 2050. The additional 2 billion will come predominantly from developing countries, while the population in developed countries is expected to remain more or less stable due to migration from developing regions, which is expected to occur at a rate of 2.4 million persons per year.

In both developed and developing regions, the workforce (25-60-year-olds) is now about 604 million and 2.4 billion respectively. However, by 2050 the developed regions will have decreased to 528 million while the developing regions will increase continuously, reaching 3.6 billion in 2050 and continuing to rise. While this presents, with great acuity, the problem of employment creation in these regions, some of the developed world will have to face a different set of complex issues, namely ageing and the sustainability of its social model, which needs adequate public policies to help keep the situation under control.

If one takes a closer look at Europe, one of the developed regions, the overall stability of the population is due not so much to immigrants, but to an increase in life expectancy compensated by a decrease in fertility (1.5 in 2010 compared with 2.19 in 1975).

Europe's population, of 732 million in 2010, is expected to register a 6% decrease, and stand at 691 million by 2050, assuming a medium variant of fertility and life expectancy; however, in the same period, the population aged 15-59 years will decrease by 30%, from 459 million to 351 million, while the age group above 60 will increase from 192 to 302 million. That is to say that by 2050 the working population will be about the same size as the senior (over 60) population group (U.N. Dept of Economics and Social Affairs, 2008).

According to the OECD, the ratio of the population 65+ to the population age 20-64 in the E.U., which is already higher than that of the United States and the OECD average, will have doubled its present value, by 2050 (Whiteford).

This constitutes the **major threat** to the sustainability of the European economy and welfare model. It could undermine social cohesion and cause generational tensions. Social security costs (pensions and health care) will skyrocket — as is already happening! — and will place an incredible tax burden on the working-age group. At the same time, welcoming and integrating the *needed* immigrants will require complex and expensive public policies, which will be difficult to explain to the public at large in times of financial scarcity.

Europe is a very diverse region, in demographic terms too, and big differences are observed, which are likely to add to the problem. Eastern Europe faces ageing, as well as huge decreases in the overall population. Countries like Bulgaria, Estonia, Latvia, Lithuania, Poland and Romania present population decline due the cumulative effects of decrease in fertility and emigration that is not compensated by immigration, whereas in Southern Europe (Greece, Italy, Portugal and Spain), the decline in fertility has so far been somewhat compensated by immigration.

Immigrants and social exclusion

In many European countries immigration and international migrants are not seen as a source of dynamism to the economy or to the innovative capacity of the country; on the contrary, they are perceived as competitors for jobs in a low performing market, leading to social tensions. Social exclusion mechanisms affect school performance of second-generation migrants who, therefore, seldom reach university, resulting in a waste of talent. Proper policies of full and responsible integration are generally needed. This in itself is an extremely complex issue very much outside the scope of this paper, hence I will concentrate only on the aspect related to the role of universities in promoting the integration of international migrants and present how the University of Aveiro in Portugal provides access to educational programmes for those who have interrupted their studies and/or have not followed a conventional educational path.

Challenges for higher education in Europe

Due to demographics and directed policies, the levels of participation in tertiary education of students from developing countries are increasing. The world tertiary student population is at the moment 150 million, with European attainment rates being exceeded by Australia, Canada, Japan, Korea and the U.S. China produces more HE graduates than anywhere else in the world, with a growing trend of about 18% in the last decade (Münz *et al.*, 2007). Labour market analysts forecast that by 2020 35% of all EU jobs will require high-level qualifications.

The E.U. 2020 **targets** of having at least 40% of 30-34-year-olds completing tertiary education, of reducing school drop-out rates below 10%, and of having 3% of the E.U.'s GDP invested in R&D&I, which translates into having another million jobs in research, can only be achieved if universities are able to respond on different fronts: as excellent knowledge producers, as education institutions (learning/teaching and behaviour role models), as part of the innovation chain and as public policy *watchers, promoters and drivers*.

Nevertheless, the huge difference in potential higher education student population across Europe is in itself a strong threat to the attainment of those targets and **constitutes the most serious problem** which, nowadays, undermines the economic development of Europe as a whole and threatens its future. In the 27 E.U. states, the 20-24 age group will *decrease* by 23.3% in 2050, but in Eastern Europe figures for that decrease are alarming, and range from 36.2% in Hungary to 60.5% in Bulgaria (Ritzen, 2009). Five countries, only, (Denmark, Luxembourg, the Netherlands, Sweden and the U.K.) have an expected increase in the 20-24 age group population.

Addressing these issues requires a modernized idea of the university as an organization with a segmented mission and clear vision; an institution that recognizes the need for knowledge creation through interaction among the different disciplines, from the hard sciences and technologies to humanities and social sciences, not with the ambition of solving all the problems, but to start addressing them in a more adequate way by pooling resources and drawing expertise from different fields.

Above all it requires institutional autonomy and appropriate incentives enabling universities to organize themselves internally and successfully address the need for reconfiguration of the HE&R&D network, to increase the quality and performance that Europe, again as a whole, needs.

The role of universities

For centuries the mission of the university has been, almost exclusively, to educate the future governing elites and to *search for true knowledge in solitude and freedom* (the Humboldt model). This ideology, which brought much academic success to the European universities, also created in academia strong resistance to interacting with the world outside its walls. Internally, a climate of persistent indifference to the importance and developments in the *other* disciplines, as well as strong competition among them, has contributed to the lack of knowledge integration. These two factors are detrimental to the quality of cutting-edge research, to its relevance and to innovation, contributing also to less efficiency in the use of resources.

Furthermore, only recently did European universities begin to include cooperation with society as a part of their mission and acknowledge the fact accordingly. But it is only through partnership with other private and public players, companies, municipalities, etc. that innovation can be introduced in the knowledge supply chain and strategic advances realized. In 2011, after a tremendous economic crisis, we start acknowledging that it is still not enough; we need to become **really** attractive to students from outside Europe, to welcome national mature cohorts, to support public polices directed to immigrant integration and family protection. The "Grand Societal Challenges" can only be addressed by a truly multidisciplinary approach in research and in education.

The questions in this paper are: i) Can a single institution, the university, respond to the demands of producing high-quality knowledge that would be available and important at global level, but also using that asset locally, contributing to the regional economic development and job creation? ii) Can a single institution educate and train research workers and citizens and, at the same time, have a policy of curriculum development and learning methodologies which responds to the needs of mature students?

The two questions have a positive answer if one is not tied to a set model of the university and if institutions are allowed to be creative in order to deliver high-quality performance in education, research and innovation. **Yes, it is possible to have differentiation within the same institution,** or if one prefers, to have a **segmented mission within a common set of values,** provided that universities are granted the appropriate degree of autonomy and use it accordingly. However, that may not be enough! An appropriate set of incentives is needed to drive change, and to transform Europe, which has some of the better universities in the world, into a vibrant region of learning and knowledge creation where multiculturalism is a reality.

Established universities, research organizations and higher education institutions must recognize the absolute need for reorganization of the landscape, be it through mergers or other, more loosely coupled, forms of association of institutions (not only HE but R&D and business) to enable a higher degree of coordination, thus maximising synergies, achieving the needed critical mass, avoiding waste and guaranteeing highest standard in the delivery of integrated research, education and innovation.

I turn to University of Aveiro (UA), to illustrate how some of the above has been attempted with reasonable success, given the complexity of the issues. To make matters clear from the start, one should emphasize the fact that UA is, in European terms, a research-led university, with 50% of the budget earned in a competitive way from different sources, national and international, and 46% of postgraduate students (Master and Ph.D.)

PORTUGAL AND THE AVEIRO REGION

I begin with the expected evolution of population in Portugal up to 2050 (Pinto). Starting from the actual 10.7 million inhabitants, of which 18% are older than 65, Portugal follows the trend of the rest of Europe: the overall population will be about the same by 2050, but with increasing numbers in the 65+ group, while the 0-14 group is getting smaller (Figure 1).

Figure 1: Population Evolution PT

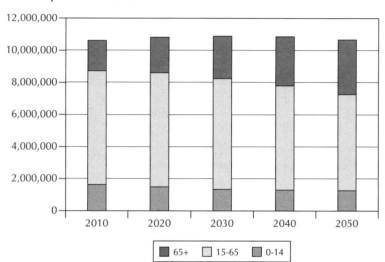

Higher education in Portugal consists of a binary system including universities and polytechnics with different missions. Polytechnics are more professionally oriented, not carrying out fundamental research, and allowed to grant degrees of Bachelor and professional Master only, (in other European countries, these institutions are called Universities of Applied Sciences [Finland] or *Fachochulen* [Germany]). Total enrolment in higher education of the 20-year-old cohort is about 36%, which is similar to the European average, although still lower than that of most industrialized regions. This has resulted mainly from an increase in non-university higher education (polytechnics), which grew at a considerably higher rate than that of university education.

Similarly to what happens in Europe, the 20-24 age group is expected to decrease by from 5.3% (2010) to 4.5% (2050), relative to the total population (Figure 2). In 2008, the Centro of Portugal region accounts, roughly, for 11% of this age group.

The fraction of total graduates aged 30-34 was 21.6% in 2008, which is low when compared to the current European average (31%) and targets (i.e.,

Figure 2: Portugal 20-44 age cohort

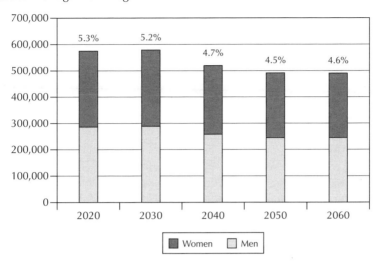

40% for 2020). The tertiary qualifications of the Portuguese population aged 25-64 are still below the OECD average. In 2008, 14% of the 25-64-year-old Portuguese population had a tertiary degree, while the OECD average was 28% (Ministry of Science, 2011). Although enrolment in tertiary education of adults aged 30-34 has increased by about 20% over the last three years (2005-2009), it is still relatively low and about 4.1% (2009) of the corresponding age group. Adult enrolment in tertiary education for the 35-49-year-old cohort was as low as 2% in 2009. Hence we face problems with the competitiveness of the country partly due to the low qualification of the working force.

THE UNIVERSITY OF AVEIRO, A DIVERSE INSTITUTION

The University of Aveiro is located mainly in Aveiro, a medium-sized city in Portugal's central region, in the heart of an industrial region and a centre for commerce and services. Integrated in the community and region, UA has a **strong research dimension** and offers a range of university bachelor, master and Ph.D. programmes, but also (since 1993) polytechnic undergraduate programmes, professional masters, and (since 2003) post-secondary vocational programmes.

Having built a profile based on sciences, engineering and technology, it includes today health-related areas including a master's in Medicine. Research-wise, Telecommunications, Electronics, Materials & Nano-sci-

Total n° of registered students (2010/2011)	14768
University:	
Undergraduate (1st cycle)	4567
Integrated masters:	2431
MSc, PhD:	3787
Polytechnic schools:	
Underfraduate 1st cycle:	2424
Post-graduate 2nd cycle (professional)	304
Post-secondary:	1050
Teaching Staff:	1000

ences, Environment & Marine Studies and Education are recognized as areas of excellence.

Why and how such integrated model?

Until the 1990s, only one polytechnic school, ISCA, the Institute for Accountancy and Administration existed in the Aveiro region. However, the available socio-economic indicators pointed to the lack of a polytechnic offer in technology that would cater for the local needs of the industry, while research results had more impact internationally (papers in high-impact factor journals, n° of Ph.D.s, patents etc) than regional relevance. This reality, together with an opening in the framework education law in 1986, led the university to propose the creation and integration in the university of one polytechnic school for Technology and Management located in Águeda, the heart of the industrial region, 50km from Aveiro City. Nowadays the university includes four polytechnic schools which cover the needs of the whole region, including not only technology, management and design, but also the health professions. In the meantime, ISCA asked to be integrated into the UA.

Thus, Aveiro University took on the challenge of becoming more than a node in the Portuguese higher education network: it **became a network in itself**. It embodies university departments, research units, interface units, polytechnic schools and a relevant vocational education network. This enables the construction of individual education paths, from post-secondary vocational education to doctoral programmes, including vocational training, 1st and 2nd cycle degrees, and different kinds of postgraduate specialisations.

In this context, the role of the polytechnic schools is particularly relevant. These schools are vocational training centres within the network and play other important roles regarding cooperation with the region. We consider this model of integration, within the same institution, of university departments (16 at the moment), research labs (16) and four polytechnic schools, although requiring strong leadership and being a challenge to the management, an asset of the University which gives us the needed instruments to help tackling the serious social problems we face one decade into the 21st century: those of retraining the workforce and so fighting unemployment, responding to shifting needs of the labour market and promoting regional innovation; at the same time ALSO producing knowledge, through interdisciplinary research teams, which may contribute to find answers to, climate change, excessive use of fossil energy production, scarcity of food, etc.

Organization and Profile

The UA does not follow the traditional faculty structure, but is organized in university departments and polytechnic schools in an almost textbook example of a matrix organization (Figure 3). This matrix structure allows it to mobilise for each education programme, research area or line of cooperation with society, the human and material resources from the relevant disciplinary domain, allowing extensive flexibility, fast response and efficiency. This structure enhances the possibility of multidisciplinary approaches in interface areas which are fundamental for tackling the challenges faced by society today.

Research

Research has always been and continues to be a central priority. The approach to research has been to focus on innovative fields, taking advantage of transdisciplinarity and **prioritising a small number** of areas.

The high standard of research is visible in achievement through international evaluation. There are now four Associated Laboratories on Campus. These have a special status awarded by the Portuguese Ministry of Science and Technology to large interdisciplinary and exceptional research units: the Centre for Environmental and Marine Studies (CESAM), the Centre for Research in Ceramics and Composite Materials (CICECO), the Telecommunications Institute (IT) and the Institute for Nano-Structures, Nano-Modelling and Nano-Manufacturing (I3N), plus another three research units graded as excellent, Mechanical Engineering, Organic and Food Chemistry and Education.

Inter-institutional agreements with other universities and RPO and protocols with companies for the realization of internships and projects support the transfer of technology, in addition to the development of applied research.

Figure 3: Matrix organisation: a) for study programmes; b) for research units

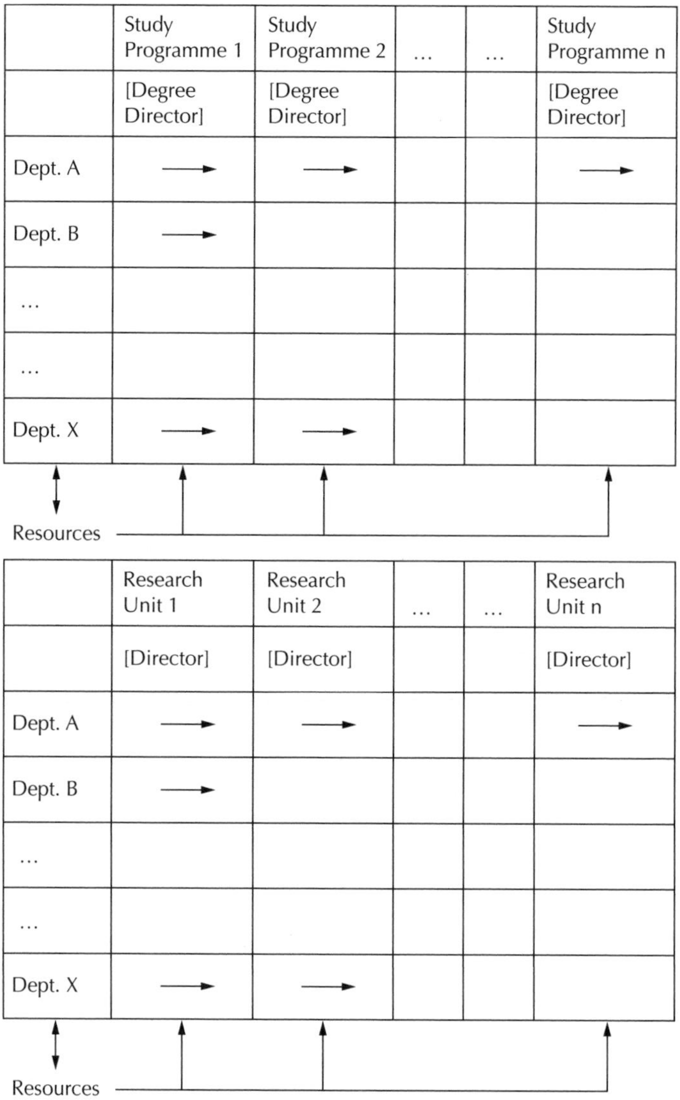

	Study Programme 1	Study Programme 2	...	...	Study Programme n
	[Degree Director]	[Degree Director]			[Degree Director]
Dept. A	—▶	—▶			—▶
Dept. B	—▶				
...					
...					
Dept. X	—▶	—▶			

Resources

	Research Unit 1	Research Unit 2	...	...	Research Unit n
	[Director]	[Director]			[Director]
Dept. A	—▶	—▶			—▶
Dept. B	—▶				
...					
...					
Dept. X	—▶	—▶			

Resources

Several research units function in collaboration with other renowned entities in their field for the benefit of research and technology transfer, in particular: the Telecommunications Institute (*IT*) (of which Portugal Telecom is an associate and shareholder). A strong relationship with companies is an important facet of UA's identity. It participates in numerous associations, programmes and projects in collaboration with business and industry, notably with Portugal Telecom (PT), Nokia-Siemens network and Martifer. The Nokia-Siemens Corporation research and innovation centre (employing about 200 engineers) is located on campus.

The UA is now (2011) once again responding to societal priorities by pooling research assets into coherent work programmes focused on: ageing (IT, I3N and Mechanical Engineering), natural resources and food (CESAM and Organic and Food Chemistry) with a specifically allocation of funds for the next five years.

Interaction with the region, boosting employment through qualification of the workforce: Making use of our polytechnic schools

The "post-secondary education" offered by UA through its polytechnic schools comprises a set of Technological Specialisation programmes (*CETs*), which are professionally-oriented programmes leading to a level 4 vocational qualification certificate. These programmes promote a training path that combines qualification and professional skills and competences with the possibility of proceeding to higher education. The main focus of each programme is placed on practical training (typically half of the total number of ECTS in each programme is attributed to work experience).

The *CETs* are delivered in partnership with secondary schools, technological centres, professional training centres, entrepreneurial/industrial associations or city councils, among others.

In promoting these programmes, UA seeks to enhance technical and vocational education among young people in areas which lack qualified personnel; to offer a new training opportunity for potential learners who are either not motivated for "academic" education or have left school too early; to encourage the return of mature persons to school (workers or unemployed) for professional re-qualification and technical training; and to modify the negative dominant view about technical education in Portugal.

In so doing, the university is strongly improving its links with the leading economic and political sectors in the region in a variety of ways. Firstly, the choice of programmes and training actions is made in close cooperation with the leading industrial sectors and reflects their priorities in terms of training needs. In addition, curricula are designed by teams involving the university

and industry; programme courses are implemented by teams made up of university lecturers, industry professionals and training experts, and there is always a significant commitment from the local authorities.

In conclusion, the CET offer not only constitutes a de-localised educational network but, by the nature of the partnerships it involves, also provides a number of opportunities for dialogue and service-sharing with the region.

UA: LINK IN THE INNOVATION CHAIN

Clusters and other innovation promoting projects

UA is strongly involved in the national programme for the implementation of "Collective efficiency strategies". We have been active agents with firms and other institutions in the setting up inter-institutional dynamics leading to the creation of clusters in the areas of energy, sea, health, food industry, information technology, communication and electronics, engineering and tooling, petro-chemistry, habitat and creative industries.

UA is currently also acting as leader for the Science and Innovation Park in close proximity to the university campus.

Joint programmes with nearby municipalities: Recently, the University has taken the lead to an innovative approach, in the link with the region, which goes far beyond the traditional focus on technology transfer and spin out activities, enlarging and enhancing the contribution that the university, and indeed research activities and scientific knowledge, can have in shaping (local and regional) public policy and development trajectories. The university and the association of the 11 municipalities of the Aveiro region, with about 375,000 inhabitants, decided to take a bold step by traditional standards: they established a partnership for the design of a regional development programme, going beyond the role of piecemeal consultancy work and aiming at a joint approach to regional development. In fact, rather than hiring a group of academics as consultants, this initiative had a dual aim. The first was to mobilize the diversity of disciplinary knowledge existing in the university to help address the problems and expectations of the different municipalities and the regional community as a whole; the second was to set in motion the process of creating a shared understanding of regional development dynamics and challenges, which indeed could and should lead to a re-interpretation of needs and expectations.

As mutual knowledge and trust were further developed between the local authorities and the university, a wider range of initiatives were taken. At the level of the Association of Local Authorities, a new programme was prepared focused on "Urban Networks for Innovation and Competitiveness", which was built around five selected topics: education, culture, health, climate change and entrepreneurship (including social entrepreneurship). A new relationship between local government, small and medium-sized firms and the university is emerging, integrating local public policy, economic modernisation and revitalisation, and multidisciplinary research activity.

Lifelong learning and tools for widening access: UA provides access to its educational programmes for those who have interrupted their studies and/or have not followed a conventional educational path. By this we mean access under special conditions for students over the age of 23 (+23s) or holding a CET diploma to enrol in full 1st cycle programmes. The UA also created conditions for candidates in general to enrol in specific modules or isolated disciplines (at the level of the 1st, 2nd or 3rd cycle).

Both the graduates from the +23s programme and from the CETs have contributed significantly to boost employment in the region.

Outside the scope of standard degree programmes, UA created two entities which contribute to the provision of continuing education programmes: the Association for Professional Training and Research (*UNAVE*), legally autonomous but controlled by UA, its main shareholder, and the Integrated Teacher Education Centre (*CIFOP*). *UNAVE* offers short-term professional and vocational programmes for university staff and the general population, while *CIFOP* provides a range of courses and programmes for teachers.

This set of continuing education opportunities is sought by working students in general, company employees who need specific knowledge and professionals of various kinds who are looking for re-qualification or to update their knowledge and skills. Continuing education is recognized through the attribution of a certificate, whether or not it leads to a formal degree.

Lifelong learning is growing and its organization is at present being rethought. Mechanisms for the welcoming and guidance of candidates, as well as for the recognition of prior learning, are being put in place.

CONCLUSION

In difficult times, creativity and initiative are attributes required of all Institutions, Universities are amongst the oldest institutions in Europe. Contrary to the belief that they do not change, I hope to have shown exactly the opposite: Universities not only change, adapting themselves to new circumstances and societal needs, but also and foremost they can lead and be drivers of change.

These changes are not consensual within the academic community. Very often such strong interaction with the outside world, be it from getting involved with high-tech companies in doing applied research (the most accepted form of cooperation) to helping design educational programmes and paths to adult learners (immigrants or nationals), is seen as not within university mission and harmful in different ways. I believe that the 21st century needs a different and more embracing understanding of the university mission.

REFERENCES

Ministry of Science, Technology and Higher Education, Portugal (2011). *A New Landscape for Science, Technology and Tertiary Education in Portugal, Sample Background Information*.

Münz, R., Straubhaar, T., Vadean, F. & Vadean, N. (2007) *What are the migrants contributions to employment and growth? A European approach*, HWWI Migration Research Group.

Pinto, M.-L. *Private communication*, Data Instituto Nacional de Estatística Portugal.

Ritzen, J. (2009). *A Chance for European Universities*, Amsterdam University Press.

Teichler, U. & Büger, S. (2005) *The Changing Numbers and Composition of Student Enrolment in Europe and Japan*, Centre for Research on Higher Education and Work. University of Kassel, Germany.

United Nations Department of Economics and Social Affairs (2008). Population Division. *World Population Prospects: The 2008 revision.*

Whiteford, P. Anticipating Population Ageing — Challenges and Responses, Social Policy Division, OECD. http://www.oecd.org/dataoecd/19/20/31639461.pdf

CHAPTER

Sustaining World-Class Universities: Who Pays and How?

Howard Newby and Alastair Flett

INTRODUCTION

Higher education is now unarguably a global activity. In a digitally connected world, where capital and labour flow increasingly freely without hindrance from national boundaries, universities are no less subject to the forces of globalization than any other part of service sector economy. Universities from all over the world now have truly global reach, are engaged in international competition and collaboration, source talent worldwide, contribute to global grand challenges, and are increasingly asked to serve as a cog in the gearbox between international, national and regional economies. Our performance is measured against institutions from across the globe with league tables and a host of other metrics.

In this contribution I will sketch out what I describe as the macro challenge of higher education funding — the relationship between the growth — or massification — of HE, in pursuit of civic and economic benefit, the quality of work the sector can offer, and how the financial burden is shared between public and private purses. I will then use the recent debate in England as to how universities should be funded as a useful prism through which this question might be considered, looking at the impacts and costs, both financial and other, that the solution arrived at will impose on the key trio of stakeholders in HE: the universities themselves, the students, and government and the wider civic society.

Before I begin in earnest though, some caveats.

Throughout, I deliberately I use the term university as convenient short-hand for the type of organization that delivers higher education. This is not to deny the role that other providers play in HE in delivering high quality tertiary education (most notably in the U.K., the contribution made by Further Education Colleges in this field), but simply to reflect what I think most of us mean by the type of institution that has the kind of global perspective I have just outlined, and judges its performance in the way I have described.

Also, for reasons of time and space, this contribution focuses very heavily on the sustainability of undergraduate learning and teaching. Again, this is not to deny the importance of other activities — indeed many of us would point to the role of research, to give an obvious example, in making our universities world class — and it is interesting to note many of the points I will make about funding for teaching may be extrapolated to cover other areas as well.

THE MACRO CHALLENGE

Despite the impact globalization is having on universities, they have, traditionally, been very much creatures of the nation state. This is most obviously true in Europe, but also in many other countries, notwithstanding the presence in some cases of a significant private university sector. Indeed, some universities were created almost as symbols of national pride and prestige. Moreover, as the 20th century progressed, they were also seen as extensions of the welfare state: the provision of higher education was, haltingly, seen as part of a more generalized welfare state provision for the education of its citizens.

Universities were traditionally rather elite institutions educating only a very small minority of their national populations. But, as we know, in the latter half of the 20th century this began to change, first in the U.S. and then elsewhere where the opportunity to engage in higher education was extended to a much larger proportion of the population. This has often been referred to as the transition from an elite to a mass system of higher education. In so far as how higher education was publically provided, this, of course, placed ever increasing claims upon the public purse. As the need for these resources grew, so governments began to examine rather more forensically the purposes of this investment. If one adds into this the growing recognition over the last 20 years that higher education is an important component of global economic competitiveness, then one produces a situation of quite immense change in the balance of the relationship between universities and the state.

This can perhaps best be summarized by stating that it was once the role of governments to provide for the purposes of universities, but it is now the role of universities to provide for the purposes of government. And this has been a quite pronounced shift which has taken place in the lifetime of most of today's academics. As the resourcing has gone up, so governments have asked more and more stridently, what are universities for? And the answer has been rather depressingly utilitarian: the purposes of universities have not been seen to be intrinsic — that is the cultivation of the student mind or the pursuit of higher learning for its own sake — but rather ulterior — the contribution to economic competitiveness, social inclusion and other non-educational goals. And slowly, as the knowledge economy argument has taken hold, so governments have come to view universities as being far too important to the pursuit of these policy goals to be left to their own devices. Governments, in other words, increasingly regard universities as delivery agencies for public policy goals.

To give my own institution as an example, when the University of Liverpool was granted its charter in 1881, it relied almost exclusively on donations from local funders who were less concerned about the higher level skills agenda, as we would call it today, than "the ennoblement of life and the advancement of learning". But, as universities became dominated by public funding, so their mission was defined in terms, increasingly, of a public policy agenda: driving economic regeneration and growth, upholding national cultures, and inculcating civilizing influences in their predominantly young student body. As far as the formal relationship between universities and the state was concerned, this manifested itself, as the 20th century progressed, in an increasing tension all over Europe between state control on the one hand and institutional autonomy on the other. We move rapidly from "the ennoblement of life and the advancement of learning" to the world of "something for something".

Yet embedded in this was a genuine paradox. Governments came to recognize the importance of higher education in the pursuit of public policy goals, and in so far as universities were public institutions, governments were called upon increasingly to provide the resources commensurate with the needs of these universities to undertake research, engage in knowledge exchange, and teach their students. And then, as the 20th century drew to a close, the forces of globalization compounded these dilemmas.

Thus governments all over the world have sought to expand their higher education systems as they recognized the need to raise the skills levels of their populations — all governments want to engage in what these days we call "massification". However, they also wish to enhance the quality of the higher education that is provided so that this massification can take place without compromising standards. And, as if this were not enough, governments all over the world wish to achieve both of these things while also, wherever possible, reducing the burden on the taxpayer.

These three factors produce a kind of force field in higher education policy which is common to most countries, even though the particular ways in which this manifests itself in practice varies according to the precise political context. For example, in some countries there has not been the level of expansion of higher education which one might otherwise have expected if it was solely based upon the needs of the population. The U.K., indeed, might be considered such a case. In other countries quality was allowed to slip, whatever public rhetoric may otherwise suggest, and this was certainly the case in some continental European countries where the quality of undergraduate higher education has undoubtedly declined over the last 30 or 40 years. And in some other countries there has been a concerted drive to reduce the fiscal burden of higher education by actively seeking a mixture of private and public finance, either in the form of increasing student fees or allowing private — whether for-profit or not for-profit — universities to establish themselves. Indeed the most common feature worldwide has been the response of the enormous social and economic demand for higher education to be met by the private sector rather than the public sector.

In this respect the United States is unusual in that many of its elite universities are private. In most other countries in the world where private higher education is common, the private sector has been created in order to take up the excess demand which cannot possibly be accommodated in the elite public universities. But whatever the particular character of private universities, most of the higher education expansion worldwide lies in this part of the sector and one only has to look at Asia, Latin America and most of central and eastern Europe to observe this.

THE ENGLISH FUNDING REGIME: THE BROWNE REVIEW AND SUBSEQUENT

Without wishing to focus exclusively on the British, and more specifically, the English experience, I know that many of you will be interested in the recent radical changes to the student finance regime there and the effects it is likely to have on the sector. As well as instructive in demonstrating the importance of communicating change effectively, they highlight through practical example a number of the issues I have raised.

Tuition fees were introduced in 1998 in response to the Dearing report's identification of a looming shortfall of funding for HE in the U.K., and since then funding for British and other E.U. undergraduates has operated on a mixed economy basis. Students pay a heavily subsidized fee (currently around £3,300) with, in many cases — depending on the subject studied — a much higher contribution to their education funded by the state, allocated to universities through the Higher Education Funding Council for England. Fees for non-E.U. students are unregulated. Through this funding model, government also controls the numbers of students entering HE, and indeed over the last couple of years has introduced significant disincentives to over-recruitment.

Students can access a variety of financial support packages to ensure they meet their financial obligations while at university, ranging from scholarships and bursary schemes run by the universities themselves, to government-backed loans and grants, the latter being dependent on household income.

However, as you will be aware, things change. We are now at a tipping point in England, where funding for teaching is shifting irrevocably from a system predominantly supported by the general taxpayer, to one where it is the direct beneficiaries — the students themselves — who will foot the lion's share of the bill.

In November 2009 it was announced that the former Chief Executive of BP, Lord Browne of Maddingley, would lead an Independent Review of Higher Education Funding and Student Finance. The review made good a promise — made in 2004 as part of the attempt to persuade Labour rebels to support the lifting of the fee cap to £3,000 — to review how much students should be charged for attending university.

In announcing the review, Lord Mandelson said that it would consider "the balance of contributions to universities by taxpayers, students, graduates and employers" to university finances. In short the focus of the review would be on who paid for higher education. It is interesting to note that at the time there was little or no appetite on the part of any of the major political parties for a broader discussion around changes to the role of HE. So, while Browne could address one element of the macro challenge I sketched out earlier — the fiscal burden generated by HE — it would not debate the other two corners of the force field — massification and quality. In fact both were taken as a given and the need to make them sustainable was implicitly offered as reasons for the review.

Securing a Sustainable Future for Higher Education, the title given to the final report of the Browne Review, was published in October 2010. In summarizing the panel's findings, Lord Browne highlighted a number of points, including:

- the continued massification of the sector in the U.K., noting that now 45% of people between the ages of 18 and 30 entered HE compared to 39% a decade previously;
- the need to maintain and improve the quality of provision, largely through the mechanism of student choice and resultant competition, including deregulation of student numbers;
- and that — and this is probably worth quoting in full as it gets to the heart of the force field I described earlier — "a degree is of benefit to both the holder, through higher levels of social contribution and higher lifetime earnings, and to the nation, through higher economic growth rates and the improved health of society", and that "getting the balance of funding appropriate to reflect these benefits is essential if funding is to be sustainable."

Of course, it was this last item that, understandably, drew the attention of the public, the media and politicians, and led to one of the more trenchant debates on higher education policy in recent years.

So, what did Browne recommend? Most eye-catchingly that the cap on fees be lifted entirely, supported by improved information for applicants, thus, when combined with deregulation of student numbers, allowing market forces to be used to improve the quality of provision. This shifting of the financial burden from state to student would occur post graduation, and only apply to those who could afford it, based on their earnings. He went on to recommend that universities needed to be aware of their social responsibilities, and, far from seeing the lifting of the cap as a licence to print money, ensure that measures were put in place, not just to avoid less well off applicants from being put off from coming to university, but to actively encourage them to do so, and to support them in making the most of their time there.

Government would continue to play a key role in the financing of HE by paying upfront for student support in the form of loans and maintenance grants, although this would in effect be funded by a tapered levy payable by universities on all fees above £6,000. Student loans would only become repayable after the graduate passed a defined income threshold, and would be written off after 30 years.

While undoubtedly it was the fees and funding elements of Browne that captured the public's imagination, it is probably worth noting here, that in amongst the more detailed recommendations perhaps the most radical suggestion of them all gained little publicity. The deregulation of student numbers would, combined with the removal of the fee cap, have led to the genuine marketization of undergraduate provision in England, albeit one backed by the government acting as the customer's banker through its provision of loans to those that needed them.

So, what happened next? In Harold McMillan's phrase, "Events, dear boy, events."

As you will know, six months before the publication of the Browne Report, Britain went to the polls. With no single party able to claim a majority, for the first time since the National Government of the Second World War a coalition between two of the three major political parties was required in order to form a government. Of course, intrinsic to the success of any coalition is the ability to compromise, and the publication of Browne and the debate over the funding of higher education that ensued are a lesson in how that process of compromise can shape policy.

Other than relatively bland statements about growth and widening access, the Conservative manifesto had, perhaps wisely, stopped short of promising anything other than "careful consideration" of Browne. The Liberal Democrats, meanwhile, had promised to scrap tuition fees. However, with the coalition's commitment to cutting the national deficit the key theme behind much of its decision-making, a position was agreed whereby:

- The HE budget would be slashed, with a 40% reduction in state funding for teaching, a figure that grows to roughly 80% once the government's frontloading of student support arrangements is stripped out of the equation.
- Continued support for STEM subjects, with the implication that the cuts in funding will be drawn from classroom based subjects.
- A fee cap of £9,000.
- Any institution wishing to charge above £6,000 would be subject to an Access Agreement and have to contribute an element of its additional fee income to widening access measures specific to the University (for example, bursaries or outreach work) and to a National Scholarship Scheme.
- Fees would be paid up front on behalf of students, with graduates repaying these loans at a progressive rate once their income exceeds £21,000. Maintenance grants would be given to those from lower income households, while maintenance loans would also be available.

So, what are the implications for this system of student finance? In examining this, I will focus in turn on the universities themselves, the students and the government and wider civic society.

UNIVERSITIES

As you would expect, I and my colleagues in England have spent a considerable amount of time over the last six months grappling with what the implications of the new student finance regime will be for universities. These seem to fall into three clear groupings: the financial impact, the fundamental redrawing of the relationship between a university and its students, and, by extension, the impacts of increasing marketization.

If one were being particularly provocative, it could be argued that in one sense, the financial impacts on universities of the new funding arrangements are negligible. After all, a reduction in funding from one source (the government) has been accompanied by an increase in available funding from another (tuition fees). However, that would be to seriously misread the situation.

As you will know, the vast majority of universities in England have now stated that they expect to charge the maximum fee of £9,000 a year. The reasons for this are clear. Rough calculations show that for any university offering a mix of science and classroom based subjects, more than £8,000 of that fee is required just to make up for the lost state funding for teaching. When the need to improve widening access activity is taken into account, along with reductions in capital funding, the £9,000 universities can charge suddenly does not sound very much.

Moreover, given changes in student expectation that the new system encourages, universities will be under increasing pressure to invest additional funds in this area, through improved student accommodation, better teaching facilities or any other of the range of factors that contribute to a student's overall satisfaction with their time at university. Thus, by changing the funding mechanism in this way, universities are encouraged to spend more in order to compete, making the sustainability equation a harder one to resolve.

What is absolutely clear is that the new arrangements fundamentally redraw the relationship between a university and its students. While already on an unsound footing, the argument for higher education as some sort of paternalistic movement, dealing out what's best for students — and by extension society — regardless of their views on the matter, has now been thoroughly decommissioned. Students, already in some senses viewing themselves as being in the position of buying a good when they come to university, will vote with their feet. If universities do not provide what they want, they will not go.

I think what is particularly interesting here is the slightly awkward way in which the market looks like it will develop as things stand. By maintaining regulatory control over the number of students in the system, an element of protection is offered to institutions. As long as demand continues to outstrip the number of places, competition and marketization will actually occur in the opposite way to that which the government intends — the applicant will be the supplier, offering their talent to selecting universities rather than vice versa. Given the funding constraints described above, there will not be the scope to impact on the market in the traditional way — by altering prices to stimulate demand.

However, it would be a mistake to assume a more marketized world is not far off. We are already seeing an HE landscape in which private providers, and indeed conceivably overseas providers, are beginning to be encouraged to test the waters, and offer "off quota" places, which may well begin to relieve the pressure in the system here. It is not unreasonable to assume that much of this provision will be focussed at the cheaper end of the market, by organizations that do not have expensive estates or research infrastructures to maintain. Slowly but surely we will see different groupings of potential students making a variety of trade offs in their mind between the cost, type and quality of education they will receive. It will be interesting to see whether the sector responds to this through an increasingly obvious hierarchy of institutions or a more diverse, niche market led approach.

STUDENTS

But how — other than through the gradual development of increased choice — will the students be impacted on? To state the obvious, the answer is in the pocket. There is no getting away from the fact that the fiscal burden generated by HE will be placed more squarely on graduates' shoulders than ever before.

In amongst the myriad complexities of the psychology of tuition fees, how they are set, and how what terminology we use for their repayment, an interesting, yet frustratingly unprovable point emerges.

By setting a maximum fee level of £9,000, what the government have done is set a guide price for the sector. Quite apart from the (very sound) financial reasons for universities wishing to charge the maximum, we can now add the fact that should you not, you are tacitly admitting that the student experience and outcomes offered by your institution are not of the highest quality. Because of this, I would argue that more students will pay a fee of £9,000, or close to it, than would have been the case had the government simply elected to remove the cap altogether and forced universities to truly analyse their position in the sector.

What is more provable is that setting the fee at the £9,000 has prevented universities from generating the level of additional fee income needed to operate a truly needs blind admissions process. At these fee levels universities need some element of fee from all of their students to survive. We could argue then that, paradoxically, the government's policy of capping fees in an attempt to widen access and promote social mobility has had the reverse effect.

There is also one other area where the impact of the funding changes will be felt by students. Although we will have to see, it seems entirely likely that the increase in fees for undergraduates, and particularly the way this is perceived as debt, will suppress demand for Masters provision, and potentially Doctoral study too. If you graduate owing in excess of £30,000 you have to be pretty sure that further study is what you want to do to defer your earning power for another year — or possibly four or five — while, in all likelihood generating further debts in order to support yourself. Will we see a situation where postgraduate study adapts to become a vocational matter — either in terms of direct entry into a profession (Law, Teaching and so on), or as a grounding for an academic career — with associated student finance packages for each?

GOVERNMENT AND THE CIVIC SOCIETY

And how will government and the wider civic society be impacted by the new funding arrangements?

In one sense, it is difficult to analyse how the U.K. government will pay for Britain's contribution to a world class higher education system, as we are currently operating in somewhat of a policy vacuum. Given the pressure to reduce the national debt, details of the revised student finance package have been agreed prior to the development of a white paper on higher education policy.

However, one impact looks — on the face of it — reasonably clear. By removing roughly 80% of the Teaching Grant, it would appear there is a significant financial saving. However, once the pump priming of the new student finance system is put into place, this reduces to 40%. These are only initial figures, though. The government's calculations have been based on the need to underwrite the costs associated with universities charging an average fee of £7,500. As what I have already said implies, this looks to be a misguided assumption.

Options are currently being discussed as to how this can be dealt with, ranging from reducing the unit of resource attributable to each student, or simply reducing the number of fundable students, and inviting universities to bid for the remainder, at least partly on a cost basis.

Social mobility is one policy goal that it appears clear those on all sides of the political divide wish to encourage, and of course, universities play their role in that. I have already alluded to how setting the fee at £9,000 might impact on that from the individual student's perspective, but I think it bears noting that not only students who come from a low income household and go on to become doctors or lawyers benefits from this. In the right numbers, all of society benefits, and we must be careful not to lose sight of this. Any dampening of social mobility caused by setting the fee at this level should not be forgotten.

Another by-product of the approach to funding proposed in England is the increasingly utilitarian attitude towards higher education it represents. In addressing a number of financial issues, the government are, of course, looking for value for money. They make this explicit by saying that, despite the major cuts in public spending, funding for the STEM and other strategically important but vulnerable subjects will be maintained. Without wishing to get into a debate about which has the most worth, a degree in Medicine, or a degree in underwater basket weaving, it does present issues to those who see diversity as one of HE's strengths, and who hold the academic pursuit as valuable in its own right.

And finally, although my focus here has been on how government aims and objectives will be impacted by changes in how HE is funded, I should also note that industry too, can expect to feel their effects. There is a logical progression from asking graduates — as primary beneficiaries — to pay for their education, to asking industry to pay an element of the cost in return for having a steady stream of ready to work graduates injected into the economy on an annual basis.

By and large, industry has remained quiet on the issue, but there are at least three obvious ways in which, encouraged by the need to incentivize the most able students to come and work for them, they might contribute. The more traditional method would be for a company to identify the more able students and offer to part fund their study in return for an agreed period of employment with them. Secondly, we might see a greater onus on industry to work with HE in curriculum design and even to contribute to some elements of provision, again in the interests of ensuring that their needs as future employers are met. And thirdly, it is highly likely that industry will increasingly cut out the middle man and, in a twist on the privatization of HE, begin to offer their own range of degrees. In the U.K., for instance, just before Christmas 2010, McDonalds announced plans to run its own foundation degree in business management for its employees. The idea of companies having their own degree awarding powers will, I think, become increasingly common.

CONCLUDING THOUGHTS

In drawing this contribution to a close, I would like to bring to your attention three key areas that, in light of changes to the funding scheme in England, and in particular a greater private contribution, will require careful thought. Recognizing that HE is both a public and private good, they strike me as areas in which effort, dialogue and goodwill will be essential in order to ensure the right balance is struck.

Firstly, in a world where students will, for better or for worse act like customers, and universities will seek greater private contributions, universities must be careful not to become slaves to the market and endlessly reconfigure what they offer simply to meet perceived demand. They must work hard to retain their unique characteristics and place they have in society. We need to think about how should we actively engage in the debate about the purpose of higher education, and convince people of our position.

Secondly, we cannot afford to think that issues of widening access and social mobility can be dealt with formulaically through the student finance package alone. Universities need to do more in terms of outreach activity, aspiration raising and so on, but it is also clear that this is not just an HE issue. More needs to be done through schools, support networks and other areas of social policy to ensure that no one is excluded from the merit based society that we all say we want. How can the linkages required through all aspects of social policy be found and resourced.

And finally, we all need to be aware that we cannot have it all. In a world of scarce resources there is an interesting question to be answered in relation to institutional autonomy and the government's regulatory position in light of the new funding settlement and where it seems to be leading us. Is it inconsistent for a sector to be pushed towards privatization in terms of its funding, but for government to retain its grip on sector policy and regulation in the way that it currently shows no sign of giving up?

CHAPTER 21

Globalization, Universities and Sustainability Effects

John Niland

INTRODUCTION

More than ever, research universities live in an environment heavily impacted by the forces of globalization. Their strategic thinking continues to be influenced by robust competition in critical areas such as funding, enrolment, recruitment and reputation, as well as by developments beyond their national higher education systems. Intensifying these abiding effects of globalization, a series of recent dramatic events, ranging from financial markets meltdown to massive cyclones, earthquakes and stricken nuclear reactors, heighten the sense of some urgency to better understand how sustainability imperatives will shape the future.

Alarm over the future of the modern research university has spawned something of a Jeremiah literature, touching on the evils of "academic capitalism" (Slaughter & Rhoades, 2004), the radical "restructuring of academic work and careers" (Schuster & Finkelstein, 2006), and the idea that "colleges are wasting our money and failing our kids" (Hacker & Dreifus, 2010). An abiding theme across this writing is the dangerous world in which universities now find themselves, although the diagnosed fault lines vary from the "blizzard of KPIs, management accounting software and the intrusion of corporate values" (Brooks, 2011) to Taylor's (2010) argument that "as with Wall Street and Detroit", American higher education "must be rigorously regulated and completely restructured". Whatever the merits of either extreme, they serve to underscore a rising unease about the very sustainability of research universities, at least in their modern form.

UNIVERSITIES AND THE IDEA OF SUSTAINABILITY

In recent years *sustainability* has become something of an issue *du jour* in corporate reporting and public policy discussions. It has many subtleties, but in essence is the challenge of how to survive and thrive, while leaving future generations unburdened by our actions. The practicalities of sustainability go well beyond environmental measures, and, with increasingly sophisticated corporate reporting required in many parts of the world, public companies have developed a keen awareness of integrated performance the idea of the triple bottom line:

"The success of companies in the 21st century is bound up with three interdependent subsystems the environment, the social and political system and the global economy... in short, planet, people and profit are inextricably intertwined." (IDSA, 2009, p. 11).

Universities are being similarly influenced, and while, globalization brings many corporate analogies knocking at their door, there are important differences. Some might even see the preservation of a *sui generis* standard as a sustainability issue in itself. In any event, for universities the idea of sustainability is best presented in two dimensions.

The **first dimension** relates to the central role of research universities in discovering and disseminating new knowledge that better informs the climate-change debate and other meta-environmental concerns. This effort ranges from "green revolution" research and teaching, embracing the basic science of climate change, through to engineering applications and on to policy development and implementation strategies. Other research contributions come from such areas as micro finance theory and application, through to national park conservation and management courses. Virtually every academic discipline can connect with the idea of sustainability, and most do.

The **second dimension** applies the idea of sustainability to the university as an institution and involves triple bottom line measurement. Here the focus primarily is on actions which serve to balance the books through time, to ensure a viable future financially as a *genuine* research university. This is not just avoiding bankruptcy, which universities seldom if ever encounter (so far!), but entails strategies designed to maintain the very DNA of a research university. Attention to sustainability brings a new awareness for universities of the need to manage operational risk, capital and budgetary risk, market risk, regulatory risk and reputational risk categories long familiar to the corporate sector, and now central to sustainability objectives in research universities as they grapple with the competitive environment engendered by globalization, the Global Financial Crisis of 2008-09 and its long echoes. Through international revenue generation, universities are even caught up now in managing risk associated with legislation covering anti-money laundering and anti-terrorism.

For a research university, sustainability means maintaining standing in the eyes of stakeholders, particularly alumni and prospective students, but donors are also important, as are international ranking bodies and credit rating agencies. This in turn raises some interesting questions: from a sustainability perspective, is a research university's standing set in a zero sum or positive sum sense? Is it relative or absolute? How will the meaning of a research university and the concept of its "standing" change over the next 25 years? What are the markers of institutional sustainability? Beyond this, many research universities now seek to be good environmental citizens, including operating with a zero carbon footprint (or some such critical environmental standard), and reporting outcomes in one of the global sustainability reporting regimes.

Looked at this way, sustainability is a well nuanced idea which invites multiple perspectives. The focus of this paper is less with the role of university research and teaching (the first dimension), and more with issues connected to institutional sustainability (the second dimension), though there are cross-over points. Particular issues to ponder are grouped under three subheadings:

1. those highlighted by the effects of the Global Financial Crisis (or Great Recession) and its continuing aftermath, especially the new funding landscape: effects arising from profound budget trauma; privatization trends; the emerging role of rating agencies and debt issuance; and the rise in Asia of cutting-edge research and universities of world standing.

2. those to do with an emerging paradigm shift in how modern research universities build international alliances, particularly through integrated branch campuses, and the active role of governments bent on nation building exercises through strategic higher education enhancement;

3. those to do with the sustainability practices of universities as institutions with a significant environmental footprint in their own right: the growing sophistication of "green and clean" campus operations; student engagement with the sustainability movement; and universities' nascent participation in public environmental reporting regimes, particularly the Global Reporting Initiative (GRI).

In each of these areas, sustainability actions and strategies inevitably impact on governance, which is taken here to mean that system of checks, balances and oversight determining legitimacy in decision-making. For a university, this involves students, faculty, academic managers and trustees. Governance operates at the level of the discipline and academic department, at the institutional level and in relations beyond the university, as with corporates, NGOs, foundations and, critically, governments and regulators. Governance effects, viewed through the lens of sustainability, are examined in each section.

SUSTAINABILITY AND UNIVERSITY FUNDING

The effects of the Global Financial Crisis (GFC) are profound, with virtually no corner of society escaping the maelstrom sweeping out of Wall Street (and now compounded by further debt drama in Europe and the U.S.) Many research universities have been hit with underperforming endowments and/or by large cuts to government funding, driven by the burden of rising State debt levels. This has come as a rude wake-up call, and, while it may be too early to be sure of the longer run implications, they are bound to carry institutional sustainability effects.

Bearing in mind that no two universities are the same, and that national contexts differ markedly, this section examines some of the possible risks and opportunities thrown up by unprecedented pressures on university financing and quite profound shifts in the funding landscape, post the GFC.

The Public Purse

A common line of response for universities beset with powerful budget problems has been to cut programs, limit faculty recruitment and increase casualization, reengineer cost structures, and sell off extraneous; assets even more challenging, perhaps, amalgamate departments and disciplines internally and contemplate merger externally. But these scenarios in the past have played out in isolated institutions rather than being system wide. This time it is different, with the GFC generating far wider and deeper effects globally than anything in living memory. And looking forward, all of this is in the context of an average national gross debt burden sitting at 100% of GDP across OECD countries, compounded by ever rising government spending-to-GDP ratios: in the past decade alone, the figure for Britain rose from 36.6% to 47.2% and for the U.S. from 32.8 to 42.2%. (OECD reporting).

Looked at through the lens of sustainability, three diverse challenges can be highlighted. For one thing, presidents and their governing bodies will need to implement the more difficult vertical budget cuts to protect areas of excellence and reprioritise, rather than the easier option of spreading the pain evenly through horizontal cuts. Another challenge will be to break down disciplinary barriers and seek out new delivery arrangements. Third, the GFC has lacerated the private pension holdings of many U.S. faculty, creating some rising concern that an academy already ageing will grow even older through delayed retirements decisions. The sustainability concern is over a lost generation of younger scholars irrevocably moving into other careers.

In contrast to the U.S., U.K. and European experience, many Asian universities seem less impacted by the GFC, and in some countries, such as Singapore, Hong Kong and China, governments are actually boosting funding in line with nation building strategies. The move in Hong Kong to fully fund, for all eight universities, a shift from a three-year British-style undergraduate program to a four-year program more common in the U.S., effective in 2012, has entailed a massive infusion of government funds. The recent report of The Royal Society (2011) highlights the rising tide of Chinese scientific research output:

"China has leapfrogged into second place behind the United States in world scientific publication rankings, having overtaken Japan, Britain, Germany and France... and is on course to overtake the U.S. within two years... China is also on course to overtake Japan in annual registrations of U.S. patents by 2028, having registered 1,655 in 2009 compared with only 90 a decade earlier." (SCMP, 2011).

The Royal Society notes, however, these figures represent quantity and not necessarily quality, as would be reflected in the recognized benchmark of citations. Yet the trend is clear and powerful.

The obvious question to ponder is whether we are witnessing a fundamental shift in the geographic axis of leading research activity. In broad terms, this would put research universities in the East on a stronger sustainability footing, and may well see a loss in some sustainability for those in the West, in a comparative if not absolute sense.

The Private Purse

Even before the GFC, most OECD countries were searching for ways to move university funding off the public purse. This *privatization effect* reflects growing pressures on the tax dollar from other big public expenditure areas such as health, community welfare and defence and national security, at a time of rising demand for student places. Given demographic effects and geopolitical reality, these pressures are not likely to lessen, and indeed are often accentuated by burgeoning public debt.

Two main non-government (or private) revenue streams are evident: *first*, a growing requirement by governments for local students to cover a significant part of the cost of their education; and, *second*, the waves of full fee paying international students driven by globalization, well evident since the 1990s, but now more intense as universities strive to keep pace with one another in a dimension important to both international rankings and credit rating exercises, not to mention funding.

Since the mid-1990s Australia has led OECD countries in developing income contingent, deferred liability student loans that enable the government to effectively shift the weight to the private side of the cost equation, for the most part without electoral backlash (Chapman, 2010). The impact of this, reinforced by the growing number of full fee paying international students, is evident in Figure 1: in 1996 the split between public and private (or at least non-public) revenue was 62/38, but by 2009 this had reversed to 45/55. This trend is unlikely to lessen, as the leading research universities lobby the government to substantially deregulate fee setting. A similar, but more aggressive, story is unfolding in the U.K., post the Browne Report (2010). Even in California, where uniform tuition regimes throughout the State system has been traditional public policy, Berkeley Chancellor Robert Brigeneau is pressing for differentiation options.

Figure 1: Proportion of Contribution to Australian Universities' Revenue by Government and by Non-Government Sources: 1995 to 2009 (constant dollars)

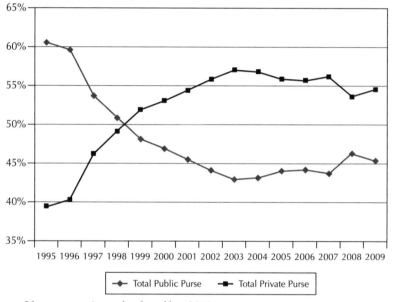

Source: Universities Australia data files, 2010.

The growth in international student fee income has been particularly strong, but more so in some countries than others. From just 600,000 international students in 1975 we now see "around 3.5 million students travelling abroad to study each year", generating more than "$35 billion a year in English-speaking countries alone" (Davis, 2010, p. 21). In Australia, about 17% of university operating budgets is contributed by international student fees, a three fold percentage increase in the past 15 years. This is more than double the OECD average, and four fold that of such countries as Sweden, the Netherlands and the U.S.

The high incidence of international study in Australia carries the implication that other national systems have some scope for expansion, should competitive pressures drive policy in that direction. But there are also risks as a university drives up local tuition and extends its dependence on offshore income. These range from shifting government visa policies to foreign exchange volatility and national financial crises; from overstretched infrastructure to resentment by local citizens that their children are being squeezed out of university places; even to the proposition advanced by Peter Thiel that a bubble is building in higher education, as happened through unsustainable price and debt profiles in the US housing market (Thiel, 2010).

The Debt Purse

Globalization, with its rising competition to maintain and advance standing, changes the mental set within which university presidents and their governing bodies think about strategy. This is now being illustrated by the engagement with rating agencies, to facilitate bond issuance and secured debt. Moody's regularly reports on universities in Australia, Canada, Singapore, Mexico, the United Kingdom and, most commonly, in the United States where "universities have been accessing capital markets directly for longer than universities in other nations". Moody's rates around 500 universities and colleges in the U.S., and for public universities there, the median debt in the pre-GFC period grew from $101m in 2003 to $162m in 2008:

"As (U.S.) universities expanded their research, educational and student-life facilities to meet rising demand for their services, they developed more ambitious strategic and capital plans. To fund these plans, they faced strong incentives to maximise financial assets invested in high-performing endowment pools in order to increase their resources to a greater level over the long-term. Long-term investment management became, in effect, a core business line of the university because it was generating institutional resources much like private fundraising and student tuition." (Moody's, 2010).

For the United Kingdom, Standard & Poor's (S&Ps) regularly reviews the credit worthiness of leading universities, focussing on those with international reputations and placed in the top 150 in *The Times/QS* rankings: "more research intensive universities (will) benefit relative to universities that do less research" due to the effects of government funding policy on full economic costing (FEC), which are likely to help entrench their comparative advantage. Similarly, the Research Assessment Exercise (RAE) exercise can "have an added significance in affecting the reputation of a university, and therefore its ability to attract prospective students and research contracts" (S&P, 2008 October). But there are risks, and a sustainability challenge:

"Maintaining global competitiveness will continue to require investment in staff and infrastructure. For many universities, this may mean accepting greater financial risk

in the short term, in the hope of strengthening their overall competitiveness in the longer term. In this more competitive and global (and therefore less regulated) environment, we would expect the credit differentials of UK universities to widen, with certain universities ceasing to exist." (S&P, 2008 October).

The point may be less whether universities assuming sizeable debt can service and repay it, but rather how this limits future degrees of freedom in setting priorities and budgeting. Put another way, research universities may be able to repay their debts as and when they fall due, but will they "be able to fulfil their missions at the same time?" This will be a critical sustainability issue over the next decade or two.

The rating agencies have signalled they will be alert to international student flows, measured not just in numbers, but in the academic strength of the first preference pool, hedged by a spread of source countries. This in turn will heighten the role of the university's offshore marketing and quality control protocols. Governance structures and practices, as well as the capacity of senior management, invariably are examined. Infrastructure management and planned maintenance, and the absence of chronic internal departmental deficits, are other declared areas for attention by the rating agencies. Standard & Poor's (2008 July) notes that even a university's international ranking is in the mix because "somewhat unpredictable movements in league tables can also have a big impact on demand for a particular university."

On the evidence publically available, universities issuing bonds and assuming debt do so mostly for quite strategic and competitive purposes, with an eye to sustaining and advancing their standing. Private sector joint ventures seem well suited to the planned debt issuance model now emerging. A target area for private sector capital-raising is student accommodation, which is particularly important in the competitive environment of international student recruitment. (Lucas, 2010, p. 57).

Governance Implications

The Global Financial Crisis, and enduring competition for standing and sustainability, is leading universities to think differently about funding strategies. Government is also more (not less) influential, a paradox captured by Moody's statement in its rating of Macquarie University: "Because higher education is Australia's third largest export and an integral part of public policy goals, Moody's believes that the Commonwealth would likely step in to provide emergency assistance to Australian universities in a crisis situation." (Moody's, 2010).

It seems inevitable that as research universities strive to compete on a global front, with less base load funding support from their home governments, the work of the rating agencies will become more important (seemingly having recovered from the reputational damage given their role in the GFC!) Their reference points and processes will come to have some influence on how research universities govern and manage themselves. Financial literacy and trusteeship values rather than representational styles are bound to figure even more prominently in a governing body's skill-mix. This, for example, was part of the thinking when the University of Hong Kong radically restructured its governing council in 2007, away from the traditional "elected" model to an "assured skills-mix" model. (Niland, 2009).

Other governance issues arise from the changing role of government. Con-tributions from the public purse may lessen, but this is unlikely to lighten their sense of fiduciary duty or interest in strategic oversight. As the role of the pri-vate purse increases, government will extend its orientation to consumer pro-tection, through quality assurance bodies, and will assume an underwriter role and brand protector. Rating agencies indicate they will take into account the preparedness of government to step in and save an institution whose bank-ruptcy could damage the nation's higher education brand.

Other governance effects can be expected from the growing presence in public universities of students making a significant contribution to the cost of their education. The demand for support services and an involvement in shap-ing course structures, if not content and standards, occurs. Higher and more pervasive fee regimes is one factor in driving new course delivery modes, rang-ing from year-round teaching to enable faster progression and therefore earlier entry into the workforce, to some online attendance for on-campus students. Ubiquitous social media facilitates campus wide communication among stu-dents, including teaching evaluation and commentary. The combined effect is to give students a stronger presence in the informal (but powerful) gover-nance networks of a university.

TRANSNATIONAL EDUCATION AND SUSTAINABILITY

One manifestation of globalization has been the international activity of research universities over the past 25 years, initially through the recruitment of offshore students and collaborative alliances between institutions. There were also isolated examples of cross border mobility of universities themselves. With a few exceptions, such as INSEAD in Singapore, branch campuses mostly entailed fly-in-fly-out arrangements for faculty, and physically were located in short term leased space in a partner university. Exit plans were sim-ple, and without any major risk issues for the home campus. Now, the sheer number of branch campuses is a major marker of internationalization in higher education: The Observatory of Higher Education counted 162 interna-tional branch campuses in 2009 (up 43% from 2006), of which three quarters came from U.S. institutions, with the remainder evenly distributed between

Australia, U.K., France and India. (Hare, 2011). We also see more cases of a long term, committed presence, with governments building into their national development strategies quite targeted arrangements to attract brand-name overseas universities into deeper collaboration.

Branch Campuses and Government Mentoring

Examples of this new transnational engagement range from Carnegie Mellon's modest branch campus in Adelaide to King Abdulla University in Saudi Arabia, where the strongly state-linked institution is actively recruiting research universities to locate onto its 36 square kilometre complex. Another model is the Shenzhen Campus Project in China's Pearl River Delta, sponsored by the municipal authorities, which is drawing a significant cross border presence from six of the eight universities in Hong Kong, with that government's encouragement. Hong Kong University, whose Shenzhen campus footprint, at 100 hectares, is double the size of the home campus, will access resourcing from Chinese authorities, not just for buildings but funding for research and academic programs as well. The Chinese University of Hong Kong similarly sees its expansion into the Shenzhen project as a sustainability enhancing move: "As a leading institution in Hong Kong, CUHKU must tap into resources outside Hong Kong to scale up the research for achieving its aspiration of excellence." (CHUK website).

The world's most intense importer of higher education expertise, experience and branding is currently Singapore. There, the approach to developing sustainable research universities, often from scratch, is to build into the arrangement "strategic collaborations and symbiotic relationships with premier institutions of international standing" with strong support funding (Tan, 2008). Prominent examples include: the deep collaboration between Singapore Management University and the Wharton School at the University of Pennsylvania and Carnegie Mellon University; the Duke University Medical School at the National University of Singapore; and the mentoring of the Medical School at Nanyang Technological University by Imperial College. "Yale brings the Ivy League to Singapore" is a recent headline about the new Liberal Arts College to be developed at NUS. The new fourth university, Singapore University of Technology and Design, is essentially a branch campus of MIT in partnership with the Singapore Government. Beyond bricks-and-mortar are many traditional alliances involving joint degree programs and shared research centres. The critical point is that all this is woven into a coherent, high energy and well funded government policy of leveraging off transnational education for national development.

Singapore, to be sure, is a special case: a city-state with a highly professional government genuinely committed to building a "knowledge-based economy where ideas and innovations generate wealth". But there may well be important sustainability implications for western research universities in this emerg-ing new paradigm of international engagement. Are research universities becoming another category of sovereign wealth funds, and how does that affect those outside this model? How big is the risk for universities which eschew cross-border arrangements, or where the home government is either disinterested in international higher education as an economic driver, or is so hobbled by public debt post GFC, they really have little choice but to go to the global sidelines? And what are the governance implications between home and host environments?

Another sign of the changing times is that more foreign students now study for British degrees at off-shore branch campuses, than in the U.K. itself. With GBP9,000 plus per annum tuition looming, "you could go to Malaysia, live it up and get a Nottingham degree" for less than U.K.-based study, further boost-ing offshore enrolment for British degrees. Such a development would also lift the standing of the offshore courses. (Labi, 2011, quoting Disney).

This may be fanciful speculation, but it carries some ring of truth and does underscore just how the game is changing for research universities now facing higher levels of market volatility. Because of the competitive environment brought by globalization, and depending on the strategies they develop (or avoid), research universities can rise or fall in fame in much shorter time than was the case 50 or 100 years ago. There is little doubt, for example, that the rankings success of the Hong Kong University since 2000 (it is now a top 25 member of the QS ranking) has brought enrolment interest not just locally (although this was always strong) but from top students in India, China and beyond. High quality research faculty also become easier to recruit. While many observers may disdain the growing role of international ranking exer-cises (Gladwell, 2011), the fact is prospective students (particularly those from offshore) do pay attention, as do governments, governing bodies and now credit rating agencies as well. Faculty are particularly alert to institutional standing, and recruitment will become a major sustainability issue in the next 20 years, given the seriously ageing academic workforce in the West, and the surge of new, high quality research universities in the East.

Governance Implications

Offshore operations invariably raise governance issues: how much indepen-dence is assigned to the governing body of the branch campus, and in what circumstances can its decisions be over ridden by the main governing body at the home campus? who determines and monitors student admission standards, faculty promotion criteria and processes, grievance handling and scientific misconduct issues? where is curriculum set? is the branch campus expected to repatriate a dividend and if so how is this determined? does the role of the offshore government in the affairs of the branch campus diminish the ideal of university autonomy? These are just a few of the potential pressure points.

Funding is a major issue, highlighted by CUHK's firm assurance to the home campus community that its Shenzhen operations will be financially self-sustainable, "with no funds from the Hong Kong campus subsidising its operation." (Yau, citing Sung 2011). But the most contentious issue in recent years with offshore branch campuses has been academic freedom. A guarantee of this has been given by CUHK's President, and a similar assurance to the home campus community was needed from the Yale President, addressing reported concerns that Yale faculty risked having their freedom of speech and assembly limited in the Singapore Liberal Arts College.

These are challenges, but they will be sorted through as universities become more experienced in negotiating the cultural and political diversity inherent in branch campuses. The obvious tension is between the felt need of the home campus to shape strategy and protect brand, and the inevitable imperative at the branch campus for independence.

Another governance factor arises from the trend toward international accreditation, such as that offered for Business Schools by the Association to Advance Collegiate Schools of Business (AACSB), as those in the accrediting network influence curriculum and research standards for promotion. Other disciplines will also face international accreditation regimes in due course, most notably Engineering through the OECD's Learning Outcomes Project. In 20 years, perhaps sooner, new governance ground rules will put collegiate decisions on content and standards into a much wider context than that of a university's own academic community. Assessment functions might be outsourced. How well a university responds to these new governance ground rules may well determine which research universities maintain their place in the major league, and which don't.

THE GREEN CAMPUS AND SUSTAINABILITY REPORTING

Environmental issues resonate with the culture and values in university communities, so it is unsurprising that these communities are actively interested in the sustainability performance of their own campuses. While the impact of research breakthroughs may be more spectacular, campus sustainability policy and practice, as well as public reporting of environmental performance, has a powerful demonstration effect throughout society and carries important educational effects on new graduates as they head out into their professional lives, with the chance to influence the culture of their employing corporates and organisations.

Many, perhaps most, research universities endeavour to implement (or at least project) a green agenda for their own operations, utilising the standard array of initiatives energy and water conservation, waste reduction and recy-cling, carbon management, green procurement, transport efficiencies, land-care principles, sustainable building design, and so forth. University websites these days invariably reflect an awareness of environmental concerns, and lay out policies and procedures for achieving high levels of sustainability perfor-mance. In Australia, five of the eight major research universities have signed the Talloires Declaration (although only two hold ISO 14001 Certification and can be said to provide strong sustainability governance structures for over-seeing and managing their sustainability commitment).

At the Chinese University of Hong Kong, the mission includes ensuring stu-dents graduate "knowledgeable about the environment and prepared to shape their lives and professions to address issues of environmental sustainability." (Lam 2005). At the University of Massachusetts, MBA students collaborated in the preparation of its third sustainability report to the Global Reporting Ini-tiative (GRI). Apart from engendering a "better understanding of the whole footprint of the campus and the environmental, societal and economic impacts", the exercise also built "some sense of belonging and loyalty to the institution and a sense of cohort cohesion." (Mehallow, 2011). Such institu-tional bonding through environmental involvement may still fall well short of the role played by college sport, but it is potentially a similar phenomenon.

The Global Reporting Initiative (GRI) has become the main vehicle for organizations to publically set out their non-financial, sustainability perfor-mance (www.globalreporting.org). Since its emergence in 1997, the Amsterdam based GRI has regularly refined the suite of principles, indicators and metrics organizations may use to report their economic, environmental and social per-formance. The global corporate trend is clearly toward more transparent report-ing of the triple bottom line. The majority of the Global Fortune 250 companies report through GRI framework. In Australia, 93 of the top 100 public compa-nies in 2010 published sustainability related information, 40 of which structured their statutory annual reports to the GRI standard. (ACSI, 2010).

Universities' participation in the Global Reporting Initiative (GRI) fall well short of that seen from the corporate sector: in 2010, only five universi-ties globally were listed as GRI compliant, but the indications are that this fig-ure will grow significantly in the next decade, if not through GRI then through internationally networked reporting regimes developed specifically by and for the higher education sector.

Although universities are seldom covered by their country's core compa-nies' legislation, one effect of globalization is that standards and practices set beyond the campus have a growing habit of penetrating university manage-ment systems and governance practices. Globalization carries a convergence effect, and this is likely to be strengthened through sustainability reporting, particularly when as it moves from a voluntary to a mandatory regime.

Governance Implications

The drive for an environmentally compliant campus engages many of a university's stakeholders, but none more so than students and those contemplating enrolment. This not only immerses students in one governance stream within the university, it provides a marketing opportunity to the university in its recruitment process.

GRI reporting impacts governance in several respects. With its emphasis on transparency, it places into the public domain details about the university's operation and its various social and economic impacts, as well as environment effects. This will extend the duties (and liabilities) of university trustees as it does for board directors in the private sector. To the extent public reporting becomes mandatory, either through peer pressure or statutory requirements, governing bodies will be further guided (or constrained) by influences beyond the university. Added to this effect will be the involvement of rating agencies, quality assurance bodies and ranking exercises.

CONCLUSIONS

The idea of sustainability, with all its layers and subtleties, provides an interesting long lens through which to view the changing world of research universities. Much of the discussion here is supported by observation and experience, and with anecdote as well, rather than by formal scholarly research, which no doubt will follow in due course. This said, five summary points arise:

First, the Global Financial Crisis does sharpen the sustainability challenge for research universities in enduring ways: *unprecedented funding difficulties* will cause many to really struggle to maintain the DNA of being a research university. Sustainability often will depend on finding new horizons, both financially and geographically. More and more university budgets will draw from the private purse of international enrolments and local students alike, reflecting a new era of government incapacity to fund universities at prior levels. A distinctive development will be the international migration of universities themselves through more substantive branch campuses, both for profile building and to tap into revenue opportunities.

Second, globalization forces will continue to *reshape the stakeholder landscape* of research universities. External evaluation will continue through the role of quality assurance bodies and academic ranking exercises, whose impact will likely grow. Two new external review and audit players bringing performance pressure onto universities are the credit rating agencies, primarily Moody's and Standard & Poor's, and global environmental reporting regimes, such as GRI. Both these effects bring to university management and governance functions new standards generated within the corporate sector.

Third, we can expect to see an *intensification of the role of government,* even in those countries where public funding is in serious decline, such as the U.S. and the U.K. Here, public policy will set ground rules affecting sustainability for the research university, to provide: how students, both local and international, will shoulder the greater proportion of operating costs; how debt issuance will be regulated, and what underwriting will be extended, either formal or implied, to protect the national higher education sector's international brand. Paradoxically, the stronger the role of the private purse, particularly where foreign currency is involved, the more government regulation and oversight can be expected.

Fourth, international competitiveness among leading research universities to hold or lift their standing, and those which aspire to a place at the top table, generates *new levels of volatility in international ranking regimes.* More now hinges on the right strategic path chosen by presidents and their governing bodies: prospective international students and rating bodies do pay attention to a university's standing, and whether it is changing. In the US and the UK, which currently account for most of the top ranked 100 universities, public debt levels and other budget pressures present distinct sustainability challenges. Contrasting this, governments in the Middle East and particularly in Asia, are funding new national development strategies which place front and centre the rise of their key universities to global standing. This creates an unprecedented opportunity for universities in the East to reshape their place in world standings.

Fifth, a range of *governance implications* arise from these developments. Inevitably, the style and skill mix of university governing bodies will shift in the wake of the Global Financial Crisis. External "oversight" from rating agencies and regulatory bodies (private as well as public), together with the requirements of offshore governments in relation to branch campuses, are just some of the many forces bringing new levels of subtlety to the theory and practice of university autonomy, even academic freedom. Many would see this as the bedrock sustainability issue for the modern research university.

REFERENCES

AACSB. (2011). *Globalization of Management Education,* Emerald Group Publishing.

ACSI. (2010). *Sustainability Reporting Practices of the S&P/ASX 200,* Australian Council of Super Investors, July.

Brooks, Peter (2011). "Our Universities: How Bad? How Good" *The New York Review of Books,* 24 March — 6 April, p. 10.

Browne Report (2010). *Securing a Sustainable Future for Higher Education,* www.independent.gov.uk/browne-report.

Chapman, Bruce (ed). (2010). *Government Managing Risk,* Routledge Taylor & Francis Group.

Davis, Glyn. (2010). *The Republic of Learning*, ABC Books.

Fain, Paul. (2010). "Moody's Report Shines Spotlight on College Leaders Amid Bleak Financial Outlook", *The Chronicle of Higher Education*, 22 November.

Gladwell, Malcolm. (2011). "The Order of Things: What College Rankings Really Tell Us", *The New Yorker*, 14 & 21 February, pp. 68-75.

Hacker, Andrew & Dreifus, Claudia. (2010). Higher Education? How Colleges Are Wasting Our Money and Failing Our Kids — And What We Can Do About It, Times Books.

Hare, Julie. (2011). "West meets East with new Asian campuses", *The Australian*, 13 April.

IDSA. (2009). *King Code of Governance for South Africa 2009*, Institute of Directors of Southern Africa, 64 pp.

Jeanrenaud, Jean-Paul. (2011). Quoted by Sarah Murray, "A meeting of minds that unites former adversaries," *Financial Times*, 11 April.

Labi, Aisha. (2011). "Hong Kong Venue for British Council's Conference Reflects Shifting Tends in Education", *The Chronicle of Higher Education*, 13 March.

Lam, Kin Che. (2005). "Environmental Report" of *Chinese University of Hong Kong website*, http://www.cuhk.edu.hk/cce/Production/index.html.

Lucas Report. (2010). *Aspirations for the Higher Education System in Hong Kong*, University Grants Committee, Hong Kong.

Mehallow, Cindy. (2011). *Universities Embrace GRI Sustainability*, http://www.triplepundit.com/2011/01/universities-embrace-gri-sustainability-reporting/

Moody's (2009). *Global Recession and Universities: Funding Strains to Keep Up with Rising Demand*, http://globalhighered.files.wordpress.com/2009/07/s-globrecess-univ-6-09.pdf

Moody's (2010). "Universities' Financial Straits: A Moody's Retrospective", Harvard Magazine, (September-October 2011).

Niland, John. (2009). *Five Year Review of Fit for Purpose*, The University of Hong Kong, May.

SCMP. (2011). "Litmus test of China's scientific renaissance", *South China Morning Post*, editorial p.A12, 2 April.

Schuster, Jack H. & Finkelstein, Martin J. (2008). *The American Faculty*, The Johns Hopkins University Press.

Slaughter, Sheila & Rhoades, Gary (2010). *Academic Capitalism and the New Economy*, The Johns Hopkins University Press.

Standard & Poors (2008, July). *UK Universities Enjoy Higher Revenues But Still Face Spending Pressures*, http://www.standardandpoors.com/ratingsdirect

Standard & Poors (2008, October). *Higher Education: A Global Perspective*, http://www.nacubo.org/documents/business_topics/GlobalHigherEd2008.pdf

Tan, Tony. (2008). Role of Higher Education Partnerships in Creating a Knowledge-based Economy Role of Higher Education Partnerships in Creating a Knowledge-based Economy, speech to the US-China-India Innovation Partnerships Conference held in Boston on 12 December.

Taylor, Mark. (2010). Crisis on Campus: A Bold Plan for Reforming Our Colleges and Universities, Knopf.

The Royal Society. (2011). *Knowledge, Networks and Nations — Global Scientific Collaboration in the 21st century*, London. http://royalsociety.org/uploadedFiles/ Royal_Society_Content/Influencing_Policy/Reports/2011-03-28-Knowledge- networks-nations.pdf

Thiel, Peter. (2010). http://www.thielfoundation.org/index.php?option=com_content &id=14:the-thiel-fellowship-20-under-20&catid=1&Itemid=16

Yau, Elaine. (2011). "Freedom vow for Chinese University's Shenzhen campus", *South China Morning Post*, 15 February.

PART VI

•••••••••••••

Summary and Conclusion

CHAPTER 22

Summary of the Colloquium

James J. Duderstadt and Luc E. Weber

T he VIII Glion Colloquium was held in June 2011 to consider the roles that could be played by the world's research universities in addressing the various challenges of global sustainability in the broadest sense, e.g., climate, environmental, economic, health, poverty and geopolitical. This included considerations not only of how research universities were adapting to the imperatives of global sustainability (e.g., social diversity, resource management, academic programs, research and scholarship), but also how they could develop new curricula, student experiences, research paradigms, social engagement and international alliances to better address the challenges of global sustainability, while producing globally identified citizens.

Participants prepared papers that were distributed in advance of the meeting to allow time for wide-ranging discussions. The meeting was divided into five major sessions, with an opening keynote address provide by Anne-Marie Leroy, Group General Counsel of the World Bank. An additional panel discussion was scheduled involving leaders of the European University associations to discuss the current state of research universities in Europe.

This summary chapter has been written to pull together several of the key points made by the participants and arising during the discussion phase of the sessions.

THE KEYNOTE ADDRESS OF THE VIII GLION COLLOQUIUM

Anne-Marie Leroy: How Can Research Universities Contribute to Fostering Sustainable Societies in Developing Countries?

In a sense, "global sustainability" is the end point along the continuum from "environmental sustainability" to "sustainable development" to a "sustainable society" and ultimately, "global sustainability". Robert Zoellick, president of the World Bank, sets the challenge as leveraging the opportunities that increased global interconnectedness offers to overcome poverty, enhance growth with care for the environment, and create individual opportunity and hope in working towards this vision of an "inclusive and sustainable globalization". At its core, this implies a sense of equity, and therefore, a prominent role for the mediating power of the law. We must learn to appreciate the law in its proper socioeconomic context and allow it to become a key and meaningful element in the development imperative.

Research universities can play a key role in working with the development community to find innovative solutions to the development challenges. Together, we must find ways of developing viable methods of analysing the law through different lenses to determine its adequacy and effectiveness, taking into account the political, economic, social and cultural contexts in which it operates.

For example, how do we help build legitimate and effective legal and judicial institutions in post-conflict and fragile situations, considering the low institutional capacity, infrastructure and other limitations? How do we design appropriate legal frameworks to deal with environmental crimes such as illegal exploitation of marine resources, wildlife poaching, deforestation, pollution and so on? How do we harness international law in order to provide answers to situations where new States are emerging (for example South Sudan) and the so-called "failed States" (such as Somalia) become fertile ground for regional instability? How do we respond to the global financial crisis through domestic and international legal and regulatory reforms? How can we ensure that land and property rights systems (including intellectual property rights) provide adequate protections for the most vulnerable and do not hinder meaningful economic development? How can the law contribute to enhance transparency, citizenship involvement and accountability?

Partnerships and knowledge networks provide an important vehicle for research universities to become engaged in international development. As a specific example, universities are invited to partner with the World Bank's Global Forum on Law, Justice and Development.

SESSION 1. ELEMENTS OF GLOBAL SUSTAINABILITY

Chair: Charles Vest
Luc Weber: Universities, Social Sciences, Arts and Humanities, Key Pillars of Global Sustainability
Jared Cohon: Values and Valuation for Sustainability
Thomas Bierstecker: Contemporary Global Governance and the Challenges of Institutional Reform

Pascal Morand: Responsibility of Business Schools to Train Leaders Sensitive to Global Sustainability

Today, there is growing evidence that an ever-increasing human population and invasive activities of humankind are altering the fragile balance of our planet. The concerns are both multiplying in number and intensifying in severity: the destruction of forests, wetlands and other natural habitats by human activities leading to the extinction of millions of biological species and the loss of biodiversity; the build-up of greenhouse gases such as carbon dioxide and their possible impact on global climates; the pollution of our air, water and land. Yet, while most attention is focused on the changes humankind is forcing upon the natural world, one must also question the sustainability of human societies themselves.

The concept of sustainability, well established in the domain of environmental protection, exploitation of natural resources and climate deterioration, is equally powerful as a wide-ranging concept pinpointing the necessary sustainability of geopolitical, economic, financial, and social structures — even the university itself — which are required for world prosperity and peace. In this sense, sustainability has two distinct dimensions: first, a natural one, focusing on planet Earth, the environment, the exploitation of natural resources, including air and water, and the climate; and second, a human and societal one, referring to the well-being of human beings and the economic, political and social organization and development of society.

Our traditional social and economic organizations, such as governments and corporations, tend to come up short in weighing the full range of issues that should influence policy development and economic decisions. Given the complex interdependence of our contemporary world, the challenges of contemporary global governance are daunting. The task is made all the more difficult because most of the international institutions we still rely upon to manage contemporary global challenges were created and designed more than 60 years ago. They were profoundly state-centric in their governance and design and created with very specific purposes in mind. Today the costs of their inability to cope with the growing challenges to global sustainability are enormous.

One of the keys to sustainability is "getting the prices right", that is, addressing externalities such as the true social costs of various options that are not reflected by the prices set by markets. For example, the dominant non-climate external effect of energy use is its damage to human health, primarily excess deaths from air pollution. But determining the magnitude of such externalities is difficult, as evidenced by the recent U.S. National Academy of Sciences study that estimated additional costs of utilizing fossil fuels to produce energy in the U.S. at $240 billion/year currently not reflected in the marketplace, a clear market failure that the U.S. government has been unable to address. More fundamentally, these are really issues of estimating "values" of different practices and options in a careful and rigorous fashion. For example, how do we value the welfare of future generations or our intergenerational responsibilities? Few would disagree that these are value questions. But who sets the values? Politicians? Economists? The public at large? Or universities?

After all, virtually every member of governments and almost all CEOs and leaders of every sort has spent some part of his or her life in our universities. Surely, we, the academic community, have contributed to the way society values nature, for good or ill, and we can help to shape how it will view nature in the future. Yet, we also must accept some blame for the absence of value discussions, since we have largely eliminated values and ethics from our schools and colleges, pushing such considerations into broader society where they become more contentious. Considerations of values and ethics have largely disappeared from our academic programs, particularly in professional schools such as business administration.

The concept of sustainability is to some extent inherently at odds with the cultural mantra of freedom, accepted widely in Western society and particularly in the U.S. If freedom or "liberty" is a core value, and it means being able to do anything you want to maximize your happiness and success, independent of the impact of your actions on anyone else, then the concept of sustainability may threaten your core values. Since business and industry play such a key role in both threatening and mitigating global sustainability, university business schools have important roles to play in providing their students with a framework of values and integrity that extends beyond profit to include environmental and social welfare.

Of course, it would be inappropriate to suggest that universities should dictate values to their students. As a starting point, we can suggest that some level of environmental literacy should be a basic goal of our curricula. Being sure that every student has some basic understanding of environmental issues and phenomena seems desirable. This requires broader considerations than the natural sciences. The social sciences are essential to the study of social organizations and communities. Some consideration of the arts and humanities must be an essential component of education if one is to acquire the perspective necessary to understand and estimate values characterizing complex issues such a global sustainability. The university is where these disciplines can be best pulled together to address the issues of global sustainability.

Today, universities have become key drivers of the knowledge society, with responsibilities to provide ever increasing educational opportunities, to perform the research necessary to address social needs and priorities, and to provide a mechanism for reasoned debate and policy development concerning major issues such as climate change. Hence, it is natural to add to these roles a responsibility to provide students with the understanding and values necessary to embrace global sustainability.

SESSION 2: THE CHALLENGES OF GLOBAL SUSTAINABILITY TO UNIVERSITIES

Chair: Heather Munroe-Blum
Charles Vest: Strategy in the Face of Uncertainty and Unpredictability: The Research University Role
James Duderstadt: Global Sustainability Challenges: Timescales, Magnitudes, Paradigm Shifts and Black Swans
Yuko Harayama: Over the Horizon: Addressing Global and Social Challenges and the Role of Universities
Ralph Eichler and Patrick Aebischer: Action Is What Counts: Sustainability at ETHZ Zurich and EPFL Lausanne

The uncertainty and imperfect predictability characterizing complex phys-ical and biological phenomena cause havoc when fed into social and political decision-making systems on issues such as climate change. It appears that democratic systems have particular difficulty dealing with strategic issues to begin with, and these difficulties are only compounded when the forcing func-tions that need to be recognized by strategies have non-trivial uncertainty.

Despite the increasing confidence on the part of the scientific community that activities of humankind are changing the climate of the planet, there remains substantial public opinion that denies the reality of both climate change and human impact. Part of the challenge in shaping both public understanding and policy concerning global climate change issues is the diffi-culty of conducting rational discussion of concepts such as severity of conse-quences and probability of occurrence. The situation that causes particular consternation is one that has a very low probability of occurrence, but has potentially disastrous consequences, such as the blowout of the BP Deepwater Horizon well in the Gulf of Mexico in 2010 or the impact of the massive 9.0 earthquake and tsunami on a Japanese nuclear power plant in 2011.

Unfortunately, many of the phenomena we need to consider today are not inherently certain, and to make matters worse, we usually have rather incom-plete information to begin with. Climate change is even more complex. Its prediction is inherently probabilistic. Even our understanding of the past and present is probabilistic. Climate change depends on nonlinear interactions of many subsystems of the climate and on various forcing functions that are com-plicated to understand.

How do we tackle these global challenges, while increasing the quality of life and leaving room for development? To deal with these market failures, tra-ditional policy tools — incentive tax, subsidies or regulation — may be mobi-lized in theory. So, too, part of the challenge is to understand better public perception and misconceptions so that issues can be reframed in terms that will engage even sceptics in a constructive dialogue. It was noted that one issue that seemed to persuade even the strongest sceptics of global climate change that the issue deserved attention was the recognition that "green energy" industries would soon comprise one of the largest economic sectors in the world. Without at least some attention to these technologies, nations would be largely left out of this marketplace.

In those rare instances in which both public understanding and scientific agreement have converged, effective policies have been developed, such as the Montreal Protocol addressing depletion of the ozone layer by limiting the emissions of CFCs. The policy development for re-combinant DNA experimentation involved a similar process involving scientists, government leaders and industry.

Yet, today, we have a difficult time in engaging in open discussion of issues such as global sustainability. Both politicians and scientists discuss whether or not they *believe* that climate change is real and if so, whether or not they *believe* that it is caused in large measure by human actions. In far too much of the discourse in the United States, *belief* has taken on a connotation of a religious-like, or ideological belief, rather than implying whether or not scientific observation and analysis are sufficient to form a basis for policy.

Our current inability to generate sufficient concern and action to address the challenge of global sustainability may be due in part to the difficulty we have in comprehending the timescales, magnitudes and paradigm shifts characterizing phenomena such as energy production and climate change. We usually think in terms of the timescales characterizing our own experiences. For example, businesses tend to function on timescales determined by quarterly earnings statements and policy evolves on timescales of election cycles. We tend to think of natural phenomena, such as climate change or biological evolution operating on very long timescales, thousands or even millions of years. But all of this is changing, with serious implications for global sustainability. While the time frame for major damage is not immediate, the necessary risk mitigation requires near-term action to stem problems that would occur decades into the future.

We also have problems with magnitudes. For example, it is estimated that over $16 trillion in capital investments over the next two decades will be necessary just to expand energy supply to meet growing global energy demand driven by the energy needs of developing economies. A second example of just how magnitudes influence global sustainability is demographics. The United Nations has recently updated its projection of world population growth to 9.3 billion by 2050 and to over 10 billion by 2100. This raises the logical question: Can we sustain a population of such magnitude on Spaceship Earth?

The forces driving change in our world — anthropogenic driven changes in our environment (climate change, declining biodiversity), changing demographics (aging populations, migration, increasing ethnic diversity), environmental impact (climate change, biodiversity), globalization (economic, geopolitical, cultural), and disruptive technologies (info-bio-nano technologies) — are likely to require a new level of knowledge, skills and abilities on the part of our citizens. In the face of these and other realities, universities have important roles in not only conducting the research necessary to reduce uncertainty, but also to help both policy-makers and the broader public to understand the nature of risk and to assist in developing better social and political means to discuss uncertainty and risk.

More generally, tackling the challenges of sustainable development requires critical thinking, innovative technologies and an open dialogue between science, industry and society. Universities can play the role as "honest brokers", providing impartial scientific information to all parties concerned, with due emphasis on the assumptions and uncertainties that are unavoidable in all scientific studies. They can also act as role models for the decarbonization of society by sharing their own operations management techniques and fostering a sustainable campus environment for working and living.

To be sure, the traditional roles of the university will continue to be important, but they also must evolve. An increasingly complex and rapidly changing world requires graduates capable of both depth in a particular discipline, as well as intellectual breadth. Universities are challenged to bring their research, scholarship, analysis and especially education — in every field, natural science and engineering, social science, humanities, and arts — to bear on the challenge of creating a citizenry, a policy community and political system better able to join together to move toward a more sustainable future in a context that is inherently uncertain.

PANEL DISCUSSION ON HIGHER EDUCATION IN EUROPE

Moderator: Howard Newby
Participants: Berndt Huber, Jean-Marc Rapp, Fritz Schiesser and Georg Winckler

The original Maastricht Treaty gave no power to the European Union for higher education. There was little that could be done to integrate higher education in the E.U. without further organizational structures. There were early efforts to create an E.U. "higher education space", such as the Erasmus program to encourage student mobility among institutions. But it took the shock of the weak performance of European universities in the rankings of global university rankings to stimulate a broader effort. The Bologna Process was launched in 1998 when the ministers of education from Germany, France, Italy and the United Kingdom issued the Sorbonne Declaration signaling their goal of achieving greater integration across European higher education.

A year later, 26 European ministers of education meeting in Bologna, Italy, followed up with a second, more inclusive communiqué spelling out their collective goal of increasing "the international competitiveness of the European system of higher education". (This effort has now expanded to 47 nations, 27 being members of the E-U.) The goal was to promote student and academic staff mobility by establishing consistent degree programs and a European-wide quality assurance/enhancement system. Courses were assigned to various levels; learning outcomes were measured; and degrees were developed within a 3+2+3 year framework for baccalaureate, masters and doctorate degrees.

The early phase of the Bologna Process was led by government ministers who believed that since language defined the states served by the universities, they owned the universities and the process. However, progress has become increasingly dependent upon non-state actors such as the European University Association (EUA) and its student counterparts, the European Students' Union (ESU) and the Council of Europe, which now drive the Bologna Process. The Bologna Process has evolved into a process explicitly linking six sets of key actors: ministers of education, university leaders, student leaders, leaders of international organizations, European Union bureaucrats, and policy think tanks that helped to define the issues and shape the agenda. But there remains very strong influence by the nation-states, in part because of the very limited mobility of students and faculties across the E.U. and vertically among institutions.

The ongoing dialogue established by the Bologna process has encouraged faculty to focus more on what students learn and the student experience. The development of quality control agencies and mechanisms has harmonized degree requirements so that degrees in the same field mean roughly the same thing across Europe. It has also prepared European nations for the different task of better differentiating among profiles and missions of universities in their effort to build institutions with world-class reputations.

There has been a similar effort to coordinate and intensify research activities across Europe through a European Research Council similar to the U.S. National Science Foundation. Yet, here there is a challenge, since so much of basic and applied research in Europe is conducted by non-university players (e.g., Max Planck Institutes, CERN). While there are moves to better position research universities in research policy development, this is still a struggle in many nations, such as Germany and France.

The EUA now includes over 800 universities (after the addition of Eastern Europe). A League of European Research Universities (LERU) was also founded consisting of 21 of the most research-intensive institutions. Both organizations are important components of the Bologna Process and the European Research Council and play key roles in shaping policy and lobbying for their agenda. They both see the current challenges as massification, demographics and mission profiling (e.g., the excellence agendas in Germany, France, and Spain).

SESSION 3: IMPLICATIONS FOR UNIVERSITY TEACHING AND LEARNING

Chair: Georg Winckler
Heather Munroe-Blum: Universities Serving As and Educating Global Citizens
Alain Beretz: Preparing the University and Its Graduates for the Unpredictable and Unknowable
Roberta Johnson: International STEM Education for Global Sustainability
Linda Katehi: Sustainability As Principle, Practice, Driver, and Culture

The "millennial" generation of students currently enrolling in universities is much more inclined toward social engagement than their predecessors as baby boomers or Generation X. Their positive attitude towards global challenges, coupled with their embrace of the revolution in technology and communications, are distinctive characteristics. How should universities adapt to educate today's students as global citizens? Truly global citizenship requires of its people three important qualities: multicultural intelligence, empathy and courage. To what extent are universities educating and training people to understand and take effective action in relation to such imperatives?

In our globalized world, one of the most important roles of universities is forging international connections. Contemporary research and scholarly collaborations often demand a scale so massive, so daring, and requiring such a wide range of expertise, that it will increasingly be impossible for any single institution, organization or industry to assemble the necessary talent and infrastructure to tackle these on their own. This provides an unusual opportunity to launch more transnational research and connected research, along with education partnerships among nations and institutions.

Universities can engage with global issues more deeply by embracing research and knowledge translation on challenges that might not be receiving attention by other institutions or sectors. For example, to what extent are universities engaging with post-disaster reconstruction, nuclear risk, aging populations, international financial regulation or business ethics?

Entrepreneurship is in the university DNA, making of our institutions great places for attraction of talent with hunger to test new ideas. This includes the transfer and application of the knowledge and technology that flow from university research. But it does not stop there. It means, for professors and students, bringing the energy and expertise of universities to bear on problems that impact society: creating and evaluating a more effective biomedical device, sharing advice with policy-makers in societies transitioning to democracy, or helping communities devise sustainable solutions to nutrition problems, and doing so via creative new approaches to teaching and learning. Social entrepreneurship has become an important theme with both local and global importance.

Here we face this double challenge: on the one hand, promote teaching that can transfer skills which correspond to an immediate demand of our society, while, on the other, the ability to face the unexpected and remain original and creative. Key here is the importance of research-based education in the construction of student skills. Research promotes in students a practice of positive criticism, adaptability, capacity to challenge, and a constructive experience of failure. Research-based education not only provides students with a learning method and technical know-how. It also provides an ethical framework, which is unique to the type of pedagogy developed in universities. These ethical principles are essential in the development of sustainable society.

The sustainability of humanity is determined by our ability to keep in balance the three pillars of society — our environment, and our economic and social systems. This broader concept of sustainability has evolved over several decades from the oil embargos of the 1970s, to the recognition of climate change in the 1980s, to the concern about political stability after the 9/11 terrorist attacks. Today, sustainability is more than a state of mind. It has evolved into a core value and strategy. It is principle, practice, driver and culture.

Sustainability has triggered a shift in thinking and reprioritization to acknowledge climate change and commit to sustainability as a practice, energy approach and commitment. Because of their commitment to service, many leading universities are embracing sustainability in their curricula, research efforts and policy studies.

Universities must act, and as they do so, they must break from the past. The traditional university approaches will not conquer the future. Behaviours and structures must change to fully embrace collaboration and multi-disciplinary solutions. The world's universities must be bold, creative, disciplined and frugal. It is possible. If universities work together as partners and collaborators, they will be the models, the living laboratories and the solution.

Yet, we face another formidable challenge. We cannot achieve global sustainability without widespread sustainability education. We need awareness on the part of the majority of the planet about sustainability. Education and global sustainability are a coupled set — one cannot achieve global sustainability without widespread sustainability education. Furthermore, education for sustainability must include STEM disciplines, as well as humanities and social sciences, and must be made available internationally, and where the bulk of the population is — namely at the primary and secondary levels — if we are to have any chance of making meaningful progress towards global sustainability.

Furthermore, because leading individuals towards sustainability involves a consideration of values, and the formation of values takes place mainly when we are young, weaving consideration of values into education across disciplines in the primary and secondary level is an essential and too-long neglected component of education at these levels. Universities can play a major role in global sustainability by broadening their educational activities to include younger students. After all, students are likely to be the most essential element of achieving a sustainability education on sustainability issues, since they not only have the openness, the energy and the will to address these issues, but their future will be dependent upon their efforts.

SESSION 4: IMPLICATIONS FOR RESEARCH

Chair: Michel Benard
Timothy Killeen: Global Environmental Sustainability: An "All Hands On Deck" Research Imperative
Berndt Huber: Research Intensive Universities in a Globalized World
Georg Winckler: The Contribution of Research Universities in Solving the Great Challenges

Human activity is changing the climate system and the ecosystem services that support human life and livelihoods. The changes are occurring at an unprecedented and often bewildering pace. Solutions will need to address both the long-term *mitigation* of deleterious effects (through, for example, building a low carbon global economy) as well as near-term *adaptation* to changes already underway (through, for example, more effective conservation of freshwater stocks globally and creating greater levels of societal resiliency). Yet, detailed solutions are not always self-evident because of incomplete, contradictory and changing requirements that are hard to recognize until after solutions have been tried.

Furthermore, there is a mismatch in cadence between the evolution of the complex emerging sustainability challenges and our evolving state of readiness to respond — a mismatch that demands a new "call-to-arms" for the modern research university. Although it is possible to ponder global environmental sustainability questions from an academic standpoint at leisure and with a sense of distance and perspective, these changes are, in fact, occurring at rates that can and will simply overwhelm some of the traditional academic processes. It is critically important that research universities play their ordained role fully: aggressively educating and empowering the needed human capital to address these historic challenges, while also identifying and driving a vigorous research agenda that address the challenges of global sustainability in a timely and effective manner.

For example, the United States is currently stimulating universities to address these challenges at three levels: the Science, Engineering and Education for Sustainability (SEES) program of the National Science Foundation; the Global Change Research Program (USGCRP), a 13-agency cross-cutting program of the federal government designed to further research in global change; and the Belmont Forum, established in the Fall of 2009 as a high level group of the world's major and emerging funders of global environmental change research and international science councils.

European universities also are heavily engaged in these issues. There has been considerable effort over the past decade to strengthen their research capability, providing them with more autonomy and less bureaucracy (e.g., ministers no longer appoint the faculty); harmonization of degrees and encouraging the mobility of students and faculty; encouraging distinct mission profiling and competition; and funding peer-reviewed research across throughout Europe through the European Research Council. While the funding of basic research lags behind applied research related to economic development, the E.U. research area is taking shape with leadership in many scientific areas.

Yet there remain many challenges. European universities continue to be too hierarchically organized, a fact that strongly hinders creativity and diminishes research opportunities for young scholars. While they continue to focus research on fundamental investigations, key to producing the knowledge that drives innovation, they must also compete with an array of non-academic research institutions (e.g., Max Planck, CERN, CEA) for funding and reputation, unlike the United States where most basic research occurs within research universities and is deeply integrated with graduate education.

Emerging technologies may overcome many of these constraints since they allow new forms of research collaboration. Massive digitization of printed materials (Google) and crowd sourcing (e.g., Wikipedia) are examples of tools that research universities are using to evolve toward an open system where information flows freely. Social computing is empowering and extending learning communities beyond the constraints of space and time. Open knowledge and education resources will clearly expand enormously the knowledge resources available to our institutions. Immersive environments will enable the mastery of not only simply conventional academic knowledge, but as well tacit knowledge, enabling our students to learn not only how "to know" and "to do", but actually how "to be" — whether scholars, professionals, or leaders — but above all, contributing citizens of the emerging global community.

SESSION 5: ENGAGEMENT WITH THE WIDER COMMUNITY

Chair: Howard Newby
Rafael Rangel: University 2.0: The University as a Driving Force for the Economic, Political, and Social Development of Society
M. S. Ananth: Sustainability and IIT Madras

Maria Héléna Nazaré: Regional Engagement and Sustainability: University of Aveiro in Portugal
Howard Newby: Sustaining World Class Universities: Who Pays and How?
John Niland: Globalization, Universities, and Sustainability Effects

Challenges such as global sustainability require universities to leave behind those paradigms that tend to limit their vision and function and move forward towards proactive schemes focused on society and its needs. The Tecnológico de Monterrey System began in 1943 as Mexico's MIT, but now its mission has broadened to become not only a "citizen oriented" university, but a world quality educational institution serving as a decisive change agent in Mexico. It is an excellent example of an evolving ecosystem for learning and engagement, based on the belief that a university must be embedded in the society it serves or it will fail.

The Tecnológico de Monterrey System is a private institution, supported through fees, grants, and auxiliary activities involving extensive outreach to society through schools, economic development, and social incubators. It has embraced a new paradigm of University 2.0 in which the traditional activities of a university, education, research and extension, are reshaped with ethically focused intents and purposes to serve society through an immense array of new activities such as technology parks, business opportunity platforms, community learning and training centers, and research and education centers. It has cast aside the traditional tendency of universities to isolate themselves from society. Instead, through this new paradigm, it has accepted the obligation and the opportunity of reducing the social gap and preventing the disintegration of the structures that sustain humanity by means of deep-rooted, replicable solutions that aim to bring education and entrepreneurship to each and every citizen.

India provides an excellent example of how an emerging economy, now the second largest consumer market with the second largest pool of scientists and engineers in the world, balances economic development with environmental sustainability. Universities play a key role in both objectives, facing both the challenge of massification necessary to handle five times the current student population, and implementing new educational, research and outreach to address the impact of a rapidly growing economy on the environment. Ironically, although the university is recognized as the most traditional of all institution, it has of late become the major instrument of change in social, economic and political systems. Hence, it is natural to look for it to play a leadership role in sustainable development by adopting a new educational paradigm based on multidisciplinary education concerning environmental issues, stressing the values of equity, justice, and cultural and environmental sustainability, and viewing the learning process itself as lifelong and adapting to the needs of a changing world.

The E.U. faces a serious demographic challenge of quite a different nature with a projected loss of 42 million over the next 30 years. This constitutes the major threat to the sustainability of the European economy and the welfare state, undermines social cohesion and causes generational tensions. Social security costs, in terms of pensions and health care, will skyrocket and put an incredible tax burden on the working age group. At the same time, welcoming and integrating the immigrants needed to compensate for a declining population requires complex and expensive public policies, difficult to explain to the public at large in times of financial scarcity. This will require many research universities to develop a broader portfolio of academic programs, including more applied disciplines similar to those of the Fachschulen and polytechnic universities.

The global financial crisis has sharpened the sustainability challenge for research universities in enduring ways: unprecedented funding difficulties will cause many to really struggle to maintain the core values, priorities and contributions of the research university. Sustainability will often depend on finding new horizons, both financially and geographically. More and more university budgets will draw from the private purse of international enrolments and local students alike, reflecting a new era of government incapacity to fund universities at prior levels. A distinctive development will be the international migration of universities themselves through more substantive branch campuses, both for profile building and to tap into revenue opportunities.

There is likely to be an intensification of the role of government, even in those countries where public funding is in serious decline, such as the U.S. and the U.K. Here, public policy will set ground rules affecting sustainability for the research university, to provide: how students, both local and international, will shoulder the greater proportion of operating costs; how debt issuance will be regulated, and what underwriting will be extended, either formal or implied, to protect the national higher education sector's international brand. Paradoxically, the stronger the role of the private purse, particularly where foreign currency is involved, the more government regulation and oversight can be expected.

During the past decade a remarkable paradigm shift has occurred in the relationship between universities and governments. It was once the role of governments to provide for the purposes of universities, but it is now the role of universities to provide for the purposes of government. As costs have risen and priorities for tax revenues have shifted to accommodate aging populations, governments have asked more and more stridently, what are universities for? The imperatives of a knowledge-driven global economy have provided a highly utilitarian answer: to provide the education workforces and innovation necessary for economic competitiveness. Governments, in other words, increasingly regard universities as delivery agencies for public policy goals.

This creates a range of implications for university governance. Clearly, the style and mix of university governance bodies are changing. Student debt burdens are rising with serious political implications. New stakeholders are challenging university autonomy and academic freedom. And the dynamics of the interaction between governing boards and the university administration are becoming increasingly difficult. These may be the bedrock of sustainability issues for the modern research university.

SESSION 6: SUMMARY AND CONCLUSION

Chairs: James Duderstadt and Luc Weber

The open discussion began with a renewed expression of concern about the serious public and political misunderstanding of compressed timescales characterizing many sustainability challenges. Even though many recognize the issues at stake, they believe that there is time to work it out — perhaps over decades, perhaps over one or more generations. However, we now have a historically unique and pivotally important race on our hands: a race between the development, dissemination and application of the knowledge needed to create a sustainable future and an opponent: the deleterious and disruptive changes, now well under way, that might/will sap our ability to respond in the future. This race is such a tight one, with the two horses running neck and neck together at this moment in history (in fact — an even more humbling thought — during our professional careers!) In an ideal world, after all, the required knowledge base could have been available and well-accepted a century or two ago. And, in a non-ideal world, we would never have had an inkling of what hit us.

Because of the need to win this race and because of their unique ability to educate and mobilize the world's brain trust across the full range of disciplines, research universities have the following urgent and specific responsibilities:

1. To *transform* education — and not just post-secondary, but the full spectrum of formal and informal education — to educate, engage, empower and energize the next generation of problem-solvers;

2. To *drive* a robust international and collaborative research agenda designed to identify, invent, test and deploy solutions designed to address the formidable challenges of global sustainability;

3. To *insist* on building both disciplinary depth and trans-disciplinary breadth of research and education, connecting science, engineering, technology, mathematics, social sciences, arts and humanities disciplines in service to society;

4. To *assess* the need for societal action, to transmit authoritative information to stakeholders and then *take ownership* of the process of transition of knowledge to application, working in new partnerships.

Research universities must respond and respond quickly to these onrushing, complex, and multifaceted sustainability questions that demand science and technology analyses, coupled with deep understanding of human decision-making processes under conditions of large — and sometimes poorly defined — uncertainty. These challenges will undoubtedly stress research universities in ways that are quite unusual and it is likely that many institutions will simply fail to be relevant to the times. Those that do step up, however, will play an historical role for the future of human well-being.

Who sets the agenda for universities? To what degree does sustainability depend on the relationship with the state? And what about these challenges to the sustainability of the research university itself, at least as we currently understand it? In fact, in order to prepare for the unpredictable, the university needs to be itself a sustainable structure. It cannot change its policies or priorities to answer to short-term requirements of governments or economical stakeholders. Long-term sustainability is an absolute requirement if we want to be able to respond quickly to the unpredictable; it implies that universities are granted enough autonomy, both on the academic and financial aspects.

A decade ago, the Glion Colloquium met to consider emerging challenges for the world's research universities. These were seen as essentially *positive* forces for change, and included the digital revolution, shifting forms of competition, collaborative research, and the new energy in "town and gown" relations. Since then, the mood has darkened somewhat. Alarms over the future of the modern research university are numerous. An abiding theme is the dangerous world in which universities now find themselves, although the diagnosed fault lines vary from the intrusion of corporate values to the argument higher education must be rigorously regulated and completely restructured. Whatever the merits of either extreme, they serve to underscore a rising unease about the very sustainability of research universities, at least in their modern form.

Hence, perhaps it is appropriate to conclude this summary of the VIII Glion Colloquium with a quote from the first Glion Declaration, drafted a decade ago by Frank Rhodes at the dawn of the new millennium:

"For a thousand years, the university has benefited our civilization as a learning community where both the young and the experienced could acquire not only knowledge and skills, but the values and discipline of the educated mind. It has defended and propagated our cultural and intellectual heritage, while challenging our norms and beliefs. It has produced the leaders of our governments, commerce and professions. It has both created and applied new knowledge to serve our society. And it has done so while preserving those values and principles so essential to academic learning: the freedom of inquiry, an openness to new ideas, a commitment to rigorous study, and a love of learning. There seems little doubt that these roles will continue to be

needed by our civilization. There is little doubt as well that the university, in some form, will be needed to provide them. The university of the twenty-first century may be as different from today's institutions as the research university is from the colonial college. But its form and its continued evolution will be a consequence of transformations necessary to provide its ancient values and contributions to a changing world" (Rhodes, 1999).

Achevé d'imprimer en décembre 2011
dans les ateliers de Normandie Roto Impression s.a.s.
61250 Lonrai
N° d'impression : 11-4601
Dépôt légal : janvier 2012

Imprimé en France